D0209092

TEMPERED ZEAL

TEMPERED ZEAL

A Columbia Law Professor's
Year on the Streets
with the New York City Police

H. RICHARD UVILLER

CB

CONTEMPORARY
BOOKS

CHICAGO · NEW YORK

Library of Congress Cataloging-in-Publication Data

Uviller, H. Richard.
    Tempered zeal : a Columbia law professor's year on the
streets with the New York City Police / H. Richard Uviller.
       p.   cm.
   ISBN 0-8092-4607-4 : $19.95
    1. Crime and criminals—New York (State)—New York.
2. Law enforcement—New York (State)—New York.
3. Criminal procedure—New York (State)—New York.
4. Police—New York (State)—New York.
I. Title.
HV6795.N5U95   1988
363.2'3'097471—dc19   88-5076
                                                     CIP

Published by Contemporary Books, Inc.
180 North Michigan Avenue, Chicago, Illinois 60601
Manufactured in the United States of America
Library of Congress Catalog Card Number: 88-5076
International Standard Book Number: 0-8092-4607-4

Published simultaneously in Canada by Beaverbooks, Ltd.
195 Allstate Parkway, Valleywood Business Park
Markham, Ontario L3R 4T8 Canada

To Rena and Daphne

CONTENTS

PREFACE:
SETTING AND VANTAGE

A few years ago, I decided to spend my sabbatical leave in the company of a group of working New York City cops. I had been teaching at the Columbia Law School since leaving the office of Frank S. Hogan, the legendary District Attorney of New York County, where I worked as a prosecutor for some fourteen years. Another fourteen years had passed since I joined the faculty, during which I taught courses on law enforcement and the Constitution. I realized it had been a long stretch since I was part of the process I have been trying to understand. I had begun to wonder whether I was building classroom theories out of stale and secondhand materials.

My Hogan years, the late fifties and sixties, had been an exciting period in the development of our American criminal process, a time in which we reshaped our ideas about the influence of constitutional restraints on the work of the police. As chief of Hogan's Appeals Bureau, I had argued a number of cases before the United States Supreme Court presided over by Chief Justice Earl Warren, and I often took the results into the trenches to attempt to explain the

Court's new sensitivity to the lawyers and law enforcement officers affected.

But standing in the middle of the eighties, reading endless pages of judicial prose and scholarly comment, I suddenly felt somewhat out of it. I realized I no longer knew how the Court's message sounded in the stationhouse and the squad car. The Supreme Court, over the last few decades at least, had been unabashedly engaging in lawmaking as instruction, a lesson beamed squarely at the nation's police officers. The course they were teaching concerned the demands of the Constitution on the process of law enforcement. I wondered: Had the imperatives of the Warren Court become comfortable with long use? Or were they bent out of shape by administrative adaptations? Perhaps they had gone dead on the shelves? And what about the more recent decisions? Were the cops awake and responsive at the other end of the pipeline? Or was our Supreme Court, its members deluded by the belief that they were keeping the Constitution alive, actually laboring to create a jurisprudence of futility?

These were important questions for a Court watcher interested in the criminal process. I realized that after all my reading and exercises of imagination, I had scant basis on which to offer even the most tentative response to these central questions—not even a good fresh parable.

My decision to put myself among police officers was an unusual choice. The customary research resource for people in academic law is the library, not "the field." Legal scholarship consists mainly of combining the writings of other scholars with the reasoning of judicial decisions, leavened, perhaps, with an occasional conjecture concerning the activities or purposes of real people and institutions. These ingredients are baked into an idea of one's own, which (lovingly iced) is gently displayed in the literature for consumption by other scholars or perhaps a curious judge or law student. I had done some work in that kitchen and enjoyed it, but looking ahead to my sabbatical retreat, I knew I needed activity of a different sort.

Examining the prefaces of works by a few criminal justice researchers who had ventured into "the field," I found well-delineated hypotheses producing well-financed projects, well-organized data, and carefully concluded results. I considered my own project; I had no hypothesis I wanted to test. Indeed, I resisted all temptations to formulate a theory to guide my investigation. I was determined to reverse the usual order of scholarship and let my conclusions, if any, follow from my research.

Moreover, the sort of observation I wanted to make does not easily yield quantifiable data. Much of the published empirical material examined the work of police in the enforcement of laws dealing with minor crimes and offenses. Traffic infractions, prostitution, "quality-of-life" violations, and the like have received the major share of attention. While the exercise of police discretion may be easier to tabulate in these cases, I was more interested in the heavier, more threatening crimes where the stakes on both sides are higher. So it became apparent that I would have to settle for impressionistic reporting.

It was just as well. Anecdote and description are more in my line. Though I spend most of my working hours trying to discover what I think about the legal mechanisms and processes of the criminal justice system, the question for me is never one of pure legal analysis. Context is the indispensable ingredient. Thinking about the criminal justice system means thinking about judges and cops.

I have a fairly clear picture of how judges work. My wife is one of them. And we have always had a number of friends on the bench. The cop, on the other hand, is an indistinct figure at the edges of my experience. True, as I read a vivid scenario in a Supreme Court opinion, I learn of the actions of a real and particular cop. But the human actor has been filtered through layers of judicial perception. And as I well knew, in law enforcement as in other human endeavors, the truth is often in the nuance, and the nuance is often lost or distorted in the historical account. So the judicial rendition of the "facts" of a case should not be taken for a true core sample of police behavior. A court opinion rarely reflects the alternation between decision and indecision, the mix of fear and aggression, the blend of caution and desire that characterize police action in the field.

Looking back, I realized that even when I was a young Assistant District Attorney my desk had been considerably removed from the streets where the troops meet the challenge, and what came my way was often perceived through the dull lens of inexperience. As a trial prosecutor, I knew some cops. But I knew them only as witnesses. They came to me after all the loose ends had been tied, when the factual picture was beginning to develop the high gloss of the coherent presentation I would make of it to the jury or the court. Like the accounts later rendered in appellate courts' opinions, the testimonial version of a police investigation tended to develop a false neatness. As recited from the witness stand, the activities of the police seem well directed and organized, purged of the uncertainty, false starts, and dangling conjectures of most human groping toward an unknown conclusion.

Could I find a way to enrich these formal versions with an infusion of reality? I knew that to continue to trust my understanding of the subject I teach, I had to get back to ground level in the criminal process. I earnestly hoped there was some way of inserting my gray beard unobtrusively into the daily pursuits of police officers so that I might get a fresh sense of how the process really works. I likened my objective to the anthropologist's. Could I set out, my naivete intact, and simply live for a time with the tribe under study?

The question I heard first and most often from friends and colleagues to whom I would describe my research plan was: "What makes you think they will act natural with you around?" They had a point. I knew that as an academic I would be cast by my subjects as a "liberal," and as a liberal I would be expected to be unsympathetic to what they regarded as the "real world" of the streets. Despite my prosecutorial credentials, despite my attitude of detachment— even sympathy—the scene they allowed me to enter might be artificial.

I will never know how well I succeeded in neutralizing

the Heisenberg Distortion, the discouraging principle that the energy imparted by an experimental procedure invariably alters the behavior of the matter being observed. But I believe that after a few weeks little, if any, comment or behavior was significantly changed by my presence. The sergeant later told me that I had broken the suspicion barrier one afternoon when, doing an impersonation of a prosecutor we both knew, I displayed a vocabulary so rich in obscenities that the cops figured I was okay. Though I never thought the police accepted me as one of their band, I certainly felt neither patronized nor resented due to my academic position. For the most part, my presence was simply ignored while police activities were in progress. At other times, the best description I can give of my interaction with the cops is convivial.

The matter of the Margaret Mead Error is more subtle. Does the preconception inevitably distort the perception? Just how far would my "objective" observations serve merely to confirm prior beliefs and equip me only for the dissemination of the preselected message? I dug for the elusive preconception. I could discover little by way of prejudice either way. I have known no cops socially nor, thank heaven, has my life or those of family and friends generated police work. I don't think I have ever been a "buff" or exceeded the usual juvenile play at white-hatted sheriffs and such. Nor, so far as I am aware, had the law enforcement officer any symbolic baggage as a negative figure of paternal authority or paramilitary oppression. If I had developed any general impression of the character of these people, it was: a civil service mentality cloaked with a high self-respect quotient. How would my faint mindsets affect my perceptions in the field? Of course, I could not know. But I hoped that the absence of strong views one way or the other would serve as functional neutrality. Besides, individualization is a great antidote for preconception.

I should perhaps acknowledge a bias concerning law enforcement itself insofar as it might color my reaction to the street situations I witnessed. I believe that the primary purpose of the criminal justice system is to separate the guilty from the innocent, and I regard it as a most serious under-taking. I am, therefore, rather less concerned than some of my colleagues with such questions as whether the suspect was accorded his full *Miranda* warnings at precisely the ap-propriate time or whether he received the assistance of counsel as he stood in a lineup. But I am extremely con-cerned that the evidence bearing directly on guilt be pursued vigorously and evaluated conscientiously.

Perhaps this orientation colored my perception of the scenes I witnessed. Perhaps it aligned me ideologically with my subjects more than is scientifically ideal. I take comfort in the rationalization that no one goes out into the world of police work without some point of view, and mine seemed no more intrusive than most others'.

The NYPD is surprisingly hospitable to the requests of the curious to accompany them on their rounds. When I went to get myself certified, a well-trodden path of bureau-cratic procedure was evident. I signed my tort claim waiver forms, got my photo taken, my card signed, and my name entered in the book as a "civilian observer," accredited to ride in patrol cars. My reception in the Sixth and Ninth Precincts, by both brass and uniformed teams, was so re-laxed, so routine, it was obvious that the back seat of the patrol car had been worn smooth by assorted writers, poli-ticians, community people, and whatnot. But those who preceded me had been strangers—tourists, if you will—passing through to see what they could see in a few ran-domly chosen hours. No one in the memory of the Depart-ment, I was told, had received such unlimited access for such an indefinite period as I. I do not know what huddles at police headquarters preceded the grant of this extraordi-nary license. I can only say that it appeared to me to be an act of exceptional openness.

I had known Bob McGuire, the Commissioner at the time I began my observation, casually for a number of years. I ran into him occasionally since he became Com-missioner, and I admired his performance in that difficult post. Bob's Deputy Commissioner for Legal Affairs, Ken

Conboy, I know somewhat better; we were friends and colleagues in the District Attorney's Office. It was to Ken that I took my budding plans for field research within the Department. We had lunch, followed by a short letter in which I sketched my unformed ideas of the project-sans-hypothesis. Unconditional approval was not long in coming.

So began my tour with the front-line troops of law enforcement—eight months of hanging around with whatever team was moving, doing what they did, listening to their relaxed but persistent conversation about the Job. My first approach was to the precinct in which I was raised and still live, the Sixth. I found a small, modern stationhouse nestled among the brownstones and stoop fronts of what has become the fashionable West Village. I met the brass and climbed into the backs of several patrol cars. That first week, I drove in endless aimless circles through the daytime and nighttime streets of Greenwich Village, learned to decipher the code of the incessant radio calls, rushed to several false alarms, and heard a great deal about days off and how vacations were or would be spent. In short, to my amazement, nothing happened.

I spent as little time as possible examining the organizational structure of the Department. But one fact of police life is inescapable: the distinction between the "white," or silver, shield and the "gold." All cops come onto "the Job" (as they invariably call it) with the silver badge and the rank formerly called "patrolman" and now termed "police officer" or "PO." In this status, the officer is commanded by sergeants and lieutenants in uniform at the precinct level, and the House is under the command of a captain or, sometimes, a deputy inspector. They, in turn, are under the command of area authorities of progressively higher rank. In his precinct, the white-shield cop normally rotates through the three tours, spending his or her time—usually with a partner, usually in a blue-and-white vehicle called a radio motor patrol car (referred to as an "RMP")—cruising hour after hour in a random pattern through his or her assigned sector. A PO may also draw a "foot post," which is often a solo assignment.

The principal mission of patrol is to provide a visible presence in the area to reassure the lawful and deter the lawless. In addition, RMPs answer radio runs. Many are complaints of loud or disorderly persons, a substantial number locate the sick or injured in need of aid, and a surprisingly large number are totally unfounded. The uniformed force, of course, provides several other services and occasionally even picks up a victim or catches a criminal.

The hours I spent in the back seat of an RMP were uneventful. Most were spent in a slow prowl around and around a sector of the Precinct, engaging in amiable conversation punctuated by containers of coffee. The officers told me of their grievances with the Department and with the "system" in general. I heard several stories illustrating the cops' perpetual complaint that either judges or prosecutors release dangerous criminals because of their own timidity or incompetence. I heard of the strain on young cops caused by the odd and constantly changing work schedule.

Conjugal resentment was hardly cooled by the addition of young and often attractive female officers with whom to share eight hours in the intimacy of the RMP and perhaps a drink to unwind after the tour. Actually, all the male cops I spoke to told me that they would not want a female officer as a patrol partner. The reasons they usually gave were that physical strength counted at times and that some of the women were inclined to use the stick or the gun unnecessarily to compensate for either physical weakness or an image of softness. Angela Amato, however, guessed that the real reason was that male cops felt more comfortable with other men "so they could do their macho number."

Talking about the Job one day with a team on patrol, I nodded without lifting my eyebrows when they remarked that police officers are highly prone to problems of alcohol addiction and marital rupture. But I was surprised when the men told me that the third major occupational hazard was suicide. Years ago, from the sociologist Emile Durkheim, I had assimilated the homily that strong group associations, shared grievances, and a sense of purpose are the best insurance against suicide. I would have thought this the one form of violence against which the Job provides better than average protection.

One way out of the RMP is by competitive examination. Sergeants are made from lists derived from a much discussed, often revised, and invariably litigated examination given after irregular and often long intervals. Many police officers spend a great deal of slow time studying for the rare Sergeants Exam. Sergeants and better wear brass badges and make more money, but most of them are in uniform, and they often have dull duty supervising patrol officers.

The "gold shield" that everyone hoped and worked for is the detective's badge. Transfer from the patrol command to the Detective Bureau and the subsequent award of the detective's gold badge is a "career path" different from ordinary promotion. It is earned by activity, not exam performance and it promises more interesting, less bureaucratic duty.

By the end of my first week, a bit dizzy from the hours of looping through the streets in the rear of a heated, closed car, I decided to visit the detectives upstairs. Detectives, I remembered, handled the more serious, more complicated cases. I had some interesting conversations with several of the officers, but the large comfortable detective room, with its well-designed lineup chamber, was all but empty whenever I came by.

I realized that at the prevailing pace, my brief sabbatical leave might be over before the first incident entered my notes. I began to look around for a dirtier precinct than the one in which I was languishing. From all I had heard, the neighboring precinct to the East, the Notorious Ninth, was overrun with crime. With some trepidation, I resolved to look in on it.

ACKNOWLEDGMENTS

I would first like to express my gratitude to Helen Whitney for her thoughtful advice concerning the theme of this book; to Carol Rinzler for her expert blue-penciling of an earlier draft; and especially to Marie Winn for her skillful editing of the final draft.

I also offer thanks to former Police Commissioner Robert McGuire and his Deputy for Legal Affairs, Kenneth Conboy (now a federal judge), for their unrestricted invitation to pursue any line of inquiry that beckoned within the Department. My appreciation too to the Abraham M. Buchman Fund for Administrative Law, whose helpful grant allowed me to devote my summer to this book. And thanks to Barbara Hettinger for cheerfully typing and retyping an early draft.

Finally, and with special emphasis, I wish to express my appreciation to the officers of the Ninth Precinct Robbery Identification Program and particularly to the squad commander, Sergeant Martin Browne, for taking me into their company and their confidence, for sharing their thoughts and feelings with a stranger during the many months I sat and moved with them.

1

THIS SHITHOUSE PRECINCT

One February morning not long ago, I put on my helmet and bike clips and pedaled over to the Ninth Precinct stationhouse. It's not hard to find a police station in New York City. The stationhouses themselves are often inconspicuous enough, wedged between other buildings of similar vintage and style, but the blocks on which they sit are the only ones in the city with parked cars angled into the curb. Vehicles, marked and unmarked, cops' and city's, are vital to the police function, and there is never enough room for them. The Ninth, in addition to the curb, boasts a parking lot across the street. It is its only luxury.

On East Fifth Street between First and Second avenues, a block crowded with low, brick-front houses hung with fire escapes and showing their age, the Ninth Precinct stationhouse stands as a broad and stately reminder of the architecture of the Progressive Era just before the First World War. In the high-ceilinged room just inside, a battered but shiny brass rail runs chest high in front of the Desk—a generously long expanse of dark wood paneling—where a lieu-

tenant or sergeant makes endless entries in a ledger. At one
end stands a large, incongruous pot of ferns. In a fading
row along the wall behind the Desk, engraved in brass, are
the names and photographs of the seven uniformed young
men killed in the line of duty in the Precinct. A portable
police radio (the electronic wonder that revolutionized urban police work) conveys its coded messages from the communications officer's desk to a seemingly unheeding audience. The whole room looks as if it were rescued from an
MGM back lot.

At the end of the Desk and elsewhere about the room,
police officers in and out of uniform exchange banter, ob-
livious to the occasional depressed or distraught citizen
standing patiently in front of the Desk waiting for the sergeant to look up, ignoring the periodic parade of handcuffed men being led through the room to the detention cell
at the rear of the House for the preliminary paperwork recording their arrest. A few of the officers standing around
are wearing T-shirts or sweatshirts with the House emblem:
under the words "Fighting 9th" appears the logo, an old-
fashioned wooden privy with a tattered banner waving
above it in defiance (or surrender). An officer cheerfully explained to me that it represented "this shithouse precinct."

On the wall opposite the Desk a bicycle and two shiny
pinball machines stand with paper forms taped to them,
waiting for the truck to come by to collect "vouchered"
(i.e., seized) property. In the small enclosure at the rear of
the room, two typewriters, their innards exposed, are
joined by a grimy computer screen and keyboard. Even
these devices manage to blend with their timeworn surroundings. Perhaps the computer is regularly used to check
for outstanding warrants on arrested people, perhaps to put
a suspect license number to the test, but I have never actually seen it in operation. The one time I watched someone
try to use it to discover the origin of an official badge taken
from a man arrested for impersonating a police officer, no
one in the House could figure out how to put the question
into the program.

The house sends out about 150 uniformed officers every

day in the usual three shifts: 8 A.M. to 4 P.M. ("days"), 4 to 12 midnight ("nights"), and 12 to 8 A.M. (the "late tour"). In addition, the building houses the detective squad (known as the PDU), a special robbery task force, a street narcotics enforcement unit, a "Conditions" unit (the function of which I never did figure out), a community relations team concerned largely with youth gangs in the area, and a unit redundantly entitled "anticrime" that sends out plainclothes officers at night to try to pounce on crimes in progress. At the time I was there, the Precinct was under the command of Captain Raymond Abruzzi, who has since been promoted to a full Inspector, as predicted by his troops.

The Ninth Precinct is .79 square miles in area but it is crossed by over 21 miles of streets. It has about 67,500 residents, of whom some 26,000 identify themselves as Hispanic, 15,000 as white, and 9,000 as black. Covering the notorious East Village, the Precinct stretches south for about a mile from Fourteenth Street to East Houston and from Broadway east to the river. It comprises the old Cooper Union building, surrounded by sidewalk peddlers of used clothing and trinkets; funky St. Mark's Place, the main drag of drag; and the hookers' corner at Third Avenue and Twelfth Street, where even the most discriminating customer can never be certain that the fast service he buys is rendered by a genuine female. The Precinct contains some prospering small, commercial establishments, such as those spread along the old Bowery, where groggy vagrants still assemble and a red traffic light brings a determined band of mendicants into the street to wipe windshields with dirty cloths.

The Precinct is dotted with restaurants, many with distinctive ethnic flavors. In addition to the usual Chinese places, Greek coffee shops, and Italian pizza joints, there are a few Ukrainian and Polish restaurants serving pockets of Old World residents from Eastern Europe and a cluster of Indian and Pakistani places that draw the faithful from all parts of the city. Other commercial establishments include many corner bodegas that also serve as social clubs for the large Hispanic community, a few craft and other specialty shops toward the western edge, and many liquor stores—some of which appear to specialize in half-pint bottles of wine and, like banks, are operated from behind panels of bulletproof Plexiglas.

Residences also cover a fairly wide spectrum. Some blocks boast rows of meticulously restored and maintained brick-front and brownstone houses inhabited by young accountants, designers, assistant buyers, and such. There are also a few scattered stoop-front houses, isolated on decrepit blocks, bravely trying to reverse the deterioration of their immediate surroundings. A large complex of public housing ("projects") stands along the river side of the Precinct. There are probably more residents of the Ninth Precinct housed in these municipal high rises than in all the rest of the Precinct combined.

Particularly in the eastern part of the Precinct (Avenues A, B, C, D, and the FDR Drive, known collectively to cops as "Alphabetland") many old buildings have been abandoned. A sizable number of these belong to the city and have been sealed with cement and cinderblock to await restoration or destruction, whichever the tides of municipal ecology bring first. Many of these derelicts have already been leveled, and the area is dotted with vacant lots. While some are strewn with litter, others have been converted into humble, makeshift gardens or play spaces, and one was actually transformed into a baseball field through diligent local effort (an anomaly cops on tour would point out to me in the early days of my residency).

Another surprising note of incongruity in the neighborhood is the abundance of large and often well-executed wall paintings. Cartoon characters, *trompe l'oeil* storefronts, an enormous, placid tropical beach—murals that seem oddly out of character with the cheerless streets they adorn. Quite a few of the standing abandoned buildings have had their cinderblock seals punctured and now shelter an unseen assortment of squatters. Others have been cleverly converted into sales outlets for narcotics.

Augmented police presence and the arrival of new and optimistic middle class residents have improved the scene somewhat, but at the time I was with the police, it often seemed that drugs were the heavy industry of the Precinct—at least in Alphabetland. The streets were filled with steerers and lookouts serving the dealers concealed behind the facades of abandoned buildings or crouched on inaccessible upper floors and serving their customers with baskets lowered through holes in the floors cut for that purpose. In those innocent days before crack became New York's drug of choice and before AIDS exploded into a plague, nearby "shooting galleries" provided drug customers (many of them suburban and middle class) with rented needles and a secluded place to inject the poison into their veins.

Out-of-state license plates on the parked and cruising cars bespeak the constant flow of buyers into a district widely known for the quality of its illegal merchandise. Graffiti on the walls crudely advertise the "brand names" of dope or coke sold from the nearby premises. A special detail of local police officers, instantly recognizable to all malefactors in the area, constantly prowls the lots, alleys, rooftops and dark hallways, surprising dealers, collaring buyers freshly supplied, making dozens of arrests every day. They confiscate a fortune in cash and stash each month. But their work does little to discourage the trade. Meanwhile, unknown and unseen undercover cops from a special command outside the Precinct patiently arrange major transactions to make cases against the bigger fish. Still, the highly profitable commerce in self-debilitation continues.

One of the satellite enterprises flourishing along with the drug business is the robbery of those who come to buy. Often alone and frightened, these targets are easy to spot. At least on the way in, they carry cash, usually $100 or more. Robbed, they are usually disinclined to complain to the police. Like yellow jackets at a picnic, robbers attracted to the area by these likely targets will strike at anyone in the vicinity. So the precinct also has many stickups of shopkeepers and muggings of ordinary residents.

Another trouble spot in the Ninth Precinct is the "Muni," or city shelter for homeless men. Among the hundreds of physically and mentally disabled men who congregate in and around the facility and the thousands of others bused in and out by the city for meals, there are inevitably a number of predators who will casually draw a knife on anyone to take his coat, his wine money, or his welfare check. Even a brandished beer bottle converts a petty theft into the felony of robbery. So the shelter is a plentiful source of robbery complaints.

After introducing myself to the sergeant at the Desk on my first morning, I asked for the detectives' office and was directed to turn left past the soft-drink machine and the open door of a toilet that might have been a men's room. I climbed a steep iron staircase leading up to the second floor and I know not what unused floors above. Down a hall lit by a single bare bulb, behind a glass-paneled door, I found the Precinct Detective Unit. The large room is filled with desks that so closely abut one another that they make an almost unbroken surface of pale green vinyl. The three high windows along the long wall are covered day and night by tattered blue shades, making it almost impossible to tell what tour is on duty. In the far corner is a frail-looking cage, about five feet by seven, with a door secured by latches but no lock. Obviously an afterthought for convenience, it is usually empty. A few times I've seen one to three men dozing on the floor or staring passively through the mesh.

On that first morning, I found four or five male detectives sitting at the desks, pecking at old, sturdy, mechanical typewriters, talking on the phones, reading the tabloids, or engaging in comradely masculine insult, home improvement advice, and raucous reminiscences unrelated to police work. They were of various ages and physical types, but all were attired in neckties and tweeds or well-pressed three-piece suits. I wondered at the quality of their dress, so noticeably different from the usual look of police out of uniform and so unexpected in their run-down quarters, until I learned that regulations call for coats and ties—the attire of rank, I surmise.

I met the commanding officer, Lieutenant Kennedy, and opened a conversation by asking how the prosecution of various crimes gets started. It turns out that most crimes become cases because some police officer happens on the scene and manages to "apprehend the perpetrator" in the commission of the crime or in immediate flight afterward—*in flagrante delicto*, as a lawyer might say. Another substantial percentage of arrests are made because the crime was committed by a person the victim or other witnesses knew and identified to the police. A similar source is the informer. A telephone call reporting that the person who stabbed his girlfriend last week is back on the corner where he used to hang out may bring police in time to make the arrest. Thus, a suspect may be arrested when someone "drops a dime on him," in the common, now anachronistic phrase.

This leaves a relatively small number of cases that are made by police investigation. Many of these, particularly those involving commercial fraud, underworld activities, or highly unusual or repeated crimes, are assigned to special agencies or task forces that may include prosecutors and experts as well as police officers. Enforcement of narcotics laws (which consumes a shockingly large slice of our scarce law enforcement resources) is also directed by a special unit. So what one thinks of as ordinary "detective work"—discovering a crime, identifying and locating the criminal, and assembling the evidence for use in prosecution—turns out to be an unusual way for police officers to initiate a felony prosecution.

That is not to say that the cases remaining for "ordinary" investigation by detectives are not a very important segment of the work of law enforcement. Murder, rape and other sex crimes, assault, arson, larceny, burglary, and robbery are among the crimes assigned to detective units for development by investigation. For reasons not always apparent, a changing selection of these violent crimes is, from time to time, withdrawn from the responsibility of local detective units and given to a specialized police bureau created for the purpose. During my time of inquiry, the NYPD had established centralized investigatory offices for narcotics offenses, robbery, sex crimes, crimes against elderly persons (sixty-five or over), and arson and explosion. There were special crime scene teams, emergency rescue units, and doubtless others. Burglary was so difficult to solve after the fact that it seemed almost nonexistent in the catalog of detective work. As far as I could see, that left homicides (including disappearances and suspicious deaths) and serious assaults as the principal crimes assigned to the precinct detective squads, with a few assorted forgeries, swindles, and larcenies thrown in.

In a corner of the spacious PDU office, across from the wire mesh cage and next to a small room containing lockers and a couple of narrow double-decker bunks, a door opens into a brightly painted office about seven by fourteen feet, with a single window giving on an alley. The door itself has a large, cracked panel of one-way glass. Inside, every scarce inch is in use. Small lockers along one wall nudge a file cabinet, which touches a tall equipment locker in the corner. Two desks and two tables with perilously wobbly legs hold each other up around the walls. Three or four chairs are pulled up to the desks, each of which has a standard PD typewriter and a phone. All sorts of things hang from nails or are taped to the wall: duty charts, folders, lists of telephone numbers, a hand-lettered version of the *Miranda* warnings, a bulletin board of messages. Shelves hang above these. Only about three by five feet of empty space remains in the center of the room.

This was the home of the Ninth Precinct Robbery Identification Program, (pronounced "nine rip" on the air), a unit of twelve officers, a secretarial aide, and a sergeant, established on an experimental basis in April 1982 and responsible for the investigation of all robberies in the Precinct. It was not uncommon to find in that small office at the same time the sergeant, the aide, four to six officers, a suspect, and a victim or two. And one law professor: me.

During the time I was with 9 RIP, it was an experimental unit not yet on the investigative career path (the supreme irritant in the unit). Its officers were a mix of white shields drawn from a specialized patrol team called "anticrime," and from the Ninth Detective Squad, together with gold shields from the PDU and from the central boroughwide robbery squad. I should add that in the unending discussions of the topic of shields, it was not always easy for me to recall who still had the white and who held the cherished gold.

I didn't expect to find such an egalitarian spirit in a ranked organization like the Police Department, but the prevailing mood in 9 RIP was supportive and comradely. However the men might have felt privately about one another, I never heard any speak a disparaging word about a colleague, and their interaction was remarkably fraternal. In fact, nearly all the men addressed each other by affectionate diminutives. We had Richie, Paddy, Izzy, Joey, Rocky, and four Tommies; Harry was Harry of course, and nothing could be done with Hiram, so Hiram Gonzalez was Gonz. Sergeants and lieutenants, however, were customarily accorded small but significant acknowledgments of rank. All lieutenants seem to be addressed as "Lieut," pronounced "Loot." And, despite all the democratic atmosphere and the rarity of "orders" in 9 RIP, the commanding officer, Sergeant Martin Browne, was never addressed or referred to by his first name. He was called "Sarge" or "Boss" and referred to as "Sergeant Browne."

Of all the officers in RIP, the one from whom I learned most was Marty Browne. Browne is a tall, handsome man with a perpetually relaxed, easygoing manner, and a large black revolver prominently strapped to his belt. At the time I met him, he had about twenty years on the Job, and his hair was whitening around his ears. He had been in a command position for some years, but he retained the street cop's scorn for paperwork and the foolish passion of the Brass for paper statistics. To Marty, the Job is in the streets, on the scene, in motion. And, except for the habitual exasperation with which he spoke of the bureaucracy of incompetents who called him to account periodically, I never saw him angry. As the weeks passed and we grew to trust one another, we found ourselves spending a good deal of time exchanging ideas on the Law and the Job. With his unusual appetite and grasp of legal principles, Marty relished the chance to share his views and hear some of mine. We still phone each other from time to time and often resume our exchanges, applying a bit of law or cop wisdom to the news and gossip of the day. Notwithstanding his customary chuckle of amusement at the daily traffic of crime, Marty really cares about the victims out there and believes in the importance of police work. Marty's twentieth anniversary on the Job stirs no yearnings in him for a new career. He says simply there is nothing else he wants to do more than what he does. And I believe him.

2

BEING A COP

I got an inkling of what it feels like to be a cop one day on my way into the stationhouse. It was about midday, and I stopped to pick up some lunch. Usually I put in my order with the others for hero sandwiches imported from Parisi's in the neighboring precinct. But the night before, I had been out with a team on a stakeout at a Chinese restaurant around the corner from the stationhouse. The family who ran the restaurant had been intimidated by three well-dressed Asian men in what might have been a simple holdup or, as the police suspected, one of a series of shakedowns by a young band of Chinese hoodlums trying to get a start in the ethnic extortion racket. I had been with the officers who talked to the proprietors, or at least to the sturdy woman who, acting as our interpreter, tried to convince the older members of her family to cooperate with us. Although I said nothing and, of course, showed no identification, they naturally assumed I was one of the officers.

The restaurant had looked appealing, and so the following day I thought I would vary my lunch fare. The family and I smiled as I entered and ordered lo mein to go. No check came with the lunch. I protested. They smiled. I insisted. More smiles. Finally, one of them gave in with a shrug and wrote me a check for one dollar. I left a five on the counter and beat a hasty retreat with my paper bag. When I reported my consternation to the cops, I got nods of recognition and appreciative chuckles at my initiation.

There's nothing like a restaurant meal without a check at the end to make you feel like a special person. In the smile of the owner waving aside your money, you learn the meaning of power. I am someone whose good-will should be curried. I am the recipient of a special form of gratitude, but, more important, my future favor is valuable. At least to merchants (admittedly, in this instance, old-fashioned merchants of a different cultural background), I am perceived as a member of a class exempt from the ordinary obligations of commerce. It is a heady salute.

Yet my appreciation of my special status was instantly accompanied by a troubling sense of impropriety tinged with a vague apprehension of danger, a whiff of corruption. The iron rule of my years as a public prosecutor came back to me: nobody pays my way. The exercise of virtue in office is more than refraining from applying improper leverage; it also means resisting and rejecting the favors thrust upon one.

I believe that among the cops who have learned, perhaps with some effort, to reject the temptations, there is little sympathy for the comrades who yield and less still for those who create the corrupt relationships. People accustomed to the exercise of power have no difficulty recognizing bribery and its more aggressive cousin, extortion. And—though the sense of corps loyalty is very strong—I hear in the tone of voice of the cops I speak to about it a sense of betrayal by the corrupt members who have demeaned the Job and made it harder for the rest to convince the public of their probity.

News of a criminal prosecution and rumors of departmental discipline against a corrupt cop travel fast. The cops talk about it, but in subdued tones as though someone had died. Discovered and prosecuted, corruption is regarded as a personal tragedy and an institutional disgrace;

the consequences are—cops think—painful but deserved.

I recall an exchange of comments among Robbery Identification Program (RIP) people one Monday morning relating to a cop from a neighboring precinct who had been suspended while under investigation for corruption. A couple of the RIP cops had encountered the officer in question at a weekend softball game and reported to the others on the general uncertainty about how to treat their clouded comrade, whether to address him as though nothing were in the air, whether to wish him luck, whether to avoid him altogether. Someone had heard that a fund was being collected for the defense of the accused officer. Another cop at the ball game had suggested that, like any suspect, their brother officer should be presumed innocent. In the RIP office, the report was greeted with some shrugs, some murmured agreement, and some noncommittal interest, but there was little enthusiasm for the defense of the accused cop, and none for the presumption-of-innocence idea. However, all agreed the incident was acutely embarrassing and extremely difficult for the cop and his family.

The RIP cops I have spoken to on the subject recognize that the opportunity for corruption, like the occasion for sexual dalliance, comes with the Job. And it is not hard to imagine the thoughts that go through an officer's mind as he counts the thousands of dollars he has confiscated from the arrested drug dealer and thinks about the couple of hundred he needs for his next mortgage payment—the small portion no one will miss. Of course, not every cop has had such tempting assignments, but virtually all are aware that they are working in a market of gratitude and vulnerability. These sentiments are readily convertible into emoluments, gladly offered to reward or to turn aside ordinary official attention.

The reaction of the police to civilian complaints of relatively minor abuses is considerably different. The officers resent having to go before the Police Department board and deny or justify their actions: "Here some bastard has just put a knife in an old woman, and I get hauled in to defend myself for arresting him," a cop once told me. " 'Isn't it a fact, Officer, that you pushed this gentleman against a car with unnecessary force when you searched him? This gentleman claims that you kicked him in the ankle causing a bruise. What do you say to that, Officer?' Christ!''

Despite those stories, I cannot say I ever saw a cop hang back from aggressive action, chilled into immobility by the possibility of a civilian complaint. Their routine response to trouble is to walk confidently into the middle of it, assert their authority, and take charge. Whatever the emotional pitch, whoever has commanded center stage up to that moment, the cops' move instantly draws attention to themselves and seeks to convert the mood to passivity.

It generally works. The sudden, aggressive move can create a moment of panic, however, followed by resentment in the people approached. But the cops carry the antidote which, if expressed properly, can swiftly repair the injury. I saw a dramatic example one night while out with a RIP team. We were hailed by three people who told us with considerable excitement that moments before two or three male blacks riding in a white Lincoln and posing as undercover police officers had robbed two people on the street. ''Be careful,'' they warned us. ''These guys have guns. Big ones!'' We asked them to get aboard to help us identify the car or the robbers, but our informants shrank back, afraid. We didn't stay to argue. We put the description over the air and cruised around the neighborhood. Soon we crossed in front of a white Lincoln waiting for a light.

We come to an abrupt stop and three cops jump out of our car, guns in hand. Standing back a few feet on both sides of the Lincoln, the cops identify themselves and order the surprised occupants out of the car. Three black men and a white driver emerge, full of indignation and protests of innocence. The RIP team moves in quickly and pats down the occupants. One of the RIP cops is now examining the driver's papers while another leans into the car; I can see him quickly run his hands into the upholstery and under the front seat. In a matter of moments, the RIP team is satisfied that they have stopped the wrong vehicle. Only now do they speak to the occupants.

"Hey, guys, sorry. Wrong car. Sorry we bothered you."

"What's going on?" one asks, mollified by the tone of voice and the cops' abrupt retreat.

"Nothing, man. Got a description of a set of wheels like yours, that's all."

"Hey, okay, man. No problem, right?" says another.

"Sure. Enjoy your evening now, okay?" the cop replies, though he does not accept the proffered handshake.

When I later commented on how smooth the operation was, and how they had managed to pull out with nary a feather ruffled, Rocky Regina (one of the RIP team) brushed my compliment aside: "Listen, we don't make trouble. We're not out there to prove how tough we are. The people understand we have to do what we do. As long as you treat them right, they don't get uptight." He smiled at his own rhyme. "You know what I mean?"

"But weren't you afraid someone might drop a complaint on you guys?"

"Believe me," Rocky Regina put in, "If I worried about that every time I made a move, I wouldn't do a thing."

It may seem surprising, but in all the moves I witnessed out on the streets with different RIP teams, I never saw an officer speak rudely to a civilian, much less push someone around. Perhaps the prospect of a civilian complaint kept them civil; maybe my presence encouraged good behavior. I prefer to believe that, in the interests of ordinary efficiency, these cops had developed a street mode that proved workable for both them and their clientele.

Almost all the RIP cops I watched on the street displayed an attitude of toughness and consideration toward the people they approached. Even a cop like Rich Abbinanti—whose normal affect is lighthearted, rather boyish, and unfailingly courteous—addresses suspects in an assertive, nononsense tone that demands respect and deference. I remember him once quietly but firmly interrupting a suspect's impassioned response to remind him that the form of address was to be "Officer," not "man." I also noticed that whenever a cop put his hand on a person—to take him into custody or to direct him into the holding cage for example, the hand was placed heavily and decisively. The gesture it-self unmistakably expressed all the authority implicit in the role.

Police officers relish respect and, in many small ways, insist on a show of deference from the ordinary folk among whom they work. They know they represent force—they are, after all, "the Force"—and they move with an air of confidence that tells the world to yield the right of way as they pass by. The manner of assured, authoritative presence and control is so characteristic I am convinced it has a functional as well as an attitudinal base. Manifest confidence begets submission, and the cops learn the firm tone and hand that informs even the normally aggressive customer of the futility of resistance. It's effective. In virtually every encounter I have witnessed, the response of the person approached was docile, compliant, and respectful.

The customary wariness with which the citizen greets the approaching cop greatly facilitates the cop's job. From stopping a speeding car to stopping a barroom brawl, the implicit threat of painful consequences serves the officer well in avoiding the necessity of using the physical and legal power at his fingertips. At the same time, we do not want our police to exploit their position of dominance to gain the corrupt rewards of office or to revel in their superiority at the expense of the citizen's sense of personal dignity. The demands of restraint must be strong enough to balance the temptations of power; the freedom and peace of mind of the community hangs in that precarious balance. And the cop is stretched between broad license and severe limitation.

I once asked Hiram Gonzalez, a RIP officer who seemed particularly adept at maintaining an easy relationship of mutual acceptance with the people in the street, how it came about. "Why not?" he replied. "I grew up among people like these. I know how to talk to them to put them at ease. They're usually pretty uptight when a cop grabs them, but when they hear me say, 'Hey, man, take it easy,' they relax a little. It makes it easier for both of us. And besides, the people around here know us. They know if they don't attack us, we won't hurt them. We'd have to be pretty stupid to ruin that arrangement. Sometimes I see people I locked up after they get out. They give me a smile and a wave—'Hey, Gonz, how ya doin', man?' No hard feelings. Sometimes they'll even come up with some help in another case. It works."

By the time a cop reaches a unit like 9 RIP, with a few years of street action under his soles, he has developed an air of casual confidence. Take it easy, leave it to me, no big deal, I've seen a lot worse—these are the phrases with which cops meet crises of the most extraordinary sort. Though several have later admitted to me that they were disgusted or frightened, on-duty cops effectively suppress those reactions, appearing to take in stride experiences that would upset most of us.

I was cruising with a RIP team one day when they pulled up at a fire-gutted building behind three or four radio patrol cars hastily pulled up to the curb and left with their crownlights flashing. The RIP guys must have picked up a radio signal that I missed. Inside it was like a stage set: the charred studs and beams intersecting in the dusty half-light, uniformed officers standing in groups of two or three—smoking, laughing, and talking in low tones. One of the RIP cops went over to a sergeant, and another explained to me that some poor bastard had hanged himself from the fire escape. Emergency Services was cutting him down. What did that have to do with RIP? I asked. Never can tell, was the answer, might be some mope we're looking for. The other RIP cop joined us. "We don't know him," he told us, "at least I don't think so. First time I ever saw a stiff that was hanged."

As we left the place, the cop described the horrible disfigurement of the corpse's face to his partner, who showed little interest or surprise. A note of wonder, little more, could be heard in the voice of the cop who had seen the corpse. The subject was dropped as we climbed back into the car and resumed our prowl.

Not far beneath the cops' professionally unexcited demeanor, however, flows a strong current of repugnance toward certain crimes or criminals. The cases that tap the cops' feelings are not always the same. For some, it may be a sexual component in the crime, for others the presence of children. But the revulsion factor is always there, ready to break through the surface. To me this spurt of police anger is a reassuring reminder that human sensibilities may be dulled but never deadened by overexposure to cruelty.

Even Sergeant Browne, RIP's commanding officer, who seemed unmoved by the daily tally of violence, had his point of emotional vulnerability. For Browne, it was gratuitous violence to helpless victims like old people. I have seen him shake his head in disgust as he recalled some brutal robberies he had investigated in the Bronx. An edge of hatred appeared in his voice as he told me of the young hoodlums who would terrorize homebound elderly poeple, forcing their way into their apartments, stealing whatever trivial amount they could find, and often gratuitously beating their victims before they left.

One day I was talking to Detective Angela Amato, who is married to Joe Dean, one of the RIP detectives. Angela is a small, attractive young woman who grew up on Long Island. She retains a suburban innocence in her outlook. After a number of years on the streets of New York City, she still finds it hard to believe the violence and racial hostility she enounters. Her father owned a linen supply company in a bad neighborhood, she explained, employing black and Hispanic workers. She described the atmosphere in her father's company as friendly and convivial. She became a police officer, she told me, so she could "give everybody a fair shake" the way her father had.

Angela likes the interpersonal aspect of police work and, after proving herself as a rookie by requesting late shifts on Forty-Second Street and serving as a "decoy" for an anti-robbery team, she asked to go to the sex crime unit—an assignment rarely requested, she told me, despite the unusual challenge and importance of the work. It was there she picked up the case that shocked her.

"Here's a woman, ninety years old, feisty woman, goes to do her own shoping at D'Agostino's," Angela began. "She gives her normal delivery boy fifty cents to deliver the groceries. Another fellow who works there part-time decides he's going to take the groceries to her apartment. The individual rings the bell, she lets him in, he puts the packages down.

"In the confession I got from him, he told me just what happened," Angela said. "In his own words, he told me he said to the old lady, 'Let me have my tip.' She says, 'I gave fifty cents to the other guy; get it from him.' At that point he says he was annoyed with her. She went and got a couple of bottles and gave them to him so he could get the refund from them. So in his words, he was insulted, she had insulted him. He asked her could he use the bathroom. And he said he made a determination in the bathroom that she was going to get hers—that's what he tells me—for insulting him. So at that point he came out, beat her with his fists, raped and sodomized her.

"He leaves from that place and continues on his route delivering groceries." Angela's voice began to rise. "At another place, he steals sneakers from the house. And that person tipped him a dollar. Who knows what would have happened if he hadn't tipped him.

"He eventually copped a plea to four to twelve." Angela reflected. "Listening to him talk, you could tell this boy was angry, and this is how he took out his anger on this woman. That really shocked me, that at that age he could have that kind of anger. He was sixteen, but he was like a little boy. And I'm talking to him, and he was very unemotional about the whole thing, and then said to me at the end, like, 'I'm sorry, sorry I did that.' " Angela paused, then added, "Sorry, but not really."

Angela shook her head, uncomprehending. Fully exposed to debased motivation, she still found it appalling that a person so young could be driven by such naked cruelty. "People do the most terrible things for no reason, I mean really no reason at all."

3

THE GOOD COP MOVES

Frustration has many shapes in the law enforcement business. For the police, there is the pervasive irritation of working within a bureaucratic organization that always seems more concerned with rules, statistics, and risk aversion than with good ideas and initiative. Then, too, there is always the unseen presence of the courts and especially the shadow of the appellate courts up to the Supreme. Remote, unseen, and often dense, judges have the last word. By these detached and unsympathetic figures, the cop's work will be judged and the judgment will be heedless—or so it seems—of the opinions of the police and the street truth as the cops perceive it. Many times I was told, "The system! It just doesn't back us up; we bring them in, but the courts won't put them away."

I was beginning to understand that the core of the problem of frustration—in fact, the essential stress in a cop's identity—is the inescapable sense of helplessness at the heart of power, the maddening inability to make the process work despite all the authority implicit in the badge. The cops have assembled a list of systemic barriers to effective performance and just results: "unrealistic" Supreme Court justices; "timid" prosecutors; "soft" trial judges; neighborhood "liberals"; and, of course, the top-heavy, dull-witted, nearsighted departmental administration. The complaints may be more or less merited, but they all speak of the frustration of wrestling with a system that seems to resist the objective to which the police officer considers himself committed.

Relations with the District Attorney's Office are particularly troublesome. Although the police and the prosecutor are united by a common purpose, the alliance is not always harmonious. Frustrated by the impossibility of their shared objective—to stop crime and to take all criminals out of circulation—and the unavoidable friction between their respective approaches to it, goaded by the inevitable public and media disappointment with their failures in the hopeless endeavor, police commissioners and prosecutors have been known to blame each other.

In the federal system, both the investigative arm (the FBI, for example, the closest thing we have to a federal police force) and the local prosecutorial arm (called a United States Attorney) are attached to the same body, the Department of Justice, and responsive to the same head, the Attorney General. Anatomical coherence tends to foster communication among the parts, though mutual suspicion between the left and the right hands of justice is not unknown even in the federal system. In a state like New York, the Police Department and the District Attorney are entirely separate and independent. The District Attorney is an elected county official, the Police Commissioner is appointed by the Mayor. Their organizational independence, while affording some built in checks and balances, encourages disharmony.

To some small degree, top-echelon recrimination filters down to the troops. But at the front lines, cops and young A.D.A.s intersect often enough that their opinions of one another are usually based on actual experience. Each member of the RIP team speaks well of one or another of the young prosecutors with whom he has had a good relationship. But everyone has also met A.D.A.s who scoffed at the cop's account of the events of the crime ("Oh, come on, Officer. Who's going to believe that the defendant just handed over the gun when you walked up to him and asked for it?"); who disparaged the police investigation ("Maybe, Officer, if you'd *looked* in the garbage cans, we'd *have* that weapon to show to the jury!"); who groaned at perceived weaknesses in a case for which the arresting officer was not responsible ("How do you expect me to try this case? *Your* eyewitness wouldn't be 100 percent sure if you showed him his own mother in a lineup!"); or who disregarded the convenience of the officer or civilian witnesses ("I know you people have been down here twice before and waited all morning, but I'm going to put this down for next week. You'll just *have* to tell your wife to have the baby on another day."). Incidents of this sort do little to improve the cop's appreciation of his prosecutorial partner.

But I encountered an unexpected and more devastating criticism of the New York County Assistant District Attorneys as a group. Considering the usual disparity in age and experience between the detective with six or ten years on the street and a number of courtroom exposures behind him and the fledgling prosecutor, flushed with his new authority but inwardly frightened by his own inexperience, I would have guessed that the standard cop comment on A.D.A.s would be "green." Instead, it was "yellow." Over and over I heard the same complaint: "They're backing away from the tough ones. If they see a problem with a case, they start looking for a way to get rid of it." "These young A.D.A.s want nothing but pop flies. They're thinking too much about that won-lost record." "Just once, I'd like to see one of them meet a challenge by trying a little harder instead of lowering the plea offer."

I've thought about the nature of this criticism. It is not that cops are against plea bargaining. Although they all have favorite stories of inexplicably short sentences in serious cases, cops seem to me quite realistic about the trial weakness of a case, and they readily see the wisdom of settling for a guilty plea calling for a year and four months to four years rather than going to trial to roll the dice for that five-to-fifteen-year stretch.

Rather than a general complaint about light dispositions, I think the criticism of the A.D.A.s must be understood in terms of energy and courage. Although I have never heard a cop use those words in connection with their own work, I have heard a number of them refer to the sudden and unknown dangers of the Job. Every time they draw their guns, fingers lightly curled around the outside of the trigger guard, every time they approach a stopped suspicious-looking vehicle, or knock on a closed door, they must be stepping over some unconscious line of reluctance. The Job, they believe, requires a little extra effort. They feel in their bones that to hold back, to yield to the sense that the prize is not worth the risk, to allow the frustration of fruitless effort to discourage action against the odds, is weakness. And if that attitude encroaches on performance, the result will be indolence and timidity—the enemies of law enforcement. "The good cop moves," Marty Browne once told me. "The guy who'd rather sit on his butt and watch shouldn't be in this line of work."

From the outside, I cannot judge the merit in the cops' perception of the young hands in the prosecutor's office. I do know a few former students in the Office, and I'm certain there are some A.D.A.s whose appetite for the fray is strong, whose judgment is sound, and whose professional energy is high. But it would be understandable if, in that office, the brass chose to allocate its comparatively thin resources to the easy and winnable cases.

It may be true that the upper stratum of the D.A.'s office keeps in touch with the activity of the troops by computer printouts. From this, the inference might be drawn that the courtroom crew try to keep their statistics bright. It is not difficult to imagine a young and eager trial Assistant, then, with a drawer full of indictments and a roomful of incoming complaints, who thinks first of the glamor and the winnability of the matter at hand. Even on a homicide, a long, painstaking, pretrial investigation of a circumstantial case may seem an inefficient trip to an uncertain conclusion.

Arduous, low-visibility, high-risk trials are rarely at the top of the young assistant's triage list.

With good reason, then, the prosecutors often appear to be gun-shy on the tough cases and reluctant in the dreary ones. To the police, this means that many of the A.D.A.s fail to perceive the value of moving energetically and re-sourcefully against the unpromising target. It is not a fail-ure easily forgiven.

In addition, cops frequently have a different take on the "facts" than the authorities further along in the process. The only sort of "truth" recognized by courts and prosecu-tors is distilled from the accounts of witnesses, blended and boiled by adversary devices, and measured against a set of social and psychological assumptions acquired far from the scene of the crime. Prosecutors and judges, like police offi-cers, usually do not have to reach a conclusion on the ulti-mate fact of who did what to whom. But for all who look into the factual brew, the temptation is strong to arrange the ingredients in a rational pattern and lean toward a just re-sult. None of the participants is truly dispassionate all of the time—nor should they be.

Among the referees, the cop believes deep down that he himself is most favorably positioned to perceive the action, understand the behavior of the players, and recognize the dictates of justice. Yet his call on the play is frequently un-heeded. Somehow, the respect by which the cop lives in the street evaporates when he gets downtown. He gets the feel-ing that *he* becomes the suspect; his actions are questioned, his tactical decisions criticized. Clearly in charge up to that point, the cop seems to lose control of the case; his view of the truth no longer prevails; his ability to effect a just reso-lution falters. The payoff on what was often hazardous la-bor is disappointing. The lesson of humility is a hard one for a cop to take, and the reaction to repeated experience with the loss of authority is likely to be frustration and dis-gust.

Marty Browne told me about a case demonstrating that, in fact, police are sometimes in a better position to discern who is telling the truth than the judges or prosecutors remote from the scene. A middle-aged resident of the neighborhood who, Marty told me, "likes his wine" was attracted to a young woman who "hangs around on the street" and invited her to his apartment. She went with him and they had sexual intercourse. Afterward, she asked him for some money. Affronted, he refused, insisting that theirs had been a purely affectionate coupling. She left and sometime thereafter met a young man she knew from the street and told him of the business. He had an idea how to set matters straight and the two perched in front of the wine-drinker's house until he came out. The young man then put a knife to the victim's throat and held him, while the girl enlightened her recent lover by relieving him of his valuables.

Some good police work by RIP located the girl, and she was arrested. The young Assistant District Attorney listened to the basic factual outline for about five minutes. "Doesn't sound like a robbery to me," the prosecutor pronounced. "Besides, he drinks." The case was over, tossed.

Perhaps the prosecutor was voicing with clear prescience the reaction of a Manhattan jury to such a case. Maybe all the jury would have had to hear was the sobriquet "wino" and the acquittal would have been in the bag. But it must also be said that the prosecutor's judgment was formed here on the most superficial impression. If the facts recited to the prosecutor justified the toss, some fairly serious rewriting of the substantive law of crime was being quietly done here, some dangerous class lines were being drawn in the enforcement of the penal law in derogation of basic and cherished principles of equality. As it was, the victim (who showed up in court sober, I was told, in a coat and tie) found himself ignored, cast out of the law's vast concern, the crime against him somehow beneath official cognizance.

At the point of entry of a case into the court system, the Assistant D.A. is generally working on a volume basis with all the crudeness of perception that implies. He or she tends to react to a blend of the superficialities of the case and the preconceptions bred of previous incomplete perceptions.

There is little or no inclination or opportunity to check out details, to look for support or contradiction for the story rendered by the first witness on hand.

By contrast, the RIP persistence, the appetite for yet another detail, usually applied to the pursuit of suspects, can be turned to the verification of the complainant without missing a beat. And the data gleaned, the bases for informed judgment, are unknown or inaccessible even to the most conscientious A.D.A. until much further along in the process, if at all. Prosecutors may be more decisive decision makers, but they are not likely to be better detail checkers. Nor does legal training enhance sensitivity to the nuance of the individual case. It must be deeply offensive to find one's careful calls trumped by hasty assessment, a diligent pursuit nullified by arbitrary rejection.

On top of the debilitating sense of helplessness as he watches the criminal justice system grind out what he often believes are the wrong results, the cop has the unfortunate duty to go back on the streets where the failures of the system are inescapable. To the cop on the street, a criminal case is not a legal issue to be contemplated from an office in the Criminal Court Building. It is an eruption, a disease of the neighborhood he moves through every day. For all his carefully cultivated professional detachment ("Relax, buddy, it's just another case"), many cops suffer the sense that all they do—the risks, the endless hours, the best they can give the Job—makes no difference. "Frustration?" Paddy Rogers once said to me. "Frustration is built into this Job."

4

"I'D KNOW HIM ANYWHERE"

O ne day Officer Paddy Rogers caught a case that looked like a cinch at the start, turned into the most dogged manhunt I ever witnessed, and ended in mystifying frustration.

Before I had ever met him, I had the impression that the most notable trait about Paddy Rogers was his short stature. During my first week with 9 RIP, I noticed a pair of baby shoes pinned to the bulletin board with the legend "Paddy Rogers's boots." Another time, as we climbed into the RIP car, the six-foot-two-inch cop at the wheel found the front seat pulled forward. "Hey!" he exclaimed scornfully as he released it and let it slide back against my knees. "Who's been driving this vehicle—Paddy Rogers?"

Paddy, I soon discovered, is a no-nonsense ex-marine whose private passions are gun collecting, photography, and sport skydiving. He is short, especially among the male cops of his vintage, but he is obviously fit and moves like an athlete. His boyish face is set off by a bristling mustache (standard cop equipment) and short, reddish hair salted with gray. Rogers's style is energetic. He takes the Job seriously and puts a high value on competence. He credits his military service with teaching him the essentials of self-reliance and teamwork that a good police officer should understand. "It was a tremendous experience," Paddy tells me, "if for no other reason than the discipline. It's kept me in good stead all the way down the line." I asked about his combat experience in Vietnam. "Battle is like being involved in battles here on the streets. Let me explain. Being in the military is like being a cop: it's mostly very boring. And then occasionally you have moments of absolutely intense excitement. War is a horrible thing, no two ways about it. But intensely exciting. Working under severe pressure, it gives you confidence.

"I don't mean to imply that every cop should have been in combat," Paddy continued, "but we have cops on the street who have never had any discipline, never had any responsibility for anyone except themselves. They're twenty years old. Most of them are probably still living at home. They've never had a serious job, never even had an automobile. They come on the Job. They're given a gun and a shield and told to go out and do a job. Now they have the ultimate authority: they can take a life. Maybe they watch television too much, which I think is a serious problem by the way, but they have no idea what this Job is really about. You take a kid from East Cupcake, Long Island, and put him down here in the Ninth Precinct—he's got culture shock, severe culture shock. It's a shame."

Rogers's case began with a "push-in" robbery of a middle-aged Hispanic woman in the vestibule of her residence. She was returning home, carrying a small amount of change after buying a quart of milk, when she was accosted by a man who held a knife. When he discovered how little money she had on her person, he told her he would "teach her to have more next time" and slashed her face, cutting her clear through one cheek. Then, crouching over her as she lay bleeding on the floor, he tried to pull a ring from her finger until her screams drove the robber off.

Aside from its unusual cruelty, Paddy's case was also distinguished from the ordinary by the remarkably detailed description furnished by the victim. To Sergeant Browne, who had eighteen or nineteen years of experience, the precision was uncanny. Among other details, the victim told the police that her attacker had a scar about four inches long on his left cheek that looked recent because it had a welt under it. "I'd know him anywhere," she assured Rogers. She also noticed that he wore a belt buckle with the name "Ronnee," in that unusual spelling. This one, Paddy felt, would be a piece of cake.

Robbery—theft by force or intimidation—is regarded by both the law and the citizenry as among the gravest crimes. The range of punishment depends on the crime's degree, which in turn depends on such aggravating features as the infliction of physical injury or the use of a deadly weapon. Punishment also depends on other factors, such as the defendant's prior criminal background, and runs from a minimum of probation without jail to a maximum of somewhere between twelve-and-a-half and twenty-five years behind bars (less up to one-third off for "good behavior"). Three or four years actually served in state prison is about the average punishment for the average knifepoint street robbery tried and convicted before the average judge in New York. Sentence would be lower on a guilty plea and higher if the robber had a prior felony conviction.

The relative severity of the punishment for robbery reflects the general fear of this sort of assault as well as the attendant risk of severe physical injury. Some rare instances of the crime of robbery, much favored by journalists and screenwriters, are carefully planned, complex "capers" posing little real danger to anyone and netting the ingenious criminals a large swag which appears to be nobody's loss. More typically, the crime is committed by a swift, highly threatening act of personal aggression against a lone individual, frequently accompanied by the use or display of a lethal weapon and the forcible removal of a wallet, a purse, items of personal jewelry, or the contents of a cash register or payroll bag. Their primary mission accomplished, it is not unusual for robbers to inflict injury gratuitously or to force a female victim to some loathsome sexual submission. In short, the street predator is the serpent of the cities.

When a robbery victim first encounters a police officer, a brief description of the crime is taken and recorded on one of the many forms by which the NYPD lives. This one, called a "61," was optimistically designed for the rapid recording of a great deal of descriptive data by any rookie in a patrol car by the light of a flashlight. The data, it was hoped, would eventually be stored in a computer bank, which would become a tremendous resource both for future investigations and for statistical study. This promising plan, however, still faces a number of high hurdles, the least of which is technological. For one thing, the basic 61 form, though made out for every arrest, is really not easy to use. As a result, the officer taking the complaint is likely to leave many of the encoded boxes blank and simply record the T/P/O (time and place of occurrence), name and address of the complainant, and a line or two of narrative detail on the event, much the same sort of information that he might put down in his ubiquitous memo book.

That familiar oversize pad, bound in black leather polished shiny by use, much beloved by cross-examining defense lawyers, is, I discovered, an accoutrement of the uniform and is not carried by officers in mufti. If plainclothes cops make notes at all—and I rarely saw it—they do so on scraps of paper and later transfer them to the form on which the progress of the investigation is recorded (theoretically), a form known as a "five." As an old notetaker who distrusts his memory for details, I was surprised to discover that the pen and pad are rarely employed as implements of law enforcement.

The victim of a robbery may come to the small 9 RIP office in any of a number of ways. He or she might walk into the stationhouse to report the crime, get the 61 taken by an officer at the desk, and be sent upstairs to the RIP people. The victim may flag a cop on the street or phone 911 and be brought to RIP by a uniformed officer. Or a RIP team on patrol may come upon the complainant shortly after the crime and take it from there. In any case, the first—and probably the most important—question the cop will ask the victim is: "Did you get a good look at the robber? Do you think you might recognize him if you saw him again?" If the answer is no, the next question is: "Did anyone else see the robbery?" If, as frequently happens, the answer to this one is also negative, the case might as well be closed right there. Unless the robber is picked up on some other crime and confesses to the closed robbery, it is virtually impossible to prove a case without an eyewitness capable of identifying the perpetrator. Even if someone is found in possession of some identifiable proceeds, such as engraved jewelry, a robbery conviction is extremely unlikely—he might have acquired the loot from the perpetrator.

If the victim gives the police some crude identifying features—clothing, race, height, build, perhaps hair color or style—the police have something to go on. At least it might be fruitful to put the complainant in the car and cruise around the neighborhood for a while in the hope of spotting someone matching the description given. It's a long shot, but I have seen it work.

If the complainant tells the police that he or she got a fairly good look at the assailant's face, RIP can bring its major resource into operation. RIP was created around the hypothesis that a substantial number of ordinary street robbers strike repeatedly in the same neighborhood. On this theory, RIP has assembled a collection of photographs of people arrested for robbery in the Precinct. These are the standard PD mug shots: a front and profile color glossy print, sharp and clear. The photos have been assigned code numbers and mounted under plastic leaves in eight or ten ring-binders, filed roughly according to sex and race. In addition, RIP has been building its own photo book of black-and-white Polaroid snapshots of people who for one reason or another have been brought into the House for interrogation and released.

When victims or witnesses indicate to the police officer taking the story that they might recognize their assailant, the books are brought out. I have been told of "direct hits" scored this way, positive identifications made from the photo. But from the dozen or more complainants I saw slowly leafing through the books, patiently studying all those faces, the best the officer got was: "This one looks the most like him" or "It could be this one or possibly that one." When the victim makes a selection, the cops look up the coded number in a large ledger and again ask the witness for an estimate of height, weight, and age. These are compared to recorded data. I remember one fairly good tentative identification where the victim estimated height at five-four or five-five and the person in the photo was six-two. The cops told the victim to try again, but I could tell from the looks they gave one another that they had lost faith in the victim's ability to select the right photo.

If the victim is unable to make a photo ID, the cop will carefully explain that the case is not lost; someone may supply some helpful information, or the perpetrator might be arrested on another, similar offense. A card bearing the telephone number of the 9 RIP and the name of the investigating officer is ceremoniously handed to the complainant, who is asked to phone at any time if he sees the perpetrator on the street again or learns anything about his identity. In most instances, however, when the witness walks out of the RIP office, card in hand, having failed to recognize his attacker's likeness among the photos, the case is closed. It may not be forgotten, and it may be reopened, but the blunt appraisal must be: another "perfect crime."

Thus, the critical first event in the pursuit of a robbery complaint is the ability of the victim to recognize a face in a photograph. If the person is a stranger—as he usually is in a robbery—the mental transposition from live and round to flat and frozen is not always an easy one to make. I may be particularly inept in this respect, but I have seen good, clear photos of persons I had observed at length in the well-lit office of the 9 RIP a day or two earlier and, in the absence of some unusual facial feature, I would not have taken an oath that the photo was of the same person I had seen. I have also been out in a RIP car prowling around the Precinct looking for a person of whom the police had a recent photo. We would have the photo in hand as we scanned the people on the streets, many of whom would stand obligingly still and stare back at us as we slowly passed by. I would see several who might—or might not—have been the person we were seeking. But, at the other end of the spectrum, I heard of an eyewitness who, having had only a fleeting glimpse of her assailant in the dark, picked out of the usual six-photo array the photograph of a man who later admitted his guilt—and between the photo and the crime the robber had shaved off his mustache.

The point of these experiences is simple and obvious but terribly important to the progress of an investigation and its likely outcome. Photo identification is a chancy business. It is extremely difficult for even the most conscientious cop to know just how good the witness's powers of recognition are in a particular case, how deep and significant are her hesitations, how trustworthy is her expression of certainty. And yet the lurking danger of sincere inaccuracy, great as it is, affords no tenable basis on which to discard entirely the procedure or to discount the apparent—and indispensable—information it conveys to the investigators.

"Ronnee's" victim tried, but she could not pick out a photo in any of the several collections she was shown. She was then taken to the police artist, who prepared a drawing from her description. The process, frequently employed when a victim asserts a clear and exact recollection of an assailant's features, has been refined to an impressive technique. The victim is given a variety of facial outlines and sets of individual features to assemble into a face. After the witness selects the closest, the composite is corrected for second thoughts: "No, I think the nose was a bit broader" or "Now that I see it, I remember the hairline was higher." Then the artist shades the drawing in an attempt to unite the assembly into a human likeness. It's a great idea, but I never saw a finished product that looked like the portrait of a real person, nor have I seen an arrest made on the basis of a sketch. Its principal utility, it has often seemed to me, is adverse use by a defense lawyer at trial who tries to impeach identification testimony by showing that the defendant bears little resemblance to the sketch the victim previously had certified as a good likeness of the perpetrator. As usual, the sketch of Ronnee never figured in the chase thereafter. However, with or without it, a major hunt was on in the streets.

All of the men knew whom we were looking for, and regardless of whatever else they were doing, they all participated in the manhunt. When things are slow in the RIP office and one of the cops gets restless, he will turn to one of the others and say, "Feel like taking a ride?" or "C'mon, the streets are jumpin' today. I need a collar." Two of them will sign out one of the two old, beat-up, unmarked police vehicles at RIP's disposal and (often with me in the back seat) go out for several hours of slow cruising through the worst blocks in the Precinct. All of the people on the street, it seems—at least all of those in whom we might be interested—recognize us at once. They stand and stare at us as we pass, affording the cops a good opportunity to examine their cheeks and their belt buckles without leaving the car. Every RIP cop was looking for scars and buckles during that time. The search went on for weeks without result.

Police on patrol, I have noticed, are remarkably observant. Try as I might, I could never get the drop on them. They were always spotting small things that had not registered with me: a person darting around a corner a block away; the outline of a small, heavy object in a nylon bag slung over someone's shoulder; a face looking over the parapet of a roof; a person crouched between two parked cars in the middle of a dark block; a man standing on the corner with one hand open and the other clenched into a fist. (They called him over to the car and asked him what he had in his hand, and when he opened it to disclose a small glassine bag of white powder, they made him drop it down a sewer.) So when one team after another, day after day, failed to spot "Ronnee" on the street, it began to look as though he was not around.

Finally, an idle bit of cop chatter seemed to promise a break in the case. It sometimes seemed to me that one of the most productive investigative techniques in 9 RIP was the incessant talk about open cases. There is not much small talk among the men, only occasional sports comment, rarely personal gossip. The casual conversation in the intimate confines of the RIP office or the car is made up mostly of queries and exchanges about cases in the office. Typically:

"Say, Joey, didn't you lock up a guy called 'Chico' over on Third Street?"

"Yeah. Took a junkie from New Jersey."

"Was he wearing some kind of headband or something?"

"Right. Beads and feathers."

"I just had a complaint. Two male Hispanics. One called the other 'Chico.' He had a headband too. Could be the same guy. How tall was your guy?" Et cetera.

In one such pot stirrer about Ronnee's evaporation, Harry Childs recalled that one of his complainants, while looking through the photo books, had picked out a picture of a person named Ronald as the man who had robbed him on another occasion. Ronald had not yet been picked up. Harry phoned his complainant to ask whether that "Ronnie" or "Ronnee" had a scar. The answer was yes. Now the team had a full name and an address in New Jersey where this Ronald was supposed to be staying with his aunt. But when they checked it out, he was gone. They also traced him to his grandmother's apartment in the housing project in the Precinct. He hadn't been seen there in weeks. The hunt was heating up. RIP cops continued to look for the suspect everywhere, this time with a photo in hand. Still no luck.

Next, the RIP cops began to "deputize" people in the street. Any good investigative bureau runs on information from a variety of field informants. The RIP cops have been developing this resource since the start of their operation. There are many reasons people in the neighborhood give cops helpful tips. Sometimes the informant is a relative, friend, or lover of the suspect motivated by anger, fear, or perhaps the feeling that the person in question should "straighten out." They might even turn him in "for his own good," to protect him from street enemies. Not infrequently, good information comes from people the cops have arrested previously. Oddly enough, many of the RIP cops manage to establish a relationship of mutual civility in the very process of locking the suspect up. Once a tip even came from a convicted felon's brother, who told the police he appreciated the decent treatment they had given his brother when they took him in. I have seen the way the cops keep the friendly relationship alive, showing a benign, watchful interest while inviting cooperation. On every patrol, two or three people—people who have been in the House for one reason or another—will direct a greeting to us; often we will stop at the curb and the individual will come up to the window of the car to exchange pleasantries, rather like a social encounter:

"Hey, Thomas, how's it goin'?"

"Good, Officer, good."

"Working?"

"Sometimes. I help out my uncle in the store."

"Well, you look good. Staying off the junk?"

"Are you kiddin', man?" Mock shock. "I'm so clean I wouldn't even *drink* Coke."

"Way to be." A long look. "Where's your kid brother? We haven't seen him around lately."

"I don't know, Officer. We ain't seen him in a couple of months." Pause. "You lookin' for Floyd?"

"Just wondering why he put himself in the wind, that's all. Well, okay, Thomas. You stay straight, hear?"

"Word." A smile and a wave as we ease away from the littered curb. The cops look at each other; I figure Floyd just went up a notch on some mental list of suspects.

When the cops decided to go public with their hunt for "Ronnee" (a risky step—information flows both ways through street conduits), they asked everyone they knew in the street, anyone brought in for any reason, "You know Ronnee? Seen him around lately?" "Recognize the guy in this photo? Name's Ronnee." To everyone's amazement, not a whisper came back. One day, two of the cops found a woman who said she knew Ronnee. She confirmed the scar, but she could give no other assistance.

Finally, when every resource seemed totally exhausted, on one of the several visits the cops regularly paid to Ronnee's grandmother's apartment in the projects, they found him there. Just sitting there, watching television, as though he didn't even know he was the object of a major manhunt.

Incredulous, the cops stared at Ronnee's cheek. Not a trace of a scar. Their confidence somewhat shaken, they brought him in and stood him in a lineup. The victim looked at him and said, "Nope. Not him."

Paddy Rogers, the officer in charge of the case, shook his head. "We're back to square one," he said simply. But it was grim; the unit had been hunting down the wrong man. The disappointment was a discouraging portent of the eventual failure of the investigation. To Paddy, however, a case with a decent opening lead never becomes insoluble because of a false turn; it just takes a bit longer. He simply refused to acknowledge what had become painfully clear to me: even extraordinary persistence and a little luck can never make a case when recognition fails.

5

THE FALLIBLE FACULTIES: DESCRIPTION AND RECOGNITION

It may seem odd at first that robbery is such a difficult crime to "solve." Unlike most crimes, it is most often committed in open, public places and usually without precautions or a plan of escape. Surprisingly, most street robbers do not even bother to conceal their features, though swift action and darkness frequently serve as mask enough. And detection should be still easier because robbers often strike repeatedly in the same neighborhood. Yet the truth is that in most cases in which the robber disappears after the crime (as he most often does), an arrest, backed by good and substantial evidence, is cause for celebration.

The simple reason for the common success of this crime becomes apparent after a few weeks in the RIP office and is readily verified from our ordinary experience. Most people, particularly when under severe stress, do not obtain an accurate or durable impression of the facial features or identifying characteristics of strangers. More than once I heard a recent victim answer an officer's question about the physical appearance of his or her assailant with a rueful "I was too busy watching his finger on the trigger to take much notice of his face."

The success of a robbery investigation usually depends entirely on the victim's ability to describe and recognize the perpetrator. Occasionally, a robber will leave behind a calling card. For example, a payroll robbery once came into 9 RIP in which the fleeing gunman dropped from the backpack he was carrying some books (for a "cosmetology" course he was taking) containing his name and address and a crude map of the area of the robbery. But fortuitous evidence of this sort or other objective traces are rare indeed. The sudden thrust of violence on the isolated target, followed by the predator's quick withdrawal, generally leaves behind no evidence but the impression it makes on the mind of the victim.

The description and recognition components of identification are, of course, related in some fashion to the mysterious process we call *memory*. Psychologists have studied with care the elusive processes of perception and recollection, along with the influence of such factors as emotional excitement, cross-racial familiarity, post facto suggestion, and the like. But we all know from experience that individuals vary greatly in their ability to retain the visual image of a stranger's face. In our own lives are instances of long and clearly recalled recognitions and embarrassing obliterations. Yet it is upon just such uncertainties of memory that a robbery investigation normally depends. And the worst of it is that in some instances no one—not even the complainant—can be sure whether the expressed identification of the perpetrator is based on an accurate recollection or on an honest error of memory, hidden by careless confidence. Unfortunate as it is to lose a felon by reason of the victim's lack of talent for facial recognition, it is much worse to set the process in motion against the wrong person owing to a false positive identification.

As I thought about the problem of facial recognition, I could identify several distinct components that combine to produce a compound difficulty so formidable that it becomes surprising to encounter an unequivocal and correct identification. First, the witness must have the skill of perception to notice identifying characteristics. Some people, even those who are fairly adept at recognition, just don't seem to pick up human features in isolation. My wife recently noticed for the first time that a friend's dark-haired son, a grown boy whom we have known since his birth, is not blond. "I guess he has always seemed a blond type," she explained, "whatever that is."

In addition to skill, registering identifying characteristics usually requires a conscious effort of will. Most of us must pause and instruct ourselves to remember a stranger's appearance. We must concentrate and search the person's features for unusual or memorable traits—drooping eyelids, perhaps, or a dark mole on the side of the nose. We must recite to ourselves a catalog of ordinary traits and memorize them: about five feet eight or nine, maybe a hundred and fifty or sixty (not easy judgments for some of us), clean shaved, a short haircut but long in back, broad nose, blue eyes. If we don't go through this recital with our subject in view, it is surprisingly difficult to do it later from the mental "photograph" we attempt to summon up while being interviewed. I have seen otherwise articulate and perceptive people shake their heads in embarrassment to admit that they just couldn't picture whether the robber had a mustache, wore an earring, etc. But it takes a cool and purposeful head to run down the checklist of recognition traits immediately after being pounced on and shown the blade of a knife.

In addition to registering the vital characteristics, a witness is asked to describe them. For many of us, the power of description does not go much beyond "sort of funny looking," or "cute," or perhaps "he looks something like Uncle George when he was younger." Even for those of us who take pride in the detail with which we can describe the furnishings of a room or the features of a landscape, the challenge of facial description is overwhelming. Just try to render a description of a person whose face you know fairly well such that someone who does not know the person

might recognize her or him in a crowd. Of course, if the
subject is thin, over six feet four, bald, with a gray beard
and horn-rims, you might stand a chance. But a useful verbal description of most "average-looking" people is almost
impossible. How many times have the cops heard, "Brown
hair, medium height, medium weight, medium build, ordinary looking"? At best, the description will eliminate the
extremes. But the cops need it to point to someone in particular.

For some people, like my wife, weaknesses of perception
or description are well compensated for by remarkable powers of recognition. I'm convinced this ability is innate. Even
in an altered context or long after the last encounter, my
wife will frequently match a person with some deeply
stored inner impression and may instantly pull from memory the full story, still rich in detail. Other people, however,
(and I am in this sorry group) find failure of recognition,
even of those we once knew quite well, a persistent social
stumbling block. So where the verbal skills are not up to
reconstruction of a face, some witnesses will easily pick out
a photo. But others, like me, might find even that talent
lacking. Inescapably, my thoughts conclude, the success of
law enforcement in capturing a street robber depends in
large measure on a mental process that often disappoints
our most urgent command for performance.

One afternoon I was watching a middle-aged Hispanic
woman slowly turn the pages of RIP's collection of mug
shots, her arm and hands freshly bandaged to conceal the
cuts she had received trying to fend off the knife attack of a
robber. She was silently shaking her head and shrugging
her shoulders at the legions of young black faces, front and
profile, mocking her from the leaves of the book in front of
her. Dozens of them must have looked something like her
attacker, but she recognized none. "I'm sorry, Officer," she
would mumble apologetically from time to time, "I just
don't remember so good."

"Let me ask you something, Professor." Harry Childs,
one of the RIP officers, broke into my reverie. "Can we use

hypnosis to help people like Mrs. Hernandez remember better?"

"Dangerous, Harry," I said. "Very dangerous."

"I don't see why," Childs persisted. "I read where people really never forget anything, it just gets buried somewhere in the brain. It's really amazing what these hypnotists can get people to remember: what day of the week they had their seventh birthday party, the telephone number of some friend from high school they haven't thought about for twenty years, stuff like that."

"We could use some of that in this business," Rocco Regina offered, getting interested. "I can't even get most of my witnesses to remember what the mope was wearing during the stickup. And the guy was looking right at him in a well-lighted place."

"That's what I mean," Harry said, gaining enthusiasm for the idea. "Facial marks, tattoos. If there were three or four perps working together, what names they called each other. With information like that, we'd have a shot at picking somebody up."

"And it would improve the evidence in court, too," Harry said. "If you were the D.A., wouldn't you like to have a witness who could remember the details of the crime, what the perps were wearing, who said what—all the little things they always forget? That's evidence, right?" The ball was in my court.

"Not all evidence is evidence," I began cautiously. "As you know, there's a lot of good information out there that might lead you to your perp or sew up your case, but the jury will never hear about it."

"You mean like all that proof the judges keep out because of the exclusionary rule?"

"That too," I agreed quickly, not wanting to be drawn into a defense of the Supreme Court decisions excluding evidence obtained in violation of a person's constitutional rights. "But how about the confession of some other perp that gives up the guy you're looking for? Or the word on the street that your informant passes along to you? That's good information to you, but we didn't need the Supreme Court to tell us it's not evidence to the jury."

"But this is different," Harry insisted. "What the guy remembers under hypnosis would be testimony from the witness himself, on the stand under oath, with all the trimmings."

Harry Childs was right, of course. Hypnotically enhanced recollection is different—but it's also the same. My point was only this: though we assert that our juries decide a case on "all the evidence," we actually prevent them from considering some information good enough to be acted on in apprehending a felon and good enough for most people in their ordinary daily decisions. The usual reason that the rules of evidence conceal facts from the fact finder is that the datum is somehow unreliable, immune from our usual forensic test of weight, and may appear to the jury as stronger than it really is. Hypnotically enhanced recollection is a particularly troublesome example.

On the one hand, Harry had a good point. The evidence coming from the recollection of a witness, subject to cross-examination in the presence of the jury, is the very essence of legal proof. And the dim recollection of any witness may be revived by almost any suggestion or exposure without detracting from the acceptability of the testimony, so long as the witness swears that his or her recital comes from genuine recollection. Of course, the evidence may be challenged as a mere construct, fabricated out of the hints and prods of counsel and unworthy of belief. But whether or not to credit the witness's claim of actual, albeit refreshed, recollection is among the classic questions for the jury to decide.

Knowing this and having learned, as Harry had, the wonders of hypnosis in the retrieval department, I had thought, as a young D.A., that I had come upon the greatest aid to effective prosecution since the subpoena. But I soon discovered one of those strange areas of conservative suspicion one encounters from time to time in law. Without logic or reason, judges shy away from some datum or device in common and trusted use elsewhere in our complicated affairs. The "verdict" of the polygraph is another good example of the law's stubborn rejection of data many other respectable enterprises find worthy of consideration.

Without formal policy, or even the customary sort of fact finding on which judges commonly insist before making a ruling, courts are spooked by hypnosis. By invoking "common knowledge" (that is, bits of this and that picked up from here and there), judges have found that the process of hypnosis puts the subject in a highly suggestible state of mind in which memory might be altered and false data inserted into the mind's recall mechanism. Moreover, the technique allows this to be done so subtly that after subjects are returned to a normal waking state, the graft is undetectable even to the subjects themselves. Thus, not only is the material recovered from the witness under hypnosis untrustworthy, but some courts have held that, because of the invisible post-hypnotic effect, all subsequent products of the memory are suspect, and cross-examination is irremediably impaired.

I fully appreciate the danger that a witness, while ostensibly testifying from recollection, might actually convey artificially implanted data that would be strangely immune to the ordinary challenge of cross-examination. But I found it hard to explain to Harry and Rocky why the hypnotically "refreshed" recollection is any different from recollection otherwise refreshed or why the jury, carefully informed of the dangers of post-hypnotic sincerity, is not fully equipped to credit or discount the testimony as the circumstances may warrant. After all, there may be cases where the witness's testimony, though hypnotically "enhanced," is corroborated by other evidence and entitled to the full force of unaided recollection. Suppose, for example, that the victim, during and after hypnosis, recalls that one of her assailants had a butterfly tattooed on his left shoulder and he addressed the other robber as "Rambo." Then suppose the police, acting on this information, arrest the two defendants. The one with the tattoo is wearing the victim's en-

graved ring on a chain around his neck, and his buddy—
known as "Rambo"—makes a full confession which is excluded from evidence on *Miranda* grounds. Is there any
sound reason to exclude the testimony of the witness, on the
stand under oath, that she now remembers distinctly the
identifying mark on the first man and the nickname by
which the second was addressed? Maybe this hypothetical
case is easier than many, but it seems to demonstrate that a
flat rule of preclusion is unwise.

"Well," said Harry Childs, grasping my rather lame explanation, "I guess that means we can't use any hard evidence we find as a result of what the guy says under hypnosis? What do you call it—'fruit of the poisoned tree,' right?"

"Not necessarily," I hedged. "I don't think the courts
have gone that far."

"But I thought if we couldn't use the testimony as evidence we can't use it as a way of getting other evidence
either," Rocky put in. "Isn't that part of the exclusionary
rule?"

"Right," I allowed. "But not every piece of evidence excluded in court is excluded by *the* exclusionary rule. Hearsay is normally excluded, but that doesn't mean that a piece
of evidence you discover as a result of something someone
says someone else told him is itself inadmissible. And since
there's nothing wrong with hypnosis as such, I don't think a
court would reject good proof simply because the police
learned about it from an hypnotically enhanced recollection."

"So does that mean that if I put some eyewitness in hypnosis and he suddenly comes up with the license number of
the getaway car, for example, and I chase down the vehicle
and find the loot in the trunk, the D.A. can put the loot in
evidence?"

"Provided you had a warrant or some other good reason
to search the car, yes. At least, I don't think a court would
keep it out merely because of the hypnosis that produced the
original information."

"Okay, if you say so. But sometimes I get the feeling the

courts are playing three-card-monte with these ideas,'' Harry said.

"I know what you mean," I said.

Mrs. Hernandez had finished the last book without success, and Harry now turned back to her, handed her the RIP card, and patiently explained that there was nothing more the police could do unless something lucky turned up. As she got up and slowly gathered her belongings, Harry tossed me a wide grin and added, "At least I now know what you do for a living, Rich: standing up in front of your class and pretending this stuff makes sense."

6

INFORMATION, JUST INFORMATION

I t's hard to say where police pick up the bits and pieces of intelligence that sometimes combine to make a case, or how good cops remember, retrieve, and react to all the information that comes their way. I have seen them solicit fragments of street gossip with seemingly idle curiosity, and I have been around when highly specific tips came in on pending investigations. Often the material is gathered in encounters unrelated to the case in which they prove useful. Of course, not all information is good information, and sometimes the wires bring in contradictory or otherwise erroneous leads that serve only to confuse and delay the investigation.

I was surprised one day when I saw Sergeant Browne, the RIP commanding officer, hand the mug books over to two bored and sullen young women as they sat shackled to each other in the small RIP office awaiting transportation to the central booking facility. But for the sneer and the pout they affected, they were rather pretty—about seventeen or eighteen, I guessed. They had been arrested, along with a muscular, good-looking boy of about the same age, immediately after robbing an elderly Chinese man in Tompkins Square Park. The cops joked that the arrest had followed so closely on the crime that even a Chinese victim could not avoid becoming a complainant. Silently, the trio smoked cigarettes, occasionally flinging a defiant glare at any cop who looked their way. The boy, his wrists manacled in front of him, lifted both hands awkwardly to take the cigarette from his lips. I could almost hear our prisoners growl. It was not until later that we learned that one of the girls was thirteen and pregnant; the other, fourteen, had a baby at home.

When I took a walk down the hall with Harry Childs, he told me that the group, and the male in particular, was an ugly lot. The boy was wanted as the fifth member—and perhaps the leader—of a marauding group of young men, four of whom had already been arrested and admitted to a recent series of armed robberies, assaults, and rapes. They had implicated our Tompkins Square holdup man. "Make no mistake," Harry Childs put it, shaking his head, "this one has an attitude. I mean a real attitude." Surly, hostile, and resentful, I discovered, is the attitude that earns the description *an attitude*.

I got a sample of the problem Harry had alluded to when I heard the male suspect (who had denied all charges up to that point) assert self-righteously to one of the RIP cops that he attacked only white people, avenging his brother's stabbing by some white assailant two or three years earlier. Though I could feel my hackles rise a centimeter or two, the police let this disclosure pass without reaction. All experienced cops know that confessions rarely come without some element of self-justification. Even the most vicious predator apparently needs to cloak his conduct in the mantle of virtue, to claim for himself the justice function (setting things right by avenging some supposed wrong) or the role of victim (if not the victim of his victim, then the victim of society or "the system"). At the very least, the confessing malefactor asserts the ethic of the group ("I only did what everybody else is doing"). It seems that only the deeply neurotic person is morally strong enough to admit to evil in his own nature.

When I saw Browne hand over the big, black ringbinders containing the RIP collection of mug shots to these three young suspects, I thought it was just a casual gesture of friendly courtesy, like a receptionist offering magazines to people waiting in a doctor's office. I soon discovered Marty had other reasons.

The transformation of our guests was dramatic. The three—who had, incidentally, steadfastly denied even knowing one another—immediately became a group of high school chums laughing over their friends' pictures in the yearbook. Each page was turned with glee, each of the many photos they recognized got a little description: "Hey, that's my aunt's old man! Ain't he the baddest?" "Look, there's Chinko. He's chilling out now." "What do you know. They got Blueboy. Wait'll Junior hears this."

As the mood relaxed and conversation became more open, we were treated to some samples of our prisoners' social philosophy. One of the girls turned to the sergeant and addressed him directly for the first time: "Hey, my whole family's in here. What are you trying to do, lock us all up?"

The other girl agreed. "The cops are putting all the poor people in jail," she said.

"If you didn't go around robbing people," Browne replied, "we wouldn't be trying to lock you up."

"Look, I got to buy Pampers for my baby," one of the girls said irritably. "Where am I going to get the money? Tell me that."

"Have you ever thought of getting a job like the honest people do?" the sergeant asked.

"No way! I been looking for a job. I have a friend been looking for work for two years. Man, there are no jobs. Not for us. Who would hire us?" She paused, amused at her own insight. "Would you?"

"Maybe that depends on what kind of work you're willing to do," Browne said. "Anyway, Welfare gives you money to take care of your kid, don't they?"

"Welfare?" said the girl with a short laugh. "I'm too young to go on welfare."

The other girl was still looking through the photo book. "Hey, there's Angelo!" she exclaimed. "He used to be my old man. They got him upstate now. Some judge gave him fifteen years or something." Then, turning to the sergeant, she asked angrily, "What right does that judge have sending that boy away?"

"He committed a crime, didn't he?"

"God will punish him if he did wrong. That's not for the judge to do. It's for God."

The first girl added, "God will punish the judges who send us to jail."

"Wait a minute," the sergeant said. "Didn't you just point to a photo and tell me that dude had been murdered and someone should punish the guy who blew him away?"

"Yeah. But I didn't mean the police."

Thrusting out his manacled wrists, the boy joined the conversation: "And God will punish the people who put these things on other people."

The matter was dropped.

Later I asked Marty Browne why he had given these people the photo books to examine. He said he thought he might pick up some information concerning nicknames that might prove helpful in the future; possibly a grudge might prompt a significant disclosure. "Information, just information," he said. "That's what we live on here. Most of it goes down the drain of course. But, who knows, it might be just what we need to make the pieces fit."

I thought I saw another benefit. "Maybe these people will convince their friends that with their photos on file here, they're sitting ducks." Marty agreed. Word would travel back to the streets—it always does. Maybe some predator might think twice before pointing a blade if he knows his victim will come straight up to our office and look through a book containing a good, clear, color photograph of him, front and profile. As Browne knew well, while capture and conviction are the daily mission, deterrence is the object.

In another case I recall, information seemed to come in from all angles and with conflicting impact. Every few nights, a cab would be directed to the same spot—the service road alongside the FDR Drive, just to the east of the Projects—where the driver would be robbed at knifepoint by a man who then fled into the Projects. Joey Dean was our expert in cab stickups. He had once driven a taxi in his off-duty hours, had been held up, and subsequently was briefly assigned to the Police Department "taxi squad" to try to catch the guy who had robbed him. He told me that a cab robber never hails a cruising taxi; he stations himself at a spot where cabs discharge passengers. Before he chooses his target, the robber wants to get a good look at him; if the driver seems like a pushover, the robber slips in behind the alighting passenger. "Of course," Joe allows, "sometimes they make mistakes. It's not the smartest move in the world to stick up a cab with a cop at the wheel."

Our guy was choosing his cabs at a lot of different places and was looking over his drivers pretty carefully. Our complainants were mostly foreign and often uncooperative. But the perpetrator was making one mistake. He was doing all the robberies in the same location. Everyone knew what our next move had to be: a stakeout. A van was borrowed from Central Robbery, and the men discussed at length precisely where it should be parked and who would sit on the plant. I think the whole team would have gone if the Sergeant had not ruled that two men had to stay behind to mind the store. The team went out (without me) and sat and waited in the back of that small van from about 4 P.M. until Tommy Longobardi finally gave up about 6 the next morning. The robber didn't hit during the night, but about three hours after the stakeout was abandoned, he struck again at the same spot. Joe Dean, apparently inured, was more amused than sore as he told me about the near miss.

Meanwhile, one of the victims told the cops that the man who robbed him had gotten into his cab on Fourteenthth Street and Broadway carrying some freshly cleaned clothes. So RIP checked all the dry-cleaning stores around Fourteenth and Broadway armed with nothing but a description of the stick-up man and a hunch that he lived in the Projects near the drive. They came up with a name and address of a man fitting the description who had picked up cleaning on the day of the robbery: Merrick Wilson on Avenue D.

At about the same time, they got another name, Lucas Jones, from an anonymous phone tip. I was not at the office the day they had Lucas Jones come in, but Joe Dean told me he knew the moment he set eyes on him that they had the wrong guy. "He was too laid-back," Joe told me. "Stickup guys are more nervous, more energetic types. This guy is so lazy, he can't do anything but pick up those good ol' welfare checks."

I asked how they had gotten Jones to come into the House. They knew that they couldn't go out and arrest him on a dropped dime. Besides, they didn't really want to arrest him at that point; they figured if he wasn't under arrest, they could "interview" him without giving him *Miranda* warnings. With the weak and contradictory stories of the cabdrivers, the cops really would have liked to get a solid confession from the suspect himself. I expressed my doubts about getting a usable admission from a person in custody in the House without advising him of his right to silence. Rich Abbinanti asked why they should have to give the warnings when the person comes in "voluntarily." He and Tommy Wray both thought the warnings would reduce their chances of learning anything useful from the suspect. The discussion was academic; Lucas Jones said nothing incriminating and was allowed to leave shortly after he arrived.

As the complaints of taxi robberies kept coming in—six or more before it was over—two other good pieces of information came with them. In one case, the driver thought he recognized the man who held him up. "Oliver Jackson," he told us. "I know him, he lives in the Projects." I was excited. The perfect complainant. "Hold it," Marty Browne advised. "That's the good news. The bad news is the driver won't sign a complaint."

Another driver was a Russian immigrant. "I don't think he'll be much help," Dean told me. "He never got a real good look at the guy. But you know, it's a funny thing. He told me it was Oliver Jackson too."

"Don't tell me this perp chose another cabbie who knew him," I said, beginning to wonder.

"He's not that dumb," Joe said. "But right after the perp ran into the Projects, some woman comes up to the cabbie all excited and tells him that she's seen the whole thing and the guy who robbed him was named Oliver Jackson."

"Well, that's something," I said.

"Nah," Joe shook his head. "The cabbie didn't get her name or anything. We'll never find her."

"You still have his story of what she said."

"Wouldn't that be hearsay?" Joe asked.

"It certainly would," I replied. "But there are about twenty-seven exceptions to the rule against hearsay evidence, and this might be one of them." Joe Dean still remembers going down to the Assistant D.A., Zack Chaffee, and proudly telling him that his case was one of the twenty-seven exceptions to the hearsay rule. But the D.A. wasn't buying it and Jackson was never charged with that robbery either.

I was with a group of RIP cops when they went out and, without incident, brought both Merrick Wilson and Oliver Jackson into the RIP office for a lineup. I watched four or five of the cabdrivers, one at a time, walk up to the window and view the same lineup. No one gave Merrick Wilson a second look. But we had a couple of hits on Jackson.

Some time later, while Jackson's case was pending, I got a call from a man who identified himself as Jackson's lawyer. He wanted to call me as his witness at a hearing to examine the fairness of the lineup procedure at which Jackson had been identified. Oddly enough, this was to be the only time I would be required to testify in court about events I had witnessed while I was with 9 RIP. And it turned out to be something of a joke. My testimony was, contrary to Jackson's position, that the police procedure had been meticulously fair. The wonder was that Chaffee, the Assistant District Attorney, did not call me as his witness. But if the defense wanted my testimony, they were entitled to it.

After checking my sketchy notes and comparing recollections with the officers, I went to court and took the oath in what I hoped was a suitably confident manner, while acutely conscious of the dim and blank spots in my memory. I glanced over at Jackson and noted that he had become a Muslim while in jail awaiting trial and had perfected the Felon's Glower, a stare of intense, albeit bridled, loathing with which prisoners in court often fix the witnesses against them, as if by sheer force of hostility they can shake the case against them. I shifted my attention to the lawyer who had begun to examine me.

Jackson's lawyer was far more uncomfortable than I. He never seemed to decide what testimony he wanted from me. His questions were inarticulate and unfocused. They were easily answered, and the answers were never helpful to his client's case. His nervousness, sadly evident when he repeatedly addressed me as "Officer" or "Detective," was aggravated by the judge, who frequently interrupted, in a voice brimming with disgust and impatience, often shouting (there was no jury at this stage), "I'm still waiting to find out why you called the professor, counsel! Please, get on with it!"

Jackson lost his motion and was duly convicted of robbery. Much later, Joe Dean—perhaps to assure me that out of all the leads, all the conflicting and uncertain information, we had gotten the right man—told me, "It's a funny thing, but since Jackson went away, we can't *make* a cab job happen in this precinct."

"We do make mistakes," Hiram Gonzalez conceded with a smile as we drove slowly around the precinct one summer day. Affable and relaxed by nature, Gonz was quick and energetic in action. A tough kid from a tough neighborhood, he wondered whether the Department would approve his moonlighting ambition: to sell cut flowers from a vendor's cart in Spanish Harlem. "Not very often, but occasionally we do make mistakes."

"What kind of mistake?" I wanted to know.

"We get bad information, or at least we don't get the good stuff until it's too late."

"And you move on the wrong guy?" I asked.

"Right. But it's a funny thing how these things work out sometimes."

I asked him for an explanation. Gonz made a U-turn and drove back a few blocks. Soon he stopped at the curb and pointed out a tall, thin, good-looking young man wearing red shorts standing on the corner.

"Take a good look at him," Gonz told me. "Now look at that other guy sitting on the steps near him—the guy in the brown shorts." I looked closely at both of them. They were about the same age, same color, height, and build. Both had well-cut, wavy brown hair and neatly trimmed mustaches.

"Look alike?" Gonz asked as we turned the corner and drove on. "Let me tell you a little story. Remember that sixteen-year-old girl who got killed over on Eighth Street last year? Hit by a stray bullet during a drug shoot-out?"

I remembered reading about it.

"Well, the guy in the red shorts, he's the one who got locked up for it. He was tried and found not guilty. And you know why? Because he didn't do it. All the people on the street started telling me, 'Hey, Gonz, you got the wrong one. It's the other one who did it, man, the one who looks just like him.' Well, after the wrong guy was acquitted, there was no way the other guy could be prosecuted, right?"

I agreed. The eyewitnesses had testified that Red Shorts did it. The prosecution could not put them on the stand at a second trial to testify under oath that, on reconsideration, they had decided it was really Brown Shorts who did it. Defense counsel would have a picnic, and no jury would believe them. It's a well-known rule: the D.A. better be right the first time—there's no second chance.

"So," Gonz concluded, "there they are, side by side on the street. No hard feelings either way."

"What if Red Shorts had been convicted," I asked, "facing a real heavy sentence? Would one of his informants have come forward and said, 'This man's innocent. Brown Shorts did it'?"

"Are you kidding?" Gonz turned and looked at me incredulously. "If he'd been convicted, the people would have just let him go away. You know why? Because they say he did three other people, so he owes one. Even if it's the wrong one."

Obviously, there was more the people on the street knew than would ever find its way into a court of law.

7

THE COP'S NOSE

Police hunches are familiar to readers of detective-story fiction, and they are not unknown in the literature of famous cases. The police themselves regard the hunch as an indispensable item of equipment on the Job. When asked why he approached the man carrying a gun and a load of narcotics in a vanity case, or why he stopped the car in which the escaping robbers were riding, a cop may say something like, "I had a feeling; it just didn't smell right." Rocky Regina, for example, prides himself on the sensitivity of his nose; he believes he can sense a crime in the making or a felon in his presence.

Among police in general, I have noticed a professional confidence in the deduction that is not always justified by the scent itself. They do not always take full account of the uncertainties of life or give due deference to odd twists of causation. Much of their reasoning is founded on the faith that the likely cause is the actual cause and that the common connection is ineluctable. A police officer will tell me with absolute certainty that a white couple emerging from a van with Jersey plates is looking to cop drugs. A Hispanic-looking adolescent standing in a doorway is the steerer for a drug-selling operation down the street. And so forth. Most of the time, the cop's surmise is correct. Sometimes it is wrong. But these errors are never taken as evidence of the fallibility of surmise. They are simply disregarded, and the professional confidence in the likely explanation remains unshaken. Along with sharp observation and accumulated experience, this characteristic causal reasoning is a useful attribute in investigation where one is always playing the odds.

I suspect, however, that this vaunted "sixth sense" is less uncanny than popular belief has it, less mysterious than the cops themselves think it is. Often it is merely a convenient cover for failure of articulation. I have pressed cops to explain just why they "smelled" trouble, and they were usually able to supply some perfectly reasonable, though perhaps tenuous, basis for their hunch: "Everyone else stood still and looked straight at me; this dude turned and walked away without looking back." Or: "He was running with one hand stuck in his pocket. Now you don't run with your hand in your pocket, do you? Unless you're holding on to something heavy in there, right?"

Paddy Rogers gave me a good example of the articulated hunch. To a devoted believer in the "nose," Paddy would seem to have perfected a truly canine ability to sniff out illegal handguns. Almost as a diversion from his assigned duties, Paddy and his partner had made over 100 arrests in a year just by walking up to people in the street and plucking pistols out of their clothing. He told me that his hit rate was on the order of 97 percent. Especially interested in guns, Paddy appeared to have a remarkable nose in his subspecialty. But when I asked him how he did it, Paddy claimed no powers of divination. Perhaps because of his straightforward nature, perhaps because he had been asked so often on the witness stand to explain his moves, Paddy described his method in prosaic terms.

Rogers had been promoted to sergeant sometime after my departure from 9 RIP and, during the period in question, was assigned to the Central Robbery unit. As in most police posts, there were slow days. Inaction made Paddy restless, so he and his partner, Greg Modica, would sign out a typical unmarked police vehicle and drive up to the "Three-Four," the Thirty-Fourth Precinct, where, Paddy told me with what I assume was rare exaggeration, four out of five men standing on the street have illegal guns tucked in their waistbands. "You take someone's parking space up there," Paddy said seriously, "you're likely to get shot through the head."

He explained his routine operation. He and Greg would slowly cruise the neighborhood, eyeing the men standing idly along the sidewalks. "Let's not kid ourselves, they knew who we were. Two white guys in a Dodge Dart—we might as well have had the red lights flashing on the roof." Paddy continued, "We were watching their hands, waiting for someone to make the move." He gave me a demonstration. Standing, he made an almost imperceptible motion with his hand as though gently pulling down the front of a shirt or jacket over his belt. "They always do it," he explained. "Just making sure it's covered when they see us looking at them. It's involuntary. But it's all the tip-off we need. We jump out and walk up to him fast. 'Police. Do you have anything on you that could hurt me?' 'Only the gun, Officer.' 'Don't touch it.' We grab it, put the cuffs on him, and that's it."

It sounded absurdly simple. I asked if that was the invariable pattern. "Once or twice I think we found the gun in a holster, and a couple times we took it off a person who was waving it around. Of course, we've found guns in cars a number of times." I asked how the car search worked. "Well," Paddy said, "sometimes we pull the car over. Of course, we have to have a reason for that," he added, "but that's not hard; in the Three-Four, most of the cars have something wrong: a taillight out, the wrong sticker on the windshield, license plate missing, something. But a lot of times, we just pull up next to them and look at them. When one of them does the dance, we know we've got something."

"The dance?" I asked.

"Yeah. It's really comical. They must think we're blind or

stupid." He showed me, squirming in his seat and ducking over from the waist.

"It's obvious. They're trying to hide something in the upholstery or under the seat. Then it's just a matter of asking them to step out of the vehicle, reaching in, and recovering the weapon, or whatever it was they didn't want us to see."

I found Paddy's description of his method completely convincing, and the high hit rate he claimed, as well as the actual arrest numbers, demonstrated that he and Greg were aiming their moves with care. At the same time, it must be said that recitals like Paddy's, made from the witness stand at motions to suppress evidence, raise judicial eyebrows. The authority of a police officer to stop a suspicious person on the street and frisk him for weapons, approved by the Supreme Court in *Terry v. Ohio*, has been abused by some cops; and, in some cases, police officers fabricate the suspicious circumstances to cover arbitrary searches. It's one of those inscrutable perplexities in court, where it is almost impossible to distinguish the sharp eye of a cop like Rogers from the artful tongue of another officer who claims the same perceptions.

I knew Paddy Rogers was not a person who avoided risks, but it seemed to me he was volunteering for dangerous duty. "You chose a hazardous sideline," I offered. "You could get killed."

"Not if it's done right," said Paddy. "Let's not kid ourselves, the object of this Job is to go home every night."

Tommy Wray, another RIP officer, pursued a protracted investigation on a hunch that yielded no objective verification whatsoever and little more in the way of articulated grounds for suspicion. Though based mainly on a feeling, Tommy's confidence was as complete as Paddy's.

The case began with an armed holdup of a take-out Chinese food place over on the eastern edge of the Precinct. As in many local stores, the employees worked behind a bullet-proof Plexiglas partition. A small opening allowed the servers to pass packages to customers and receive the cash. When a gun was thrust through the opening one day, the server handed over the contents of the cash register without protest. As the robber was leaving the store, for reasons the police never learned, he turned and fired two shots at the opening in the transparent partition. Both bullets lodged chest high in the plastic, one of them about an inch and a half from the opening. Fortunately, no one was hurt.

Wray went back to the scene of the shooting several times to talk to the proprietor and the other witnesses. This was no simple matter, since none of them spoke or understood English. In fact, we were never certain whether they were Chinese or Korean, and although we tried, we were unable to come up with an interpreter from within the Department. Our only interpreter was a jovial, rotund Asian gentleman who—presumably summoned by the owners—suddenly appeared as we stood in the clean, spacious kitchen helplessly trying to communicate in Basic English with anyone who would flash us a sign of comprehension. Our volunteer materialized in a bright orange jogging suit and affably lifted the jacket at once to reveal a police revolver in a holster at his belt. He proudly told us he had once used the gun to capture two men who were robbing a restaurant in which he was dining. He described himself as the owner of a liquor store in the neighborhood and related somehow to the proprietor of the take-out place. Wray was so glad to see him and obtain his services that he accepted without question the man's assurance that he had a license for the gun and asked him nothing whatever about himself.

Although our interpreter was less than perfectly fluent in English, we were able to ask the people in the place a few important questions. Tommy wanted to know who was standing where and who had seen the face of the robber. But more important, 9 RIP had heard from a neighboring store owner that someone from the "Chink joint" had chased the robber into the street with a gun. As Tommy had explained to me, this fact had probably been omitted because the gun was unlicensed and the proprietor might not be a citizen. He also reminded me of the usual reticence of Chinese witnesses. So now, through our seemingly helpful interpreter, Wray sought to reassure his witnesses that the police were not interested in making trouble for the victims of the stickup, but the proprietor insisted that he had pursued the fleeing felon into the street brandishing only the meat cleaver from the kitchen. A deck of photos was also exhibited to each employee, to no avail.

Tommy Wray and I declined a tempting sample of the establishment's wares (not easy for Wray, whose legendary appetite is aroused by wilted and forgotten half-sandwiches and ossified "donuts") and got back into our car. "Seems like a decent guy," Tommy said, when I asked what he thought about our orange-suited assistant, "but I don't know. It's funny that he's got a liquor store and I've never seen him before. I thought I knew every booze joint in the Precinct. I just hope he wasn't telling those guys to keep quiet about the gun. I sort of wish we had our own interpreter, but I still can't figure out what language they were talking, can you?" I couldn't. "A mix," our interpreter had answered with good-humored evasion when I had asked him.

On the same day as the take-out holdup, a young man with a gunshot wound in his finger had been brought to the hospital by a friend. From the hospital he phoned a complaint to the Ninth, claiming he was the victim of an attempted robbery on the street a couple of blocks from the Chinese place. No connection was made until Tommy Wray, while conducting a hospital interview with the supposed gunshot victim, suddenly thought: "This guy could be my perp." He fit the description of the robber and his story of how he had been shot was not entirely convincing. Most important, Tommy just "had a funny feeling."

Anyway, once Tommy got the idea that the man who was shot was the guy who had held up the Chinese food place, it stuck. He kept finding features of the two cases with which to confirm his suspicion. But he knew he could not hang a case on the slim reed of suspicion alone. He needed an identification of his wounded suspect by one of the people in the take-out shop. It was a delicate matter to expose the suspect to the victim without suggesting to the victim the officer's suspicions. And for several reasons of caution and stealth, Wray was not ready to alert the man who still lay as

a "victim" in a hospital bed, free to talk to Tommy, lawyer-
less and perhaps a bit overconfident. In addition, Tommy
was reluctant to do anything that might scare him enough
to put himself "in the wind"; Tommy hoped every day to
unearth probable cause for the collar.

First, Wray managed, on some pretext, to get a blurry Polaroid photo of the suspect, shuffled it into a deck of eight or
ten other blurry pictures of young men of similar appearance, and returned once again to the Chinese food place.
None of the witnesses picked it out or showed any sign of
recognition whatever. Tommy was disappointed but unshaken. He had to set up a face-to-face confrontation, but
with no hint of prearrangement. He hit on the scheme of
asking both the Asian proprietor (with an interpreter) and
the suspect qua victim to come into the RIP office at the
same time to view some additional photos of possible suspects in their ostensibly unrelated cases.

I wish I had been there when the two walked in. Tommy
describes it as a scene of unmistakable recognition by the
food shop victim and considerable nervousness on the other
side of the table. Several cops have told me about eyewitnesses betrayed by their autonomic nervous systems which
revealed recognition as clearly as words. The cops convinc-
ingly reenact the witness's reactions as he approaches the
one-way glass window to view a lineup: a twitch, halted
breathing, and a momentary, fixed stare at one of the people
in the lineup, followed by a too-rapid turn away from the
glass. All the RIP cops seem to believe that the manifest
clutch of rekindled fear is more reliable than whether the
witness claims or denies recognition. Perhaps so; the signs
are subtle and I have never seen the revelation.

From the reaction of his participants when they saw each
other at the House that day, Tommy felt certain he had figured it right. But neither of his people gave Tommy the
overt confirmation he needed to make the collar. And nothing he did—though he worried the case for weeks afterward—could bring his hunch closer to fruition.

"I tell you," Tommy complained to me one day, "sometimes I think I must look like Darth Vader to these people.

Even when I'm trying to help them, they won't tell me anything."

I smiled to think of Wray, cheerful and forthright, as the figure of evil. "Maybe they just don't trust you," I offered.

"I know," Tommy said. "I wonder sometimes, if I were a fireman, would they tell me how many kids they had in the burning building?"

Lack of trust was only one reason police often felt deflected when they tried to get information from complainants or witnesses. Sometimes, I felt they assumed that people knew more than they actually did. What appeared to a diligent cop as willful withholding or evasion might be, in fact, genuine ignorance.

So another laborious investigation was finally closed, another crime without solution. Except in Wray's own mind, of course, where the case was as firmly resolved as though the perpetrator had been convicted by a jury of twelve. Persistence rewarded is the unvarying lesson of fictionalized crime detection from Baker Street to Hill Street. Persistence frustrated is the usual reality.

8

DEADLY FORCE

D id you ever have to use your gun?" I asked Joe Dean one day recently. I was sitting on a bar stool, having a beer and talking to Joe in his small, comfortable apartment in the West Village, a few blocks from where he had grown up. His wife, Angela—also known as Detective Amato—sat in a deep chair nearby, so attentive one might have thought she didn't know how Joe would answer.

Guns, especially revolvers, are a part of the Job, of course, and I often wondered what the cops thought about them. Many cops, especially those with a few years on the Job, had been in military service, and they knew guns and had used guns of one sort or another for years. One might guess that with such long familiarity, the weapon would lose its special character. Yet, from the strong feelings guns arouse in most of us, I doubted that cops treat the weapon as just another piece of equipment like the handcuffs or the radio. For one thing unlike other gear, the .38 is always within reach and usually strapped to their bodies. Even off duty, most cops carry a gun most of the time. And, from the way they handle it, I sensed that the RIP cops rarely forgot that the gun was the ultimate badge of their authority. As Angela put it, "I am always conscious of having the gun when I'm carrying it. It's a terrible responsibility."

There is something about a revolver that draws the attention. I felt a certain prurient lure myself as my glance rested on the guns around me every day. Some cops become fascinated with the gun and, like Paddy Rogers or Lieutenant Kennedy, get the magazines and begin collecting an armory. I was tempted to think it had something to do with the masculine psyche, and Angela agreed. But as she thought about it, she remembered women who were as attracted to guns as any male cop. That reaction, of course, would only fortify the suspicion of psychological symbolism in any good Freudian. But to me it indicated that the gun is a gender-neutral scepter of the trade. Joe, for example, had little interest in guns, Angela told me.

As far as I could observe, most of the RIP cops seemed purposely to keep their weapons out of sight. Marty Browne, to be sure, wore his large pistol in a holster strapped to his waist by the belt of his trousers, the handle jutting up under his elbow in a way that would be uncomfortable, I imagine, for anyone who has not lived with it for many years. And occasionally I would see one of the men with his gun slung under his armpit from a shoulder holster, a device requiring a lot of harness. But for the most part, the men kept their service revolvers nearly out of sight. A few, like Richie Abbinanti, kept a small gun in a holster clipped inside the waist of his pants with only a hint of the handle visible. Most chose to carry their weapons in a manner that I guessed would be bothersome and not very accessible, in a holster strapped to the ankle under the narrow leg of their jeans.

"Doesn't it make you feel funny, having one leg heavier than the other?" I asked once.

I got a puzzled look. "Doesn't bother me."

"And how do you run?"

"Running with a gun in your holster is never easy," I was told. "Anyway, the gun is usually in your hand when you're chasing someone."

The men rarely spoke of the guns, almost never handled them or even touched them. When Tommy Trepcyk came to work carrying his leather shoulderbag and had to transfer his weapon from the bag to a body holster, he did so almost surreptitiously, as though he were breaching some unspoken code against the display of the hardware.

So when I asked Joe Dean directly how many times he'd used his gun, I almost felt as though I might be opening a taboo subject. Of course, Joe answered quickly and easily, and it occurred to me that my own imagination was running in high gear. Cops are not embarrassed by their guns. They are discreet, aware of the powerful impact of the sight of an unholstered gun, as well as sensitive to the hazard presented by casual display of the weapon. They know the pistols are not toys, and they are too professional to flaunt their firepower.

"Three times," Joe said. "A couple of them were real old-fashioned shoot-outs. One time we'd pulled this car over, and before anyone could get out, they started pumping slugs at us. We fired back. They took off; we pursued. Both of us were firing, it was really noisy in there. I couldn't hear for a week."

"Anyone hurt?" I asked.

"I thought I was hit. Their bullets were hitting our windshield. But it turned out they were being deflected up over the top. It was sort of a miracle. The second time was even more miraculous."

"What happened?"

"There was a stickup team doing hotels in the Bronx. They would come in, show a badge and say they were cops, and then hold up the place. One of them was a railroad cop of some kind, I think. Well, we had a description of their car, and one night we saw it and pulled them over. We told them to get out of the car. One of the guys is standing only about four feet away from me and he says, 'Hold it, hold it! I'm on the Job.' He reaches into his pocket, and I think he's going for the Shield. He pulls out a gun and starts firing at me. I shoot back. We both miss. And the funny thing is we're standing so close that I just keep moving forward till

I grab him by the shirt and hit him on the head with my gun. The gun did me more good as a blackjack!"

"What happened next?"

"There were a lot of shots fired that night. I still remember, I could see the bullets coming out of the guns. You really can see these little red streaks. There must have been thirty shots fired, at least. This was a crowded street, too, one of your typical streets in the south Bronx—children playing and everything. And thank God, the only person who got hit was one of the bad guys."

"I can see why you say there are no marksmen in a shootout."

Joe laughed. "Everyone's too scared to shoot straight."

"So what was the outcome?"

"They got twelve to twenty-five. Attempted murder of a police officer."

"What was the third time you fired the gun?" I asked.

"It started as a purse snatch. A guy had knocked this old lady to the ground and grabbed her bag. We'd been watching him, so as soon as we saw it happen, the three of us chased him. He jumped into a car he had waiting. We approached as we usually do: I was on the driver's side, the other cop was on the right side, and my partner was in the rear. We told the perp to get out of the car slowly, and instead this guy suddenly throws the car into reverse and hits my partner—had him right up on his trunk. We opened fire. I was holding on to the door handle with one hand and firing into the car with the other. The most amazing thing about that night was that we didn't shoot each other.

"He shook us loose and took off. We later heard a guy checked into Elmhurst General Hospital with three slugs in his chest. Me and my partner went out to identify him, and the punch line is, when we got out there he was gone, escaped. Hasn't been seen or heard from since."

"So twice you fired in self-defense," I summed it up, "and once you used the gun to try to capture a perp?"

"Who was trying to kill my partner," Joe finished my sentence. "Right. I had no choice."

Like Joe Dean, Paddy Rogers had escaped unscathed from a shoot-out. He and his partner, Greg Modica, had stopped a suspicious-looking car, when it suddenly took off at high speed. Rogers and Modica pursued. The fleeing car (which, it later turned out, had been stolen) struck an abutment. One of the occupants jumped out and got away. The other two fled on foot with the police officers chasing them. In flight, one turned and fired at the officers, missing. Paddy—for the second time in a fifteen-year career—fired his weapon, also without effect. (The previous shot Paddy fired had been lethal: he killed a pit bulldog that attacked his own dog as he was walking the animal near his home.)

The gunman was later arrested and charged with attempted murder of a police officer, among other crimes. He was acquitted of the most serious charges but convicted of possessing a gun with intent to use it unlawfully.

Paddy accepted the outcome philosophically. "We knew we had a problem going in," Paddy told me. "No gun recovered. No bullet holes in any object or in any person. The jury wasn't there; how could they know for sure what happened? But I'm absolutely certain. I've been shot at several times in this country and overseas, and I know when a gun is being fired in my direction. No doubt in my mind whatever. But I knew there might be some people who would think Greg and I made up the whole thing to cover firing my gun. The perp got five to fifteen. Under the circumstances, I have no complaint about the result, none at all."

Paddy was too forgiving. While lack of corroborative physical evidence presents a problem, a prosecution based on the sworn testimony of two police officers is not a loser. In fact, as I later learned, the verdict was the result of a different problem. Eleven jurors were for conviction on the top count, but they bowed to one who was for acquittal. The holdout later told someone she wanted to vote "not guilty" because all cops are "lying scum bags." She finally compromised because, as she said, she feared that on a retrial the defendant would not be fortunate enough to get another juror as perceptive as she.

The law regarding the cop's right to shoot to kill has gone through a few changes in my professional lifetime. The old "common law" rule—and until very recently, the law in several jurisdictions—allowed peace officers (a category that includes police officers along with game wardens, court officers, sheriffs, and such) to use deadly force (force capable of inflicting death or extremely serious injury) to prevent the escape of a person they had reasonable grounds to believe had committed a crime of the felony grade. This rule—which I have always called "the fleeing felon rule"— was still the law in most places when I became a prosecutor in the fifties. It expressed a clear policy choice favoring capture, and while it certainly was not intended to return law enforcement to the bad old days when virtually all felonies were capital offenses, the law sternly warned suspected felons that disobeying a police officer's command to halt might be their last antisocial act.

When the State of New York reformed its Penal Law in 1967, the Revision Commission thought permitting a cop to shoot a fleeing pickpocket (technically, the pickpocket commits the felony of grand larceny from the person) puts a disproportionate value on a purse as against a human life. So the legislature divided ordinary force from deadly force, authorizing peace officers to employ less-than-deadly physical force to the extent they reasonably believe necessary to effect an arrest, prevent escape, or defend themselves or others from the imminent use of force against them. Deadly physical force, however, could be used for such purposes only when the cop reasonably holds one of three beliefs:

1. the person being arrested has committed or attempted the crimes of kidnapping, arson, armed burglary of a dwelling, or any felony that involved the use or threat of physical force against the victim;
2. the person being arrested has committed or attempted any felony and is, at the time of his resistance to arrest or attempt to escape, armed with a firearm or other deadly weapon;
3. regardless of the offense for which the arrest is made,

the use of deadly force is necessary to defend the cop or another person from what the officer reasonably believes is the use or imminent use of deadly force.

Since private persons continue to enjoy their common law right to make a citizen's arrest, the same New York statute goes on to provide when a civilian may use deadly force. Simply stated, the ordinary citizen may use deadly force to defend against deadly force or to accomplish the arrest of a fleeing person who has actually committed the crimes of murder, first-degree manslaughter, robbery, or forcible rape or sodomy.

There matters stood for many years. Each state could choose the circumstances in which it considered deadly force justified. Then, on the night of October 3, 1974, police were dispatched to investigate a neighbor's complaint of a burglary in progress in a residence in Memphis, Tennessee. One of the officers who responded went around to the back of the house in time to hear a door slam and see a figure dart across the dark yard. He called out to halt, but the figure scrambled up a chain fence and was about to disappear into the night beyond. The officer raised his gun, fired at the figure on the fence, and shot him through the head. The dead burglar turned out to be a young man named Edward Garner. A purse and ten dollars taken from the house were found on his person. Though the police officer was clearly acting lawfully under Tennessee's fleeing felon law, Garner's father brought a lawsuit against the state claiming that the use of deadly force under those circumstances violated his son's civil rights.

The case eventually went to the United States Supreme Court and, in 1985, to the surprise of many—and especially those who like to think that the era of judicial concern for the constitutional rights of criminals is over—the Court held that the fleeing felon rule violates the Fourth Amendment. The decision was surprising to me also. I had been studying the Fourth Amendment and teaching the law of search and seizure for some seventeen years, but it had never occurred to me that a police officer firing at the back of a retreating felon might be making an unconstitutional search and seizure. I knew, of course, that an arrest was a Fourth Amendment event as a "seizure of the person," but I never thought of that deadly shot as a means of effecting an "arrest." Of course, now that it has been explained to me, I see the connection and I appreciate the necessity for confining the seizure-by-gunshot within reasonable limits, as language of the Fourth Amendment dictates.

The constitutional limits on the use of deadly force elected by the Supreme Court in *Tennessee v. Garner* are very close to the statutory limits chosen by the State of New York almost twenty years before. To be sure, Justice White's opinion for the Court leaves a number of intriguing questions. What, for example, does he mean by deadly force? A high-speed automobile chase could be as lethal as a bullet. And when he holds that the use of deadly force is reasonable where the officer has reason to believe "that the suspect poses a threat of serious physical harm," does Justice White mean *immediate* danger only? Or can a cop shoot to capture a person believed to be responsible for a series of brutal crimes and likely to strike again if allowed to escape? But, apart from such uncertainties in the reach of the decision, the case is basically gratifying. It recognizes a principle of proportionality between the severity of the crime and the price of capture. And that idea does seem to be important enough to be implicit in the Bill of Rights.

"The last shooting I was involved in was in 1977," Joe Dean told me. "I didn't use my gun on that occasion, but shots were fired. We were up on Eighty-Sixth Street. There were two kids outside Thom McAn's, and we thought they were going to boost the shoe store. As it later turned out, this was their fourth Thom McAn job. We walked over to them, and I told the bigger guy to take his freakin' hands out of his pockets. He bolts. My partner, Larry, goes after him. I grab the smaller guy. I throw him in the car and handcuff him to the steering wheel. Then Larry yells to me, 'Joey, this guy's got a gun, he's got a gun.' So I put a thirteen over the air and took off after Harry."

The code "10-13" is the highest priority distress signal; it indicates a police officer in a gunfight. Joe continued, "I left the kid cuffed in the car, and ran over toward Third Avenue. As I come around the corner, I hear a pop—one shot. I look and here's a guy wearing practically the same clothes as Larry lying dead on the street. I thought it was Larry at first.

"It turns out that what happened was, there's a bar on Third and Eighty-Sixth. An off-duty cop coming out of the bar recognizes Larry from when they used to work together in the two-three. He sees this big kid drop a hammer on Larry, and it misfires. The off-duty cop puts one shot in the kid, just like that, right through the heart. He was dead before he hit the ground.

"Now there was a deal where Larry should have shot the guy. He had his gun drawn. He was a marksman and everything. But somehow he didn't shoot."

"Why not?"

"I wondered the same thing, but I just don't know."

I remembered that Dean had told me that he himself had once been in a similar situation himself: gun drawn, facing an armed criminal, unable to shoot. "Larry holding his fire should be no mystery to you." I reminded him.

Joe laughed. "That's a story and a half. I was moonlighting, driving a cab, when some guy tried to rob me. From the time he got into my cab, I knew this was either a farebeat or a stickup. I tried to draw him into conversation all the way uptown. He stayed out of sight. I kept adjusting my rearview mirror, he kept moving. So I had drawn my gun just in case. When he got out of the cab, he had his hand in his shirt. There is no doubt in the world he had a gun, because I later found out he had done four other cabs with a gun. Suddenly, he opened my door and said, 'Get out of the cab, motherfucker.' When he pulled open that door, I had my gun in my hand. We both just looked at each other. We were both too scared to shoot, I guess. I think I figured even if I hit him, he was going to shoot me by reflex action, so I hit the gas pedal instead and crashed my cab into a radio car that had pulled over thinking something funny was going down. I remember when I hit it, my first thought was, 'Holy shit, he's got a backup car!' But then I saw the blue and white, and I just yelled out, 'Hey guys, I'm on the Job. Give me a hand.' By the time they pulled me out of the cab, the sonofabitch got away."

"But you got him, didn't you?"

"It wasn't hard. I just went through some records of cab jobs and came up with my man. Three days later, I bagged him."

"So you really don't use the gun, even when you are legally entitled to?" I asked.

"That's the bottom line," Joe said.

"You mean you wouldn't fire on a fleeing felon even if you knew he'd committed a violent crime and he'd get clean away if you didn't shoot?"

"Not even if he'd killed someone," Joe said seriously, "unless maybe he'd killed a cop. And I think I speak for every one of the guys. It's not worth it. Look, we had one like that in the precinct only a couple of weeks ago. Perp popped some guy right out on Fifth Street. Was running down the street with the gun still in his hand. A cop was chasing him; I don't think it ever occurred to that cop to shoot. I know I wouldn't. Unless he stopped and turned on me."

"You'd let the killer escape."

"Let him go. It's just not worth it."

I was interested because, like everyone else, I had read so many stories of cops who fire on unarmed suspects, perhaps in exaggerated fear of aggression. I believed anxiety, uncertainty, or hasty misperceptions (perhaps fueled by racial stereotyping) tightened the cop's finger on the trigger. Here was Joe Dean telling me of cases when fear froze the aggressive reaction, or consideration of inconvenient consequences discouraged use of the weapon even where legally justified. I asked Joe why he thought the shot was not worth firing.

"A cop can get in a lot of trouble when he fires his gun," Joe said. "Stray shot hits a passerby. The perp claims he's the wrong guy. Lots of things. Cop has to go to the grand jury—I went down every time. Maybe a departmental investigation. It's not worth it." Joe repeated with conviction.

"Joe," Angela said, "how many times have I said that I can do this job without a gun?"

"I don't know about *that*," Joe said. "Not that you use the gun that much. But the fact of the matter is a lot of people stand up and take notice because you have it."

"I guess what I'm saying is I just don't *like* guns," Angela said. "I don't like them at all. I wish we could do this job without having to carry the gun." She looked at me. "I never carry the gun off duty. I guess I just don't want to believe that this city is an armed camp."

"But it is," Joe said. "You just don't want to face the facts. You think this is Shangri-la."

Angela laughed. "You're right."

"But I know what you mean," Joe said. "I take the gun whenever I go out of the neighborhood. I wouldn't want to live in this city without it. But I hope I never have to fire it again. Aside from everything else, let me tell you it's not that easy to shoot a person. I've been in Vietnam, I know what I'm saying. Some of the guys go hunting. I can't even shoot a deer."

9

MAKING AN ARREST
TO MAKE AN ARREST

As I became familiar with the usual sequence of events from the initial complaint to the arrest of a suspect, I discovered legal questions I had never noticed before. Strictly as a matter of law, a police officer may arrest a person for a felony when he has information that provides a reasonable basis for thinking the person committed the crime—*probable cause* in the jargon of the trade. Sources of such information are several and various and do not necessarily include an eyewitness actually pointing out the suspect. I learned, however, that 9 RIP had a policy that no formal arrest would be made unless a witness (usually the robbery victim) made a positive identification of the suspect in a face-to-face encounter (normally, at a lineup). How positive, I wondered, did this positive identification have to be? And, more importantly, how did the police bring the suspect into the House for the live identification without making an initial arrest? Were the police, in the interests of caution, making an illegal arrest in order to make a legal one?

The subject came up one afternoon while I was sitting in

the tiny RIP office with Marty Browne, Harry Childs, Joe Dean, and one or two other officers waiting for action. Joe told me that he'd had a lineup the previous evening on a series of rape-robberies. With some satisfaction, he related that he'd had "two sure hits, a 90 percent and a couple of 75s." I was interested in the mathematics of certitude.

"So how many cases are alive?" I asked, genuinely puzzled. "Two, three, or five?"

Joe laughed, "It all depends on how you look at it."

"Seriously," I said, "what do you guys consider a positive ID? Suppose a witness takes a good look and says, 'I think probably it's him' or 'If this guy were a little heavier, I'd say it's him.' Is that good enough to make the collar?"

"Do you mean on the photo or on a lineup?" Marty wanted to know. "It's different."

"It is?" I asked. "How so?"

Marty explained, "At a lineup, I wouldn't lock anybody up on less than 90 percent sure. But I'd go out and pick a suspect up on a lot less than that on the photo ID. I have to go out and bring that person in here for the lineup, and any halfway decent indication from the photos, or anything else, will do for starters. But that's not the arrest, you understand. For the arrest, I want a lineup if at all possible."

The others agreed. "Sometimes a victim who's very unsure of the photo turns out to be 100 percent the moment she sees the mope in the flesh," Harry noted.

I mused on Marty's distinction between "lock him up" and "pick him up," obviously a clear line to the others as well. It was a topic Marty and I would discuss many times. I would try to persuade him (perhaps I finally did) that the law—and particularly the Constitution—recognizes no such differentiation. Any significant, authoritative interference with a citizen's freedom to move about at will constitutes an "arrest" or, in constitutional terms, a "seizure of the person."

Normally, and especially if a person is transported to a different location or detained more than a few minutes, the seizure of a person must be supported by probable cause. At the same time, probable cause does not mean 100 percent, or even 90 percent certainty. Probable cause has been variously defined, but it is a degree of belief somewhere along the gradient between mere suspicion and the certainty ("beyond reasonable doubt") required to convict. In terms of a percentage, I think it is probably below the more-likely-than-not point—say, 40 percent sure. A strong possibility, scrupulously derived, sounds to me like an adequate working definition of the term *probable cause.*

Like my law students, Browne was surprised when I recited the leading Supreme Court case defining probable cause. In this case, called *Peters v. New York,* an off-duty police officer named Lasky had heard "a noise" (not further described) outside his apartment door and, looking through the peephole, saw two men "tiptoeing" in the hallway. He emerged, brandishing his pistol, whereupon the men ran down the stairs. Lasky gave chase and grabbed one of them. In his pocket, the officer found a case of lock picks—burglary tools illegal to possess. Even the prosecutor arguing the case to the Court hesitated to call the officer's slim grounds "probable cause" adequate to support a lawful arrest (and thereby to justify the incident search).

But, upholding the conviction, the Supreme Court held that the arrest had been lawful, based on probable cause. Surely, I urged my dubious students, the Court could not have thought that those facts made it more likely than not, much less 75 percent or 90 percent certain, that the strangers were in the process of committing some nameless crime in the hallway. Tiptoeing in the second degree? Up to the moment when he grabbed the man on the stairs, what facts had the officer observed from which he could reasonably infer criminal activity? An elementary principle precludes retrospective reasoning to justify an arrest by the product of a search that accompanies it, so the discovery of the lock picks must be disregarded in considering the legality of the arrest. Wrung dry, the situation at the time of the arrest yields precious little in the way of evidence of criminal activity. In this light, the Supreme Court's decision must be read to hold that probable cause may be founded on a highly suspicious combination of circumstances giving rise to a strong possibility of criminal activity. And even this construction is generous.

With *Peters'* low standard of certainty in mind, then, don't the hesitant, equivocal, conditional statements of recognition offered by the RIP witnesses constitute a valid basis for a full-scale arrest? Shouldn't they be deemed the cautious, conscientious equivalent of "That's him," more than enough to provide probable cause?

Perhaps a legal basis for arrest is not enough. Perhaps the conscientious police officer should not leap to make the collar on an uncertain ID simply because it measures up to the minimal constitutional mark. The consequences of initiating a criminal prosecution are considerable; what more than bare probable cause should the scrupulous cop require? Does a tentative ID of a photo, for example, count for less than a tentative lineup recognition? And is a tentative lineup ID sufficient to start the machinery rolling?

However these questions might be resolved in the abstract, I was interested in seeing how the police actually deal with the dilemma. In fact, as Marty Browne indicated, before putting a person into the system, police normally want a witness to assert confidently that he or she recognizes the perpetrator after seeing him in the flesh, a procedure I call a *corporeal identification* or a *corp ID*. It's difficult to tell whether 9 RIP requires a 90 percent certain corp ID because of conscientious policy or by reason of misinterpretation of the constraints of law. It's strange, but I have seen the same sort of thing often enough to phrase it as an axiom: Law enforcement agencies tend to overestimate restrictions on their authority.

But perhaps the instinctive inclination of the cops in RIP is sounder than the law. Perhaps the law and the Constitution should recognize and approve a relatively low standard for the brief and minor intrusion entailed in compulsory attendance at a lineup. Perhaps something better than hunch but far less than 50-50 certainty—call it *reasonable grounds*—might satisfy both the Fourth Amendment and the requirements of investigation. Then the law (were it as clearheaded as Marty Browne & Co.) might insist on a considerably higher degree of certainty for the "formal arrest" that puts the suspect on the path to prosecution. Not 100 percent certainty, of course, but a very strong basis for the police belief. It might be derived either from the "90 percent sure" report of the witness viewing the suspect or from the combination of fairly certain recognition and other known evidence, physical circumstances, or self-inculpatory words of the suspect.

However heartily lawyers may commend Browne's customary practice of obtaining face-to-face confirmation of any photo ID, the next question still troubles me: How can conscientious cops obtain the corp ID without a seizure of the suspect? If police believe they need a corp ID for a valid arrest, and arrest must be made to obtain a lineup, we have the makings of the proverbial Catch 22.

My problem with the arrest to put the suspect into a lineup is not pervasive; conceivably police might be able to get a confident suspect to come in voluntarily to face a lineup. For example, Ernest was a young man who had come over from New Jersey to buy drugs, but he was "not a dirt bag," I was assured by the cop who interviewed him. On his way to a dope joint called the Cobra Club, he was accosted in a hallway and shot in the thigh as he was trying to run away. From his hospital bed, Ernest described one of the stickup men as a white Hispanic, over six feet tall, good build, with a mustache and stubble on his chin. From this unusual—and unusually good—description, RIP cops soon spotted Morales on the street, asked him to come in to the House, and got his name and criminal history. Marty Browne assured me they had no trouble getting Morales to come in to furnish his pedigree; he had virtually insisted on it himself, certain of exoneration.

Browne may be right in Morales's case; the suspect's evident frame of mind may have amounted to true consent and, had Ernest been on his feet, might have served to get Morales into a lineup with no need for official constraint. Commonly, however, police invoke the myth of consent— the idea that a suspect waives his rights if he doesn't actively assert them—to justify their exercise of authority over the liberty of some person who is not independently motivated to cooperate.

Understandably, perhaps, of all the various constitutional imperatives affecting their work, I found cops weakest on the doctrine of consent. Here is one notable instance where the axiom of overconstruction of adverse rules does not operate. Consent is a tempting excuse, a particularly convenient bypass around the obstacles of constitutional observance. In addition, from the police perspective, ready acquiescence to a polite request seems very much like genuine consent. If two cops, guns securely holstered, ring a doorbell or stop a vehicle and casually ask, "Do you mind if we have a look around?", and if they receive an unhesitating wave, "Go right ahead; be my guest," they may understandably believe they have been freely invited to inspect the interior. The hassle of getting a warrant has been comfortably avoided.

Courts, however, take a very different view. Of all the excuses for interfering with a citizen's privacy or freedom of action, consent is the most arduous for the state to establish. The law starts from the realistic premise that a confrontation between a citizen and a police officer is an inherently unequal interaction. A police request, however gently phrased, is likely to be taken by even the toughest citizen as a command. Refusal of requested "permission" is thought by most of us to risk unpleasant, though unknown, consequences. Accordingly, the cases have held that the state bears the burden of establishing that the suspect actually consented freely and with understanding of the consequences; "mere acquiescence to apparently lawful authority," the courts have emphasized, will not do. Moreover, "burden" is not a "mere technicality" of proof. It means that where the fact finder—judge or jury—is unsure of what really happened, the side that bears the burden of proof loses. Normally the defendant, by moving to exclude harmful evidence, assumes the burden of showing that it was unlawfully acquired. Where consent is the prosecutor's theory, he takes the burden. And if the facts are a bit obscure—as they often are—the burden may well bring the prosecution down.

Despite the courts' skepticism concerning a claim of consent, cops will often go to some lengths to establish the appearance of voluntary cooperation. They will avoid the use of handcuffs, a generally perceived symbol of an "arrest." They will take care to "request" that the suspect come down to the precinct house "to clear something up," leaving the consequences of refusal veiled in ambiguity. They may specifically tell the suspect that if the victim does not identify him they will give him a free ride home if he wants it.

Many suspects, claiming innocence, take the police up on the offer and, for some few like Morales, their agreement to stand in the lineup may well be a truly voluntary choice. But though the police officers may persuade themselves—and even convince an occasional suspect—that the trip to the House is simply a mutually convenient excursion, all the amenities will probably fail to satisfy a court that the amicable felon, toughing it out with the cops, truly and freely agreed to expose himself to the substantial risk that his accuser will pick him out of a lineup.

Although the suspect is not legally entitled to withhold or conceal the item of evidence itself—he has no privilege to refuse to incriminate himself by displaying his physical appearance—he is entitled to have the police follow lawful means of obtaining the evidence. In this instance, that means requiring police to cite reasonable grounds for taking him into custody or to obtain advance authorization from a judge. Consent, while a recognized alternative, is a much narrower route than police generally suppose.

On the other hand, the police actually have considerably greater power to arrest than they believe they have. (My axiom at work again.) Because probable cause is a lot less than virtual certainty, police may lawfully effect an arrest even on a somewhat uncertain photo identification. Thus, we have the curious anomaly that the police, believing they have no legal basis for arrest, think they have obtained from the suspect valid consent to accompany them to the stationhouse. A court, however, looking at the same scenario would probably conclude that the "consent" was "mere acquiescence to lawful authority" and, as such, inoperative but that the tentative photo ID, or whatever led the police to the suspect, suffices as grounds for a lawful arrest.

Of course, the "arrest" necessary to bring the reluctant suspect into the House for a lineup is not the irreversible commencement of prosecution that police sometimes seem to think the term implies. If the victim is unable to recognize the arrested suspect in the flesh and the police or prosecutors, with good reason, are reluctant to "put into the system" a person who has not been positively identified at a corporeal confrontation (notwithstanding probable cause), the suspect can be un-arrested—that is, the arrest can be nullified without the offices of the magistrate and without undue risk of lawsuit.

In many instances, however, suspicion simply cannot be focused or amplified to amount to probable cause. Without the "consent" dodge, how are the police to obtain access to the suspect's body in order to inspect and examine its characteristics for comparison to the known features of the criminal? In addition to the configuration of his face, police may want to view the suspect's fingerprint, footprint, voiceprint, or even—someday—his DNA print.

Imagine Agatha Christie's famous situation: a person is strangled on an isolated island on which there are only ten people. Now suppose that a fingerprint (not the deceased's) is found on a lens of his eyeglasses. Is there any lawful way to obtain the prints of the ten suspects? We have no probable cause to "arrest" any of them; as things stand, suspicion on each one is exactly 10 percent. Yet for the group as a whole, we have something close to perfect certainty that the murderer is among them. In this fix, the law surely will not leave us helpless. But under a conventional analysis, there seems no lawful way to do the obviously sensible thing.

In 1969, the Supreme Court had a case called *Davis v. Mississippi* in which police, acting on the victim's description, had obtained fingerprints of twenty-four Negro youths, including one whose prints matched those taken at the crime scene. The Court reversed his conviction because they found that the defendant had been illegally held for printing. But in the course of the opinion, Justice Brennan dropped a broad hint that there may be "narrowly circum-scribed procedures" whereby a judicial officer can autho-rize the brief detention required to obtain physical traits such as fingerprints without offense to the Constitution even though probable cause is lacking. It was an eminently well-considered suggestion; it clearly indicated a realistic level of judicial tolerance for the sort of minimally intrusive investigatory procedure that might provide the only solu-tion to a solvable crime. The decision affirmed that the Fourth Amendment, which purports to be founded on rea-sonable standards, is itself not less than reasonable in tight places. Some few judges, taking Brennan's hint, have im-provised orders for the acquisition of physical evidence of identity, even going so far as to order that a suspect submit to minor surgery for the removal of a bullet that might, un-der ballistic examination, prove his presence at the scene of the crime.

Lawmakers took the hint and drafted legislation dealing with the problem of a sub-arrest detention for the purpose of obtaining some identifying evidence from the body of a suspect, including—in addition to facial features—urine, blood, saliva, and hair samples. Under the proposed proce-dure, the investigators might go to court with their equivo-cal photo ID or other evidence and obtain a "non-testimo-nial identification order," a warrant of sorts that allows physical submission but not interrogation. Although the order requires the suspect to present his body without his consent, it is not deemed the functional equivalent of an arrest and hence probably need not be predicated on proba-ble cause.

The idea of the non-testimonial identification order would caulk a significant gap in the law, and bills have been presented to both Congress and state legislatures. But the bills die. The idea itself is all but dead. The statutory framework still seems both intelligent and constitutional.

The need for a regular, lawful means for producing identifying data is as clear as ever. Yet we still have no law authorizing a procedure for the physical identification of suspects; it remains an extraordinary device for the exceptional case. Without a statute, translated into police regulations and accessible to courts and prosecutors, even a necessary procedure can wither from disuse. Most judges, like cops, are not adept at improvisation.

After Morales, the six-foot suspect in the Cobra Club case, gave his personal history, he was released. On the personal data he furnished, RIP got a mug shot out of the police files and brought it, in the usual photo deck, to Ernest's bedside. The complainant picked Morales's photograph without hesitation as one of the men who had robbed him, although not the one who had shot him. Because the victim would not be on his feet for a week or so and the suspect had no stable address, the officers had no choice but to arrest and book him and let the corp ID await the complainant's recovery. So when Ernest was discharged, the RIP cops did not have the problem of finding some legal means of bringing the suspect's body into the injured victim's view; Morales had been booked and was already in the system on the basis of the photo. All that was required was a court order to produce him from detention for purposes of identification. These orders are easily and routinely procured by the District Attorney's Office.

Of course, since the defendant normally has an attorney from the moment of his first court appearance, such an order to produce is obtained on notice to counsel. In this instance, the Legal Aid Society had been assigned as counsel and when they received notice of the impending exposure at the Ninth Precinct House, Keri Gould, Esquire, was dispatched.

10

"TRY AND LOOK ALIKE, YOU GUYS"

One afternoon I arrived at the House to find a group of RIP cops, relaxed and rather more charming than usual, entertaining an attractive young woman who looked like one of my law students and who was, in fact, no more than a year or so removed from the lecture halls and law library. Keri Gould had arrived to represent Morales at the lineup. Morales, the tall, Hispanic man suspected of participating in the robbery of our customer from Jersey, was again in the cage in the corner where I had last seen him about a week before. He was still steadfastly maintaining he was the victim of an erroneous photo identification and predicting he would be vindicated as soon as the victim saw him in the flesh. The cheerful group in the small RIP office was awaiting the arrival of the complainant from New Jersey. The cops, I sensed, for all their gallantry, were running dry of small talk. I was introduced and could not resist asking Ms. Gould what she hoped her professional presence would accomplish for her client.

"Well, for one thing, Professor," she said confidently, "I

can try to get a group where my client doesn't stick out like a sore thumb."

"Aside from the fact that the cops, not you, select the fillers," I said as gently as I could, "let me ask you this: Do you really think your man stands a better chance of acquittal if he's picked out of a lineup of people who closely resemble him? Wouldn't that strengthen the D.A.'s case? Or do you think you can persuade the cops to scour the city to find someone who looks so much like your client that the eyewitness might not be able to choose or might pick out the wrong guy?"

"That's the other thing," she continued, unfazed. "My being here keeps the cops from telling the victim whom to identify."

"Assuming that is their inclination," I replied, "your presence only keeps them honest in your presence, right?"

Ms. Gould was not discomfited by my professorial tease. But our exchange was soon cut off. A telephone call announced that the victim had arrived from New Jersey and had checked in at the Desk downstairs. One of the RIP cops immediately left to intercept him and make sure that he did not catch a glimpse of the caged defendant before we had the lineup ready. First, Morales was moved from the cage into the RIP office and the door shut. Then, with Ms. Gould watching, the victim limped into the sergeant's room at the other end of the PDU room and his door was closed. Morales was then returned to the detention cage. I walked into the sergeant's office to get a look at the complainant.

I found a rather pleasant-looking young man with curly, reddish hair, accompanied by a tall and slender young woman. It was a warm summer day, and both were lightly clad. They seemed like decent, attractive, stand-up people who would make good witnesses—at least if they were dressed to cover the brightly colored flowers and butterflies tattooed on their shoulders.

The victim was idly leafing through some collections of photographs to try once again to spot the shooter in the group that had robbed him. He pointed to one of the photos and said to Rogers, "As I told you before, this guy was there. I saw him in the street. I recognized him from before when I came down there to cop. I asked him if the Cobra Club was open and he told me it was. That's why I went into that hallway. As I said before, when I got inside I saw a guy who asked me did I want dope or coke. I told him I was going to the Cobra and he said the Cobra was closed. It was when I was trying to leave the building that this other guy with a gun came up to me and tried to get my money. Anyway, this is the only one of these photos I recognize." We left him to think harder.

Three RIP cops then left the House, and—to my amazement—returned in less than half an hour with five young men who strongly resembled Morales, except that all were considerably shorter. Undismayed by this major disparity, the cops cheerfully announced that the lineup would be conducted with all participants seated, five of them on telephone books. Such adjustments are not uncommon. I heard of a case in which the suspect had a noticeable facial mark that could not be duplicated. The police went to the local pharmacy for a box of adhesive bandages, which they placed over the suspect's mark and in the same place on the faces of the fill-ins.

Occasionally, RIP picks up a person so bizarre in appearance that a citywide dragnet would be necessary in order to assemble a group with five similar types. I remember one suspect in a cab stickup: an albino black man with a sparse, reddish-blond beard and mustache and a bad case of facial acne. The usual pool for stand-ins is the streets, particularly those around the Municipal Men's Shelter, where the necessary types may usually be found willing to give an hour for the few dollars the police are authorized to pay them. If the description calls for a type different from what the streets around the House will yield, cops on patrol duty are also available. But even among the scruffy sorts in plainclothes and undercover assignments, a search beyond our own House would have been required to obtain someone whose features approximated the suspected cab robber's, and even then success would have been doubtful.

The whole purpose of the lineup, of course, is to give the witness a hard choice. Where the prime suspect has highly unusual features, the careful composition of the line seems both more difficult and less important. It is not easy to round up, say, five 6-foot-2-inch Asian men with one blue eye and hair cut in a mohawk, because there are not many people around who look like that. For the same reason, strictly as a matter of probability, the likelihood of arresting the wrong person fitting that description is considerably reduced. So, one might conclude, the importance of a hard-choice lineup is reduced as the exotic nature of the suspect's appearance increases. Yet even matching highly specific or unusual features does not guarantee a positive identification at a lineup. And if there are only three people in the entire population of the East Village who have the characteristics the witness describes, the chance of arresting the wrong person is still two to one.

So lineups remain an essential part of the preaccusatory screening of suspects, regardless of the uniqueness of the suspect's appearance. And lineups imply a choice among people who resemble one another as closely as possible. I have gone out with the police to pick up the ordinary fillers, but I have not had the occasion to observe how they forage for the matching stand-ins when they are unfortunate enough to catch a really weird-looking suspect.

One of the unusual aspects of the lineup involving Morales was not the suspect's physical stature but the presence of Keri Gould. Contrary to what "Hill Street Blues" might lead one to expect, this was one of the very few times I saw a defense lawyer on the police premises. Why was she there? What could a lawyer do for her client in the unfamiliar routine of a police station?

Generally, whenever a lawyer can advise a client in need of advice—such as, for example, an arrested person about to undergo police interrogation—the Constitution guarantees access. And a decision called *Miranda*, as almost everybody knows, requires that the police advise their prisoner of his right to consult counsel then and there if he wishes. But an identification procedure is different. The suspect is asked nothing. The only thing required of him—to show his face—he cannot legally refuse. Having no choice, he needs no advice from a lawyer. The role of counsel is simply to be there.

The defendant's right to the presence of counsel at a lineup originated in a deep concern in the courts over the outstanding horror of the criminal justice system: the conviction of an innocent person. A book by Pat Wall, a well-regarded criminal defense lawyer, and some forceful advocacy brought home to the appellate courts what we all knew all along but discreetly avoided discussing seriously: that eyewitnesses are sometimes mistaken but sure in their identification. The corollary to this axiom is: As the process progresses, the witnesses become more certain in their erroneous belief, and the fatal error becomes more difficult to detect and dislodge.

In many cases, the testimony from an eyewitness is not merely the strongest evidence—it is the only evidence. People get convicted of major crimes on the basis of a single eyewitness's evidence alone. Once a jury chooses to believe the eyewitness (and even good cross-examination rarely shakes the testimony of a convinced, though mistaken, witness), the convicted defendant is without recourse, for the matter of witness credibility is insulated from appellate review and usually not susceptible to any other post-conviction attack. It is undeniable, therefore, that in some unknown number of cases, innocent people are convicted of serious crimes by irremediable misidentification.

The Supreme Court simply could not allow this intolerable injustice to stand as the sad but inescapable cost of a testimonial system of justice, a system that is necessarily imperfect. Nor could the Court bring itself to reject eyewitness evidence as a basis for conviction in order to shield the occasional innocent who was wrongly inculpated. Clearly, too many valid judgments would have been sacrificed, far too high a cost. Besides, of the various sorts of inculpatory evidence—principally confession, accomplice testimony, "circumstantial" evidence, and the testimony of an eyewitness—the latter is generally considered the most reliable.

Ultimately, in its search for a remedy, the Supreme Court focused on the critical moment between the crime and the courtroom testimony concerning it, when the eyewitness is exposed to the suspect in custody or to his photograph for identification. At that moment, wittingly or unwittingly, the prosecution agents may convey to the uncertain witness the suggestion that there is reason to believe that the person he sees is the one who committed the crime. That suggestion may take root, encourage the initial identification, and influence all others thereafter, including the all-important one made at the trial by the witness's testimony.

Regrettably, it is true that in times past many routine identification practices were indeed suggestive. Often several witnesses, in the same or similar but unrelated cases, would view the suspect together and hear one another's accusations. A rape victim, for example, hearing other rape victims identify a particular man as their attacker, may be led to believe that he is the one who raped her too, though she would be uncertain of her identification without the unwitting guidance from the other victims. So too a one-to-one confrontation with a single suspect in custody (termed a *show-up* in distinction from a *lineup*) says to the witness, in effect, "Here is the person we think did it. What do you say?"

The Supreme Court did not, however, simply rule out these or similarly suggestive exposures. They really couldn't. They couldn't partly because the possibly suggestive situations are too many and too various. No *rule* could hope to describe the forbidden methods in all their subtlety. Inescapably, the question of whether a witness's courtroom identification of the defendant is the result of improper intervening suggestion remains a question of fact for a judge or jury to resolve in the particular circumstances of the case at hand. No *rule* could or should remove that responsibility.

Another reason the Supreme Court declined to express a simple prohibition was that, at least as to state court proceedings, it lacks the constitutional prerogative to make rules for the conduct of criminal investigations and trial. In controlling state criminal investigations, the Court is restricted (rather loosely, to be sure) to expounding and applying a few highly specific phrases in the Constitution.

The specific constitutional provision that the Supreme Court elected to press into service for averting the tragedy of misidentification was the Sixth Amendment's guarantee to every person accused of crime that he will have "the assistance of counsel for his defense." It was not the only time the constitutional right to counsel was applied to protect a person from the development of incriminating evidence. A case aptly titled *Massiah v. United States* accorded accused defendants the right to have their lawyers present during interviews with law enforcement agents. But the lineup decisions were the first insertions of a defense lawyer into a conference between police and an accusing witness.

For those to whom the role of a lawyer in such a situation was unclear, the Court explained, first, that the lawyer, by his or her very presence at the encounter, would discourage unfair or unduly suggestive procedures, although the lawyer could assert no direct control over the proceedings. Second, the lawyer, by having been present to observe firsthand the way his or her client was exhibited, could more effectively present in court any claim of unfairness. Thus, it was hoped that lawyer's serve to "assist" in their clients' defense by preventing or revealing circumstances that might have induced a possible mistake in the ineradicable first identification.

Unhappily, the device was flawed. Apart from the discomfort some defense lawyers feel with their duty to strengthen the prosecution's case by enhancing the probity of the identification procedure, and apart from the fact that any police officer who wanted to "set up" the identification outcome could readily communicate the nefarious suggestion out of the presence of the witnessing lawyer, other serious limitations impair the utility of the method chosen to achieve the worthy objective.

One major limitation became explicit several years after the Court had announced the rule, catching a number of local jurisdictions by surprise. The Sixth Amendment by its language accords the right to the assistance of counsel only to those who have been "accused" of crime. That status is reached, the Court reminded us, only with the commencement of legal proceedings by the filing of accusatory documents in court. Most lineups and other investigatory confrontations for identification purposes are conducted before the case gets to court. So the Sixth Amendment's right to counsel does not apply, and the protection (such as it may be), is nullified at the point at which it is most commonly required.

A second significant anomaly, unnoticed by the courts as far as I have been able to detect, was quickly seen by Harry Childs as we sat around one night after the Morales lineup. I was trying to explain the development of the law culminating in the presence of Keri Gould in our shop. "Wait a minute!" Harry exclaimed. "Even with a lawyer here, and even with the fairest lineup in the world, the complainant could still be mistaken. Maybe the complainant just recognizes the guy in the lineup from the photo he picked out. Or maybe he just picks a mope who looks like the perp. But anyway, if the complainant is mistaken about the identification at the lineup, he will still identify the wrong person in court whether or not a lawyer was present."

I agree with Harry. The presence of counsel may have been an appropriate constitutional response to overt suggestion or obviously suggestive procedures in exposures conducted after formal accusation, but I believe that the real and frightening prospect of injustice arises at the preaccusatory confrontations, where the unsure eyewitness may pick a person resembling the perpetrator—most probably without any hints from the police—and thereafter repeat the initial error with increasing and unshakable certitude. If this is indeed the real problem, the provision for counsel at the lineup is a useless gesture masquerading as a true remedy.

Real protection against the danger of misidentification is available, of course, within familiar conventions of legal doctrine. Simple legislation could provide that no person shall be convicted of a crime on the identification testimony of a single stranger without some other evidence tending to connect him to the crime. We already have such a rule requiring corroboration of the testimony of an accomplice. Because it is thought that the admitted participant in the crime may falsely name another as his partner—perhaps to reduce his own culpability, perhaps to settle old grudges— we require some other evidence of the accomplice's participation. If we believe the identification evidence of the single victim/witness to be likewise unreliable where the two were previously "strangers" by some defined standard of acquaintance, a similar corroboration rule might be imposed. Although the idea has much to recommend it, I know of no American jurisdiction that has chosen to adopt it. Because the idea is hardly exotic and its corrective potential is obvious, its neglect must be attributable to the deliberate choice of our many political bodies to accept the risk of misidentification rather than endure the loss of all those single-victim/witness crimes where corroboration simply is not available. Under these circumstances, the Court's awkward pretense at a constitutional "solution" is all the more lamentable.

I doubt if Keri Gould would agree with my disparaging view of the professional service—yea, constitutional duty— she was about to perform for her client in the lineup 9 RIP was carefully constructing for Morales. At least, she pursued her assigned task with care and skill. Actually, the only assistance Ms. Gould could have rendered her client at that juncture had nothing whatever to do with the assignment envisaged by the Justices of the Supreme Court. She should have made a note for the trial attorney who would take over the case (and perhaps she did) that the victim had ostentatious tattoos on his shoulder and upper arm. The trial attorney might find a way to show these to the jury and paint the victim as some sort of "hippie" unworthy of belief. As any good defense lawyer has learned, you never know when some morsel will fall onto your plate to be converted by the skill of advocacy into a sumptuous feast for the jury. Such fortuitous discoveries as the victim's tattoo might not have been contemplated by the rule requiring counsel's presence, but where criminal defense is concerned, and the meaty evidence is scarce, you take your morsels where you find them.

Now that all necessary parties had at last been assembled, the cops lined up six chairs in a row, completely filling the RIP office, and seated Morales and the five fill-ins, each with a large numeral drawn on a card held in front of his chest. Ms. Gould thoughtfully inspected the array. She conferred in whispers with her client. She asked Morales to remove the long-sleeved satin shirt he was wearing so that he, like the others, would be clad in a T-shirt. She noticed that one of the fill-ins wore a small gold ring in one of his earlobes and asked him to remove it temporarily, which he did without protest. She did not like the position of her client, Number five, directly in front of the one-way glass panel in the office door, so she had him change places with Number Two.

During these ten minutes, Rocky Regina stood in the doorway holding the office Polaroid camera, waiting to get a photo of the lineup as it was posed for the victim's viewing. At his slightest murmur of impatience, one of the detectives watching from the adjacent PDU office would glide by and, by frown or gesture, hush Regina. "Let her have it her way," the detective offered behind a cupped hand. "She's only helping your case." When Ms. Gould could think of no further modifications and Regina got his photo and showed it to her, she turned to leave the crowded office. Only half in jest, she advised the row of numbered men, "Okay, you guys, now try and look alike."

The door to the small RIP office was closed, the shades drawn tighter and the lights extinguished in the adjacent PDU room to enhance the one-way nature of the one-way glass in the door panel. Clearly, a moment of drama was at hand. At this point, Paddy Rogers, the RIP officer in charge of the case, who had excluded himself from the preparatory stage at Ms. Gould's request, emerged from the sergeant's room with the complainant on a cane beside him. As they approached the window, he stopped the complainant and, with Ms. Gould dutifully listening in, instructed the complainant very precisely and in accord with a firm and unvarying formula: "Now listen carefully to what I tell you. When you approach the window, I don't want you to say anything. Just look at the people through the glass. They will not be able to see you. Take your time and look very carefully. Don't say anything until I ask you whether you recognize anyone. Do you understand?" Upon a nod of assent, we all proceeded to the window. Paddy Rogers and Keri Gould stood on either side of the complainant, a few of us clustered close behind. I thought I saw the victim give a small nod the moment he looked through the glass, but, as instructed, he said nothing. The seated row of men inside were clearly visible and, I thought, looked reasonably alike behind their placards. After a few long moments, Paddy went into his routine:

"Do you recognize anyone?" he asked.

"Yes," replied the complainant without hesitation.

"Which one do you recognize?"

"It's Number Two."

"When did you last see that person?"

"He's the guy who robbed me in the hallway."

"Any doubt in your mind?" Paddy asked the last question in the catechism.

"None."

The event was over. Keri Gould bid us farewell, and I asked her whether she was satisfied that the lineup had been fair. Professionally loathe to concede a point, she countered by asking whether I wanted to see her list of objections. I smiled and declined to call her bluff. She left. The five fill-ins were thanked, paid, and sent on their way. Morales shook his head in disbelief when informed that he had been positively identified. He was returned to the cage to await a ride back to the courthouse and from there back into the system. Since I heard no more of the case, I could only assume that Morales was indicted and eventually convicted, perhaps by a guilty plea—a disposition that would have required nothing further of the arresting officer. Maybe Keri Gould's presence to witness the victim's sure and swift recognition contributed to her client's decision to plead guilty (if he did). It's pure speculation, but if that was the outcome, it would have been a notable instance where the application of a defendant's Sixth Amendment right to counsel proved a boon to the economy of the system of justice as well as to the interests of the defendant.

11

CONFIDENT MISUNDERSTANDINGS

I noticed that when the RIP officers escorted a witness to the glass panel to view a lineup, they always repeated the same form of words, including the unvarying phrase "Do you recognize anyone?" One day I asked several of the RIP cops where it came from. With some surprise at my ignorance, they all informed me that the form was required by law and that any variance in the phraseology would automatically result in exclusion of identification evidence from the trial. "Do you mean," I pressed, "if you asked a witness, 'Do you see the person who robbed you?' instead of 'Do you recognize anyone?' the answer would be inadmissible in court?" Paddy Rogers insisted, "That's correct. The law is clear. I have to say it just that way."

Paddy and the others are mistaken. There is no ritual form of words prescribed by law for the identification procedure. All that the law requires is that the officers not signal to the witness their own belief that the perpetrator is among those being exhibited or, more important, that they believe one is more likely to be the perpetrator than the others. Thus, a triumphant phone call to the victim informing her, "Good news! We picked up the man who mugged you in the park last Wednesday, and we'd like you to come down and pick him out of a lineup" or such advice as "Take another look at Number Five before you say definitely no. Doesn't he look an awful lot like the man you described?" might well pollute the procedure with the very sort of suggestion it was designed to eliminate. But to say that the police conducting the lineup must take care not to compromise their neutrality is a far cry from prescribing a particular form of words deviation from which spells loss of the evidence in court. And the difference between "Do you recognize anyone?" and "Do you see the man who robbed you?" is insignificant.

This was not the only time I encountered what I venture to call the confident misunderstanding of ministerial rules. Police, like many rulebound agencies, develop a routine for handling recurrent situations. The origins may be departmental regulations, vaguely recalled legal instruction, or simply an evolved "common law" of common experience. But the human mind being what it is, these routine practices are often embedded in an articulate "rule" which is then readily cited to explain or justify the action. Sometimes these *ad hoc* rules fail to withstand close scrutiny and eventually they may be overruled judicially, usually to the agency's complete surprise.

Oddly enough, this phenomenon usually pertains only to minor ministerial procedures. In matters of considerable subtlety affecting the major constitutionally secured rights of suspects and important limitations on police discretion, the RIP cops sometimes show a remarkable appreciation of the limits of their authority. Here reason or principle rather than rule governs behavior.

I remember one night, for instance, as we were patrolling in one of RIP's unmarked Plymouth Volarés, the officers became interested in an ordinary-looking car ahead of us. As we followed closely behind, the occupants seemed to notice our attention and drove more and more slowly. (I thought that was suspicious in itself; had I been driving that car and looked in my rearview mirror, I would never have thought I was being tailed by cops.) The two RIP cops looked at each other. They shrugged and nodded, touched the siren lightly, and the car ahead immediately pulled over. The cops got out and approached cautiously on either side, guns drawn and pointed downward as usual. I saw one of them talk briefly to the driver and examine some documents. Then they both returned to our car, got in, and we drove off. ·

"What was that all about?" I asked.

"No problem. Papers in order. No weapons."

But why had they stopped them in the first place, I wanted to know. Had I noticed, they asked, that the trunk lock had a reinforcing metal plate around it? No, I hadn't, but what if it did? Well, they told me, people down here don't usually put those on their cars, especially old heaps like that one. This is about the hour for drug deliveries; thought we'd check it out. Then why hadn't they looked in the trunk, I persisted. "Don't you think, Professor, that might have violated their constitutional rights?" was the answer I got. Scholars might debate the point; the important thing to me was that the cops thought of it at all. They appreciated the governing principle and felt its restraint upon their actions. Mere mechanical rules, in contrast, are arbitrary by nature and therefore easily misunderstood.

Cops are not the only ones who tend to expect the law to act by formula alone. Many otherwise intelligent citizens, including first-year law students, embrace a similar false faith in phraseology. They want to think that "the law" endows certain words and phrases with magical properties to dispel risks, transfer property, alter relationships, and so on. Law school initiates the novices into the dark area of incantation, many believe, so that they will emerge speaking casually of "contracts of adhesion," "TRO motions *in limene*," "fee simple conveyances," and "*res ipse* torts." And these unintelligible locutions are taken as further proof that the law invests words with mystical properties. It is comforting to believe that in the law, at least, a set of rules and rituals may be found by which some aspects of life can be ordered.

For centuries, the law was in fact cluttered with forms and formulae, and strict conformance was a necessity. Although in modern times the fair result seems a more important objective than technical purity, a number of old ways survive, some with their ancient clout intact—the oath, for example. But for most other sorts of "legal" phraseology, symbolic value or convenience is the only surviving feature. The wordings of leases and wills, for example, have become customary, but the same transactions may be made by other drafts in more common, and often clearer, language.

Something in us mourns the loss of legal magic. We want to think that saying "With this ring I thee wed" makes the marriage. We need to believe that when the contract we sign is laden with legalese, sprinkled with terms like "party of the first part," "in consideration whereof," and "as hereinafter more particularly described," a binding obligation has been created by reason of the document's tedious form alone. We still crave the security of a simple, predictable relationship between a gesture and a future outcome, and we still expect the law to accomplish it.

Another instance of the police officers' confident ministerial misunderstanding concerned the sort of case in which police are permitted to exhibit a suspect to the victim in a one-on-one exposure called a *show-up*, a procedure that is normally deemed impermissibly suggestive.

Police Officer Jennifer Horr made the arrest. At the time, she was a rookie assigned to patrol duty with a unit that covers the southern half of the borough of Manhattan, which includes the Ninth Precinct. Jennifer is an unusually attractive young woman of Asian ancestry. She stands about five-feet-two in her thick-soled black cop boots and looks like she weighs about ninety-eight pounds soaking wet. She must have carried 30 percent of her weight again in uniform and equipment. All the standard gear looked too big, too bulky, and too heavy for her slight frame; giving her a rather comical look. With her standard black nylon, wool-lined, outer jacket, Jennifer wore a turtleneck pullover, and under that, a bulletproof vest. The vest, of course, enhances the unisex aspect of the uniform—though I doubt that is its primary purpose.

I have often thought the NYPD and other uniformed services should welcome their growing female contingent with a somewhat modified costume. The standard outfit for a patrol cop was designed with the male body in mind. The male uniform was probably chosen for women to proclaim the modern policy of equal assignment and to break with a sexist past in which "policewomen" were considered fit only for duties appropriate to the "weaker sex." But the skirts, reduced equipment, and other symbols of the "ladies' auxiliary" need not be revived. All that is required is a slightly different cut of the tunic, a different hat, perhaps a different blouse and necktie—just enough so that female officers don't have to walk around looking like fake men, like women unsuccessfully masquerading as "real" (i.e., male) cops. Female cops should look like female cops, and clothes designed specifically for them would help. When men became flight attendants, they weren't dressed in skirts and high heels.

From her waist, Jennifer had slung the standard gear: a holstered revolver that hung almost down to her knee, a nightstick that swung below it, a pair of handcuffs, a five-inch, wood-handled, brass-tipped, single-bladed clasp knife, a small, black cylinder of mace, and several closed black leather containers holding extra ammunition and I know not what else. Stuffed into her rear trouser pocket was the familiar, large, shiny memo book which all patrol officers are required to carry in order to provide defense counsel with ample material to harass and embarrass them, should they ever take the witness stand, by confronting them with the omissions and discrepancies the book inevitably contains.

Despite all this heavy-duty cop gear hanging from her narrow waist, Officer Horr seemed as comfortable as a veteran cop twice her size. As she sat at a typewriter filling out the still unfamiliar 61 describing the arrest she had just effected, assisted by friendly and entirely collegial advice from the RIP cops on hand, she seemed relaxed, pleasant, and, I think, rather pleased with her collar.

Because the arrest was for a robbery in the Ninth Precinct, RIP had the responsibility for "enhancement," even though the collar had been made by an officer not attached to the House. Enhancement is a relatively recent idea in the NYPD and one of the principal reasons for the existence of the RIP units. By seeking and interviewing peripheral witnesses, examining the scene of the crime for physical evidence, and otherwise trying to develop evidence while it is fresh, the RIP unit is intended to enhance the strength of the prosecution's case.

Normally, when a street arrest is made, the arresting officer conducts a fast and often poorly recorded interview with the victim on the scene, laboriously completes the paperwork, and then turns the prisoner over to the detective unit, which may interrogate him before taking him downtown and "putting him into the system" for booking and arraignment. Many months later, an Assistant District Attorney may find that the case must go to trial—a comparatively rare event, even for serious crimes, in this day of universal plea bargaining; she calls in the officer and the witness and begins to go over the facts in detail. Too often, the prosecutor discovers to her dismay that the investigation was superficial, that vital facts are no longer remembered, that possible additional witnesses have disappeared without a trace, that physical evidence, overlooked at the scene, is lost forever. In short, the prosecutor has a weak and incomplete evidential picture to present where, with more careful, expert investigation and recording at the time of the arrest, she might have had a strong and convincing case. RIP's enhancement program is designed to prevent that weakness.

Detective Joe Dean and P.O. Tommy Wray were on hand to do the enhancement. They got the essential facts from Jennifer Horr. As she and her partners were cruising in the area at about 8:30 P.M., they picked up a radio run on a robbery at Twelfth Street and Third Avenue and there found

Raymond Botchik, the victim. He told them that while walking home to his apartment on West Thirteenth Street, he had been approached by a woman who appeared to be a prostitute. As she spoke to him, a man came up behind him and showed him a knife. Both then forced him into a nearby cellar, where the man took Botchik's gold bracelet and ripped a thin gold chain from his neck. The two then ran up the stairs and Botchik immediately phoned 911 to report the crime. Jennifer and her partners responded, took Botchik into the patrol car, and slowly circled the vicinity of the robbery for a half hour or so without spotting the perpetrators. At that point, the officers permitted the complainant to go home, promising to phone him at once if anything further developed.

Botchik had given Jennifer an excellent description: white female, about five-feet-four or five, dark, straight, shoulder-length, pageboy haircut, heavily made up, wearing a black leather jumpsuit, accompanied by a short, heavy, male Hispanic. A short while after releasing the victim, Jennifer spotted the female suspect with her male companion. She stopped them and looked into the bag the female wore; it contained a clasp knife similar to the one Jennifer herself carried and a broken gold neckchain. Jennifer brought them in and telephoned Botchik to come to the 9 RIP office.

Dean and Wray took one look at "Marilyn," as she identified herself, and reported to me, "That she is a he." When confronted, Marilyn told us with no embarrassment that his name was Marvin. He readily described his occupation as "prostitute." While he denied committing a robbery, Marvin did admit to an "altercation" earlier in the evening when, he claimed, he had gone with a john down into a basement hallway at Twelfth Street and Third Avenue. The customer had tried to avoid paying him for the sexual service he had obtained. Marvin told of a scuffle but vigorously denied taking any jewelry from the john and refused to acknowledge the presence of his Hispanic friend. He described the recalcitrant customer as tall, over six feet, blond, and heavyset.

I fully expected that the ambiguous sex of this physically attractive creature in our custody, compounded by the gender of the arresting officer (to say nothing of her name), would be the cause of some masculine merriment. It's not so long ago that New York cops harassed and abused male homosexuals without mercy. I could just imagine their attitude toward transsexuals. But I am glad to report that not so much as a half-concealed snicker escaped any cop in the House.

The sexual ambiguity of our prisoner did create some moments of confusion, however. Apart from the unsolvable pronoun problem which continued to afflict us long afterward when discussing the case (the men referred to it as "the he/she case"), we had a more immediate, practical dilemma. Because only one of the two items the victim had reported stolen had been found on the arrested persons, it was obvious that a more thorough search would have to be made. Joe Dean looked worried as he studied the physiognomy of the person seated disconsolately in the RIP office. "Who's doing this strip search?" Joe inquired of no one in particular.

I looked at the prisoner more closely. Even at close range, it would have been difficult to discover Marvin inside Marilyn's skin. The face, neither too strong to be female nor too delicate to be male, appeared wholly innocent of any growth of beard. A head of shiny, luxuriant, straight black hair hung down to the shoulders, except in front, where it was severely cut in bangs above the eyebrows. The skin of the exposed arms was very white and hairless. Neither shoulders nor hips were noticeably broad, and beneath the zippered, black leather top and pants, it was impossible to detect either a masculine or a feminine shape. "Maybe Jennifer should do it," Tommy Wray offered tentatively. Jennifer immediately turned away and went back to her paperwork at a remote desk in the PDU office. Very serious, Joe

Dean stood in front of the chair where Marvin/Marilyn was seated and looked intently at him. "Listen," he said quietly, "how far has this sex-change thing gone?" Marvin/Marilyn looked at him blankly. "I mean," Joe persisted, "have you cut it off yet?"

The prisoner looked at the floor, momentarily shy, and shook his head in the negative. "Well," Joe shrugged, looking over at Tommy, "I guess we're elected." I joined Tommy and Joe in the RIP office with the prisoner, and the door was firmly closed behind us. "All right, take off everything," Joe told him.

Wearily the prisoner removed boots and then the leather outfit, handing each piece to the officers. Joe or Tommy took each article, holding them gingerly in their fingertips, as though they might be contaminated. They shook out the garments, opened zipped pockets, turned them inside out looking for the missing bracelet, other contraband, or anything else of interest. A perfectly legal procedure, incidentally.

Nothing was found. The officers did not ask the prisoner to remove entirely the ripped, black pantyhose, but he was asked to lower his underpants. No genitals were visible. The triangle of dark pubic hair and hairless thighs made me think at first that we were doing Jennifer's job after all. Joe later explained to me that transvestites have a way of gluing the penis back up between their legs so that it is all but unnoticeable. But even these seasoned cops, I was glad to see, were not inclined to probe the intimate recesses of their prisoner's body for so insignificant a trinket as the bracelet.

As I looked at Marvin/Marilyn in the few moments before he put his clothes back on, it was clear—and somewhat disconcerting—that he had female breasts. Not well-developed pectorals, nor gynandromorphic folds, but unmistakably female breasts, small but well-defined. Marvin was no mere transvestite. He was a genuine—albeit chemically assisted—hermaphrodite.

Soon we were notified that the complainant, Botchik, was downstairs at the desk. Tommy and I met him at the head of the stairs outside the PDU room. He was a young man of average height and build with dark hair, quite a different physical type from the recalcitrant john that Marvin/Marilyn had described. Tommy asked the victim a few questions about the encounter, verifying the account we had received secondhand from Jennifer.

Still holding Botchik in the hallway, Tommy presented him with a "lineup" of gold chains. He placed the chain recovered from the suspect's bag among a group of similar chains he had borrowed from his colleague's necks and presented them all to Botchik, draped over his fist. Botchik smiled appreciatively and immediately picked out his chain, exposing the broken link as he withdrew it from Tommy's hand. Botchik asked, incredulously, "How'd you find it?" Wray did not answer but asked him to wait in the hallway a few minutes until we had things ready inside.

Perhaps in strictest compliance with the lineup procedure, Tommy should not have shown the chain until after the suspect was identified so as not to suggest to the victim that the perpetrator was in fact in custody. But I thought the device was an excellent "enhancement," and I was very impressed by Tommy's wise refusal to reply to Botchik's question. His silence—not his premature chain display—demonstrated how the police had internalized the basic ingredients of a fair lineup.

Inside, Joe Dean had Marvin/Marilyn and his short Hispanic companion seated in the RIP office facing the one-way, glass-paneled door. I ventured, timidly, "Shouldn't we try to put a few other people in the office with them?" Only rarely—and then reluctantly—would I offer advice on the conduct of police procedures. But in this case, I thought the men were buying future trouble. Several PDU detectives, overhearing our discussion, assured me that because the exposure was taking place within two hours and two miles of the crime, a show-up rather than a lineup should be held. I asked for the source of the rule and was told it was well established and well known. The issue was resolved when word came that "a boss" (read: a sergeant) had said a show-up would be okay if the crime had occurred within two hours and two miles of the scene. Outranked, I subsided temporarily.

We stood in the PDU room, both suspects were seated in the darkened RIP office. Botchik walked up to the glass panel. Nobody bothered to go through the familiar formula used by Rogers and the others at a lineup. "That's her," Botchik said without hesitation. Then, almost as an afterthought, "And that's the guy who was with her." We thanked him and sent him home.

I later pressed the point with several officers and bosses. Where had the two-hour/two-mile show-up rule come from? Some said it must be in the Patrol Guide, the Bible of police procedure. Others said they were sure they had seen a bulletin from the Legal Bureau. Still others said it was in the Guidelines. All had complete confidence that such a rule was clearly established, though some thought it was a one-hour/one-mile rule.

I kept saying, "Show me the source." Finally, weeks later, one of the men triumphantly exhibited a departmental publication that correctly stated that there may be circumstances in which it is impractical to hold a lineup and a simple one-to-one exposure may be used instead. As an example (again correct), a situation was described in which a felon was apprehended in flight, within a mile of the scene of a crime, and was immediately returned to the scene, where the victim identified him as the perpetrator, all well within an hour of the crime. From this example, the police had readily created the one hour/one mile rule, enlarged by the normal process of word-of-mouth distortion to the two hour/two mile rule cited to me.

The translation of the loose, narrative example into a rigid departmental rule lost the good, commonsense core of the principle. Like most law, the rule on show-ups, when properly understood, is somewhat flexible and most readily stated in terms of its purpose rather than its mechanics. Exposures of live suspects (photos, too, for that matter) for identification purposes should be done in the manner least likely to influence the witness's selection. While bringing a witness in to view a group of people in a lineup may convey the suggestion that the police believe one of them is the perpetrator, exhibiting a single person standing alone shows the witness exactly whom the cops suspect. Confirming the evident police belief is a lot easier for a shaky witness than choosing the right one from several who resemble him. In general, as we have seen, the law prefers the hard choice.

The law recognizes, however, that there may be a few situations in which the lineup is impractical or unnecessary. If, for example, the victim reports that she was raped by her Uncle Ralph, it may be prudent to show her the man the police believe is the person she described, but it would surely be foolish to assemble a lineup and ask the victim to pick out her uncle. So, too, if a merchant comes running into the street shouting robbery and pointing frantically at a fleeing person, and if a passing cop car gives chase, catching up with the running man when he dives under a parked truck, it is only natural for the cops to bring him back to the irate merchant to ask, "Is this the guy?" before taking him in. And to require an instant lineup of passing pedestrians would be ridiculous.

The law does not always look askance at what seems perfectly sensible to the rest of mankind. So the show-up is permitted where the confrontation is so immediate that memory must be fresh and clear and the lineup procedure is either unnecessary or impractical. That sort of rule, however, becomes disfigured by any attempt to put it in rigid form. If the witness has left the scene and the case is in the stationhouse, where it is entirely practicable—indeed, routine—to assemble a lineup (as in the he/she case), the justification for the inferior show-up evaporates.

As for the hermaphrodite, Marvin/Marilyn, like so many of the cases I visited briefly as they passed through the RIP office, I never learned the outcome. More likely than not, he pleaded guilty and received a light sentence (the term depending largely on his record); the identification was solid, physical injury nil. If, for some reason, he did go to trial, the judge might well have excluded evidence of Botchik's recognition of the suspect in the 9 RIP office, since the two-hour/two-mile rule cuts no ice in the courthouse. And if Marvin/Marilyn, while awaiting trial in jail, was able to clean up his act sufficiently to confuse Botchik when he was asked on the stand to point out the person who had robbed him, who knows—Marvin/Marilyn might have walked away from it. Partly, at least, he might have owed his deliverance to the police officers' confident misunderstanding of the ministerial rules regarding show-ups.

12

TRUTH AND THE TEMPTATIONS TO PERJURY

One subject on which I could not induce the cops of 9 RIP to share any firsthand experience was perjury. Police perjury is the demon in the criminal process. We all know it's there, lurking just outside the radius of proof. Fundamentally pernicious, police perjury threatens the integrity of the entire process of criminal justice. The demon can easily make a mockery of our constitutional design and a charade of all the earnest and arduous efforts of adjudication to reach a just result in accordance with law. Yet police perjury is extremely elusive, almost impossible to identify with certainty in a particular instance. Suspicion, sometimes amplified by skepticism, is the best perjury detector we have been able to devise—the best only because it is virtually the exclusive index of whether a sworn police officer is telling the whole truth.

Not that civilian witnesses do not lie in court from time to time. A cynical friend of mine once praised the courts of this great nation as places where ordinary people from all walks of life may come and lie under oath. Even for people without a real stake in the outcome, the urge to make one's perception a bit sharper, one's recollection more certain, or one's actions under stress somewhat more heroic is sometimes irresistible. But amateur liars are more readily discovered. Impulsive perjurers may find their testimony contradicted by other credible evidence, they may be snared by inconsistencies between their trial testimony and their prior statements, or the amateur's awkwardly fabricated account may simply fail the test of ordinary likelihood, which juries apply as a matter of course to test the credibility of all witnesses. It's not perfect, but we do trust the trial process to reveal the commonplace liar.

When cops lie, however, detection is apt to be difficult. In many cases, the cop steps up to the plate as the heavy hitter, badge shining, tone official, demeanor cool. Without apparent strain or bravado, the cop on the stand may appear as a modest hero, a competent collector of evidence, a precise narrator of the critical events. The incidents the cop relates are usually known only to one or two other cops, who might coordinate their recollections. Even when possible to procure, contradiction of the cop's version from other witnesses is often weak and flawed by bias. If the defendant decides to offer his story, his patent interest in the outcome usually mars his credibility.

Not only is police perjury frequently difficult to detect, its effect is often devastating. On police testimony depends the admissibility of vital evidence acquired by search and seizure, confessions, or an eyewitness identification. Pretrial motions to suppress such evidence frequently turn on details of police observation, the sequence of minor events, and the words spoken to or by the police officers on the scene. Did the officer actually see the defendant throw a small package between two parked cars and walk rapidly away? If so, the gun taken from the paper bag is admissible in evidence. Or did the police officer simply grab the defendant as he stood on the street and take the bag from his hand? In that case, the weapon will probably be suppressed as the product of an illegal search and seizure. Did the officer give the defendant his full *Miranda* warnings before he asked him whether he knew the homicide victim or after the defendant told him that they had been drinking Thunderbird together on the evening of the murder? If the warning was delayed, the important admission—and quite possibly post-warning statements along with it—is likely to be excluded from the trial evidence. Did the officer bring the defendant to the lineup in handcuffs as the victim looked on? If so, the prosecutor will face serious trouble putting the victim's recognition of the defendant before the jury.

In addition to the importance of the cop's testimony in getting disputed evidence through the pre-trial challenge and into evidence, the police witness frequently will be the source of trial evidence going directly to the issue of guilt. Just what did the defendant tell the police officer as they sat together in the squadroom waiting for transportation to court? Did he actually say, "The bastard had it coming to him, he insulted my sister"? And how about this sharpened screwdriver with the defendant's print on the handle; did the officer really find it in the vestibule where the rape occurred or did he take it from the floor of the defendant's car when he arrested him?

The integrity of the criminal process hangs largely on police witnesses' spontaneous motivation to tell the truth from the witness stand. And it is a perilous dependence. For we know that in this system even the conscientious cop is often tempted to bend the facts to reach what he believes to be the just outcome. Somewhere out there among the 27,000 New York cops may be some moral viper who will fabricate evidence to frame an innocent suspect. And I suppose there are a considerable number who might "improve" the substantive evidence to help the jury convict a defendant they honestly believe is guilty. But the major temptation to perjury, I believe, is the desire to evade the effects of constitutional rulings that seem to nullify good, honest police work.

Nine RIP's sergeant, Marty Browne, told me of a case that raised just such a tempting opportunity to serve justice by shading truth. RIP got word that a person they had been searching the streets for had been seen in his old neighborhood in the Bronx. They must have really wanted this one bad, because Browne himself went along with the team who went up to check it out. From someone in the street, they got the tip that their man had just been seen going into his mother's apartment. On their way over to his mother's address, they suddenly stop and think: didn't the Supreme Court come down with a decision saying that police cannot make an arrest inside a residence without an arrest warrant? (It did: *Payton v. New York.*) Does that rule apply when the perp is inside someone else's home? (Unclear.) If that someone else is his mother, is it the perp's residence too? (It might well be.) Is the lack of a warrant excused if police are in "hot pursuit"? (Probably yes.) If so, is this pursuit hot enough to qualify for the exception? (Maybe yes, probably no.)

The police posse look at one another. Hey, hold it! This is not the cinch we thought it was. Anybody ever have one of these before? Where do we go from here? We could park in the hall and wait him out. Yeah, for how long? All night? All week? Maybe we could give him some kind of funny phone call and smoke him out—you know, "Hey, man, wise up! The cops are on their way over, make tracks." Then we scoop him up when he crosses the threshold. Or, better still, why don't we just knock on the door and say, very politely, would he like to come back to the Ninth with us to clear up a little misunderstanding? No cuffs, nothing. Hmm, what do you think the Professor would say to that idea? He'd probably say, "Get a warrant." Hell, by the time we got a warrant—even if we could find a D.A. who would okay a warrant, which I doubt—our man would be in the wind. I'll tell you one thing: I don't know how, but I'm not going back empty-handed.

The men would be right to think that they would probably not be able to get an arrest warrant, although the Supreme Court has required one for residential arrests. New York is anomalous. By an odd piece of legislative oversight, New York courts are empowered to issue an arrest warrant only after the filing of a formal instrument of accusation—an indictment, for example. And prosecutors are reluctant to indict before arrest, since the accusation deprives the police of an opportunity to converse with the mirandized suspect in the absence of an attorney.

I don't really know how much of my imagined debate was actually articulated as the RIP people headed for the apartment in the Bronx where they thought their man was visiting his mother; I wasn't out with the cops on that occasion. But Marty Browne phoned me about it, and I got the flavor of his misgiving, the hesitancy, the uncertainty of the law's leeway, the dictates of necessity. I witnessed the development of the immediate strategy, formed in new and unclear territory, outside the familiar routine. I also heard later from Marty how they worked it out.

"These are Spanish people," he explained to me. "Good people. Mother works, father works. They know we're looking for their boy. And they know why. So I decide, we're just not saying anything. We'll just stand there and see what happens." Marty chuckled at the recollection.

"So that's what we did. We rang the bell, and then we just stood there. The mother took one look at us. She knew who we were and she knew what we wanted. We didn't have to say a word. She went back into the apartment, and pretty soon who comes out of the bedroom but our man. He just says, 'Aw, shit' and starts to get dressed. He packs his little bag for Rikers Island, he knows where he's headed. We're still just standing there talking to each other about nothing. He kisses his momma goodbye, he kisses his grandmomma goodbye, he tells his little sister to be good, he comes out in the hall and tells us he's ready, and that's it. No one said, 'What right do you have?' or 'Lemme see your warrant.' I think those people were just as glad to see him go. They know he's bad news."

It worked. But without Marty Browne's educated common sense, the others might have been caught between the conflicting demands of action and restraint. I have no data to illustrate it, but my suspicion is that out of just such circumstances is born the most common form of police perjury: the *instrumental adjustment*. A slight alteration in the facts to accommodate an unwieldy constitutional constraint and obtain a just result. How easy it would be to go into the flat, grab the suspect, and later say you busted him as he was leaving his mother's apartment to get a six-pack at the corner bodega. Same difference. Who will believe this stickup guy if he takes the stand and testifies, in his own interest, to the contrary? And ironically, the perjured version is, on its face, probably more credible than the actual events as Marty related them to me.

By the same logic, cops may insert a little invention to fortify the probable cause upon which a fruitful search was predicated. Add a small but deft stroke to the facts—say, a visible bulge at the waistband of a person carrying a pistol. Just enough to put some flesh on the hunch that actually induced the officer to give the man a toss; it might make all the difference. Or a police officer, understandably eager to have the jury hear the bad guy's full and free confession, might advance slightly the moment at which the *Miranda* warnings were recited to satisfy the courts' insistence that they precede the very first question in a course of interrogation. That sort of thing. Although no one admitted it to me in so many words, I think most police officers regard such alterations of events as the natural and inevitable outgrowth of artificial and unrealistic *post facto* judgments that release criminals. The prevalence of this sort of perjury leads some cynics to suggest that the principal effect of the Supreme Court's carefully crafted interpretations of the Constitution on the behavior of those to whom their words are directed is to teach the police what they should say on the witness stand rather than what they should do in the streets.

Of course, there is no justification for perjury, whatever the "ultimate truth" that may be advanced by the instrumental lie. And when the lying witness is a police officer, the social gravity of the offense increases. Even the common "trivial" lie of convenience (which officer put the cuffs on, who was the first cop the complainant spoke to, etc.) must be regarded as a serious threat to the underlying premise of the adjudicatory mechanism.

Yet I cannot confidently contradict the idea that some varieties of perjury, if not exactly virtuous, are less treacherous than others. Surely the creation of evidence of guilt—putting self-inculpatory words in the suspect's mouth or incriminating evidence on his person—even to enhance the likelihood of conviction of a guilty person is a significantly graver offense to the system than the falsification—such as a timely *Miranda* warning or a revealing observation—that allows some otherwise probative item of evidence to be considered by the judge or jury. The jury, as fact finder, is supposed to have all the relevant evidence before them when they undertake the inordinately difficult job of deciding whether the defendant did the criminal act of which he is accused. Perjury that creates artificial evidence distorts the data being considered by the jury and perverts the basic premise that twelve citizens, not the police, should make the determination of whether the person on trial is the culprit. But lies that result in a more complete picture of the events on trial contribute to the accuracy of the verdict.

The only principled basis for sacrificing ingredients of a verdict that reflects historical truth is a demonstration that the ends of constitutional justice are higher than those of criminal justice. Courts, seeking to enforce constitutional restraints on police power, consciously sacrifice the correct result in a particular case on trial. As Justice Cardozo frankly said: "There is no blinking the consequence. The criminal is to go free because the constable blundered." From the exclusionary rule down to the petty piece of courtroom dissimulation, the object must be justified by higher goals and the distortion must be found to advance those goals. Police perjury, then, is pernicious despite its instrumental virtue because it subverts the higher goals of the rule it seeks to circumvent. Simply put, if the cops lie about how they got the murder weapon in order to survive a motion to exclude it as the product of a search and seizure violating the Fourth Amendment, that perjury is justified or not in direct proportion to the supremacy of the interests of enforcing the Fourth Amendment versus the interests of convicting the murderer.

The Supreme Court has, of course, answered the question, and the answer rings loud and clear in all the court-houses of the nation. But in the stationhouses and on the street, the answer is not entirely convincing. Many mor-ally—even religiously—dedicated cops find themselves in a difficult spot. They want to do what's right, and they are alarmed to discover that what appears to them as clearly right is illegal. They feel somehow betrayed by the law they are sworn to uphold. Especially if they sense that the consti-tutional constraints imposed upon them are unrealistic or unrelated to their own ideas of fair play, the temptations to evasion are almost irresistible. And for those officers who take equally seriously the oath of duty and the oath to tes-tify truthfully, the dilemma is deeply troubling.

13

PROTECTING THE RIGHTS OF THE BAD GUYS

The temptation to alter incidental facts to achieve a seeming compliance with the law is probably greatest in that area known as *search and seizure*. Here the Fourth Amendment to the Constitution sets the balance between the evidentiary need for objects that indicate guilt and the importance of personal privacy. And, as one might expect, the Constitution establishes the scale with Delphic imprecision, giving rise to many close questions of interpretation. Red meat for the Supreme Court.

Sometimes the cops would challenge me on the Court's resolution of those constitutional ambiguities, trying to put me on the defensive.

"I just don't think the Supreme Court is giving the people the protection they deserve," Sergeant Browne was saying to me one day. "I mean, they've gone too far in protecting the rights of the bad guys, and the good guys are left out in the cold."

"Let me ask you something," Rocky Regina addressed me. "Does it say in the Constitution that if we get word that some perp we're looking for is holed up with his girlfriend, we can't go over there and scoop him up?"

"It doesn't," I conceded. "Not in those words. But that's one way to read it."

"Where does the Supreme Court get the right to tell us how to read the Fourth Amendment?" Marty sounded exasperated. "Who do they think they are, the College of Cardinals?"

"Interesting question," I said. "Actually, the Court does not get that power directly from the Constitution. It is a function the Court assumed a long time ago. Chief Justice Marshall, in an otherwise very boring case called *Marbury* against *Madison*, simply took it upon the Court to review the legality of actions taken by the other branches of government. The Constitution is the supreme law of the land, and the Court is the self-appointed keeper of the word." I realized my explanation was not entirely convincing. "Anyway, they've been doing the job of interpretation for about 200 years now, so it's a bit late to object."

The entire Fourth Amendment is one sentence long: "The right of the people to be secure in their persons, houses, papers, and effects, against unreasonable searches and seizures shall not be violated, and no Warrants shall issue but upon probable cause, supported by Oath or affirmation, and particularly describing the place to be searched, and the persons or things to be seized." One important question unanswered by the language of the Fourth Amendment is the consequence of violation. The law does not take abstract entitlements very seriously (at least outside its academic groves), and lawyers recognize that a right without a remedy for its violation is like one hand clapping.

The unwritten law of practice that we inherited from England—the so-called *common law*—governed the question of consequences in this country for a century and a quarter: evidence that would help resolve the issue on trial was admitted in court regardless of the manner of its acquisition. In this condition, the right itself languished, and few occasions arose for the courts to address the underlying substantive issue: the correct interpretation of the concept of an unreasonable search and seizure. Then in 1914, in *Weeks v. United States*, the Supreme Court created a remedy for violations of the Fourth Amendment: illegally acquired evidence may not be introduced in trials in federal courts—the so-called *exclusionary rule.*

For almost fifty years thereafter, we lived with a different rule in the federal courts from the common law which still governed trials in state courts. Some few federal cases reached the appellate courts and produced some interpretations of the reasonableness clause, but the bulk of criminal prosecutions at that time—before Congress and the U.S. Department of Justice got into the anticrime business in a big way—were conducted by the states. Then in 1961, in *Mapp v. Ohio* (a case that many people erroneously believe created the exclusionary rule), the Supreme Court reread the Fourth Amendment to require the exclusion of illegally acquired evidence in state as well as federal courts. The result was a veritable explosion of cases defining and redefining the nature of the protected right of security.

In this litigation, an important question arose concerning the relationship between the constitutional guarantee of security against "unreasonable searches and seizures" and the definition of a lawful search warrant. You can read the single sentence of the Fourth Amendment a hundred times and the relationship between its two clauses will remain mysterious. The Supreme Court, however, has constructed a connection: it has chosen to define "unreasonable" searches as, among other things, searches without benefit of a search warrant. Thus, in effect the Court has constructed a rule that ordinarily prefers searches made under the authority of a warrant to warrantless invasions—what might be called the *warrant preference rule.*

Justice Potter Stewart, who was the Court's principal pilot through the treacherous waters of search and seizure law, believed that, in the absence of a warrant, no invasion of the citizen's privacy is "reasonable" except in certain carefully described, exceptional circumstances. In this reading, the Court's major task became the recognition and description of the exceptions to the warrant preference rule. Justice

Stewart wanted to construct a list of designated categories defining those searches and seizures that are lawful without prior approval of a magistrate. Under this categorical approach, he hoped to provide street cops with a rulebook that would guide their future conduct. A number of such categories emerged under his careful craftsmanship, known by such tags as "incident to lawful arrest," "by voluntary consent," "in hot pursuit," "by stop and frisk," "plain view," "automobile," "inventory," and so forth.

The alternative reading of the Fourth Amendment language—championed by Justice Byron White, for one—is that each case before a court should be judged on its own "facts and circumstances" and measured only by a standard of educated judicial tolerance. Thus, the "unreasonable" search and seizure prohibited by the Constitution is not one that fails to fit within a previously described category but rather an action that, upon all its peculiar circumstances, strikes a reviewing court as unjustified.

The virtue of Justice Stewart's categorical approach, of course, is predictability. (Justice White's "pure reasonableness" theory can claim the virtue of flexibility.) And the principal virtue of predictability in this area, it seems to me, is clarity of instruction to the police in the field concerning the constitutional limits on their investigative authority. Until Justice Stewart's resignation from the Court, his purpose dominated the landscape. The Supreme Court's message, albeit mediated by lawyers and judges on intermediate benches, was beamed to control the behavior of street cops.

The first major difficulty with Justice Stewart's admirable design of prescriptive control has become increasingly apparent in the traffic of cases on appeal: frequently the Court's instructions are far from clear. Indeed, in the vital category of searches and seizures of vehicles and the containers they contain, the Court's decisions and dissents reached the embarrassing proportions of a colossal jurisprudential joke. Until a recent effort to bring some order to the subject (the success of which cannot yet be told), the courts—including the Supreme—wrestled to find similarities and distinctions between plastic packages in the rear of a van and the pockets of a jacket flung across the back seat, between a heavy footlocker in the trunk on a stationary automobile and a suitcase in a moving taxi.

What did the police make of the Court's instruction? How have the field officers reacted? This was one of the questions that sent me out into the field initially. While the cops I spoke with are not familiar with the tortuous evolution of doctrine or the internal inconsistencies of theory behind it, they certainly appreciate the bare fact that the rule changes and that its various forms almost always provoke a division of votes on the Court. "How am I supposed to know what to do," Rocky Regina complained loudly, "when nine justices can't even agree about what I did wrong?"

The message is also somewhat bent in the process of transmission. Training films, departmental lectures, and official directives are seldom models of juristic clarity, even when the subject matter is fairly simple to start with. (It should be noted, by way of exception, that the NYPD has made a series of films on these subjects that are good enough to use in a law school classroom.) The best that can be said for some of these departmental directives is that to the extent they are easily ignored or forgotten, they do not substantially impair the good sense of the officer on the spot. For as far as I could see by watching the RIP cops, the troops understand the basic principles of search and seizure law as expounded by the High Court. Understand and accept, of course, are two different things. Their notorious efforts to alter the facts to fit the rules are evidence of both the fact that the cops grasp the essence of the Court's message and that they reject its wisdom.

"I don't know," Marty Browne concluded, "but when I have to stand there and watch a robber walk out of court a free man because the judge didn't like the way the cop took the knife off him, and I figure there are old ladies out there who could be held up by this bum the next time, maybe stabbed, I just think the Constitution should give those old ladies a fair shake too."

14

IF YOU ONLY HAD A WARRANT, YOU COULD WALK THROUGH WALLS

Many of the men of 9 RIP seemed to think that the constitutional decisions of the Supreme Court are somehow designed to deter searches and seizures. They believed the courts were essentially hostile to the efforts of the police to bring convincing evidence of guilt to the trial court. I tried repeatedly to persuade them otherwise. The whole point of the Fourth Amendment and the exclusionary rule that enforces it, I emphasized, is not to prohibit searches and seizures but merely to encourage police officers to get search warrants.

Of course, getting a search warrant means presenting a judge with a fairly good reason—*probable cause,* as it is called—for wanting to conduct the search. But the probable-cause requirement is not a major obstacle. What seems a good reason to a good cop is usually good enough to satisfy a judge. With good reason for the search and a fairly clear idea of what they are looking for and where they hope to find it, police can easily get a warrant. And evidence that would have been excluded if obtained without warrant will nearly always be admitted when the search and seizure was made with one.

The search warrant itself is a short, straightforward document; the application for it is simple to make out. In view of its importance and plain form, I expected to find the warrant in common use. Actually, I learned that 9 RIP rarely employs warrants. I discovered what must be a New York City corollary to a general axiom: Simple design does not mean simple operation, and nothing ever goes through a court without hassle.

Here's the way it's supposed to work. A law enforcement officer—preferably the line cop with some personal knowledge of the case—sits down at a typewriter and pecks out what he is looking for, where he wants to look for it, and what makes him think he'll find it there. The officer then takes the piece of paper (the affidavit) to a neutral and detached "magistrate" (who may be a judge but who, in many places, is a lay justice of the peace) and swears to the truth of his account. If the magistrate agrees that there is good reason to believe that the item will be found in the designated place, he or she signs another piece of paper (the warrant) that simply says the officer is authorized to go into the specified premises to look for the specified item of property and, if he finds it, to take it and bring it back to the court.

It's easy to say that the whole routine is a sham: magistrates are not actually neutral or detached but just as closely associated with the prosecution as the cops; they don't really read the affidavits pushed across their desks; and even if they did read the affidavits, many of those exercising the authority would not know the difference between probable cause and potato chips, much less the complexities of the law regarding the reliability of third-party informants who supply the hearsay on which the cop's belief may be founded.

However much truth there may be in such assertions, it has always seemed to me that the real values of the search warrant procedure are: (1) It makes the officer pause in his pursuit and reflect on whether he has a good reason to go into someone's private space; (2) it requires him to make a record of his reasons, recording what he knows about the case before he makes the move; and (3) his recorded reasons stand immutably for review by a knowledgeable judge after the fact, at trial, and again on appeal, if the search is challenged. In the enforced hesitation, recorded articulation, and prospect of true review, the objectives of the Fourth Amendment are well served.

The Supreme Court recently reduced these three virtues of the warrant by removing the third one. In 1984, in a case called *United States v. Leon*, the Court held, in effect, that the exclusionary rule was designed to educate police officers, not judges or magistrates; hence, searches conducted pursuant to all but the most flagrantly illegal warrants are virtually immune from the exclusionary rule and hence from meaningful *post facto* review. A police officer who relies in good faith on the facial authority of a search warrant cannot, the Court reasoned, be deterred from future illegal searches by excluding the evidence seized by what turns out to be an improperly issued warrant.

In my opinion, this exception for warrants lays rather too much emphasis on the supposed neutrality, detachment, and education of the magistrates who issue them. In fact, the liberal State of New York simply rejected the holding of *Leon* and refused to allow defective warrants to stand above judicial review. Though it may seem curious, our federal system allows any state to extend federal as well as state constitutional constructions, such as the exclusionary rule, more (but never less) generously than the scope drawn by the Supreme Court.

Before the warrant method, with its built-in protection for the citizen, can become normal field procedure, it must be made swift and relatively smooth. In San Diego, a procedure has been born out of the marriage of will and simple electronics that looks so good and serves so well that it has been copied onto the books of a number of other jurisdictions around the country, including New York. It simply substitutes recorded oral statements for written ones. The Constitution says that an officer's recitals must be under oath, but an oath may be spoken as well as written. It is only custom and statute that call for paper affidavits to support a search warrant. And what statute provides, statute may modify.

As I understand it, the simple California modification works like this. Using his radio, the cop on the scene calls in at any time of day or night and immediately gets switched into a three-way hookup with a prosecutor and a judge-on-call, while a tape automatically records all that is said. The judge puts the cop under oath and hears his reasons, asking questions as necessary. The prosecutor registers her position, and the judge, as appropriate, orally authorizes the cop to fill in the blanks on a form warrant the cop carries with him and to affix the judge's name to the bottom. The warrant may then be executed according to its terms and exhibited as authority to anyone encountered along the way. The taped exchange, meanwhile, is transcribed and available for subsequent challenge, if any. The procedure makes it easy to go the warrant route, loses none of the protection of the constitutional method, and actually strengthens the element of judicial supervision, since the judge, who might not read the written papers, must listen to the oral recital and perhaps even think for a few moments about whether to authorize the search.

Because I was one of the local enthusiasts who promoted New York's legislative acceptance of the California model, I had a paternal interest in its implementation. Sad to say, I was consistently disappointed. For one thing, the departmental bull on the subject instructed police officers that the oral search warrant was available "in exceptional circumstances." That phrase, I learned, is read by cops on the line as "forget it." Everything in police work is ordinary routine; no circumstances are ever certified as exceptional. In addition, so far as I could determine, the facilities were not in place. No blank forms were printed and distributed, no hotline number with automatic taping was set up, no rotating roster of A.D.A.s and judges was established on the other end of a beeper call system. Although the three-way recorded conference was a theoretical possibility, it would have to be patched together on an *ad hoc* basis. (Again, pronounce "ad hoc" "forget it"). There may have been some case where the oral search warrant was applied for and issued, perhaps a couple in the outlying counties of the state. But I never saw one, and the RIP cops I talked to had never even heard of the option before I asked about it.

As I looked into it further, it seemed to me that the major obstacle to making this innovation a part of ordinary routine was the District Attorney's Office. To get a search warrant in New York today, the officer must take his affidavit to an Assistant District Attorney for review before presenting it to a judge. This is a sensible idea, since the D.A. is the lawyer who will have to defend the warrant if it is later challenged, and the A.D.A. may elicit some additional material to bolster a weak affidavit or may refine an overly broad application. But from some of the precincts, the trip to the D.A.'s office and back may itself cost an hour or more, even in light traffic. Then the Assistant District Attorney must be found and plucked from his or her other (always more pressing) concerns to edit and approve the affidavit. Too, the young A.D.A. may be unsympathetic, possibly due to ignorance, and a supervisor must be found and enlisted. More time, more hassle. If the hour is right, the judicial phase of the project is relatively easy, but before 9:30 A.M., between 1:00 and 2:00 P.M., or after 4:30 P.M., the search for a willing judge adds still more time and grief. All in all, the cop from an up-county precinct who tries to do it the way the D.A. wants it done may easily spend three or four hours and considerable energy before she finally brings the document back to her hamstrung partners. The D.A.'s office, which should have welcomed and encouraged a procedure for reducing the vulnerability of searches by increasing the proportion of searches by warrant, actually frustrated the establishment of the oral warrant method. "Go for the warrant once," a cop confided to me, "and you'll think of some other way the next time."

The case on which I decided to go to the mat with the D.A. was this. The victim of an armed robbery reported that following the crime, the robber had gotten into a parked car and, after sitting there for a few minutes, got out and walked away. Someone hailed a passing sector car, and the cops arrested the man and searched him without finding the gun. A uniformed P.O. was posted at the car, and the cops came into the House to ask what to do next. A couple of hours had passed by the time Marty Browne and I heard about it. The tour was changing, and the Precinct commander was complaining that he couldn't tie up a footman sitting on the car all day. To the uniformed cops, the whole thing seemed sort of ridiculous. A gun was in that car. The car was on the street. The keys were on the desk. What do you do? Are you kidding? You go out there and recover that weapon before some other dude comes along and drives off with it.

It's possible that this view was correct and, after a lusty court battle over the issue, the police action might have been upheld as a reasonable search and seizure on some application of the "automobile search" exception to the warrant preference rule. On the other hand, a vacant car, parked and locked at the curb, is not quite the "fleeting target" that gives life to this categorical exception, and directing the cop on the scene to await the arrival of a person who will put the car in motion before moving in for the search seems a bit contrived.

To Marty Browne and to me, the case sounded like a good one for the oral search warrant method. The Assistant D.A. we got on the phone disagreed. No extraordinary circumstances, she said. Send the officer down with the typed affidavit in the usual way. But, we protested, it's four o'clock now. By the time we get the thing typed and down there, by the time you find a judge and all that, the car will be gone. Not to worry, the A.D.A. said, we'll try to expedite it—if possible. Thanks a lot.

I wrote a letter to Robert Morgenthau, the District Attorney, asking what the Office policy was on these oral warrants and, a few weeks later, got a reply setting up an appointment with Roger Hayes, a respected senior assistant. Marty and I went down and met with Roger and one of his associates. We had a polite but vigorous disagreement. The upshot of all my urgent advocacy was that the D.A. would not be moved: the Office obviously didn't like the oral warrants and would not approve one unless the case for it was overwhelming. Pressed, Hayes could not think of an example of circumstances sufficiently exceptional to be overwhelming.

Why so grudging? They wanted the cop in person in the A.D.A.'s office, affidavit in hand, before the application got to a judge. But why? The best I could make of an evasive explanation was that they were afraid they would "lose control" of the warrant procedure if the matter became one principally between cop and judge. My inquiry concerning the authority for such control was unanswered, my argument that the warrant procedure is designed to be an exchange principally between cop and judge fell on deaf ears, and my claim that the San Diego sequence does not bypass the prosecutor made no dent. They were not even persuaded by the argument that the real alternative to an oral warrant—a warrantless search on an improvised theory—costs them control completely.

There it stands. The D.A. does not trust cops and apparently has no greater confidence in the judges to produce valid warrants. So the oral warrant, so promising as a meeting point for exigency and constitutional constraint, is virtually a dead letter in New York County.

Though sometimes troublesome to obtain, the search warrant, once properly issued, is a powerful tool in the hands of the executing officer. It allows him to look as long and as deeply as he wishes, provided only that the places he looks are possible repositories for the item he seeks. He cannot look in a desk drawer for a stolen car. But if the item is small, the officer can look virtually anywhere and examine every other item that falls to view in the process.

Destruction as well as disruption may be the result of a really thorough search. Not long ago, a house was dismantled shingle by shingle and board by board as a bulldozer ploughed the yard in a lawful search for counterfeit bills. Wrongly, I think, our warrants do not hinge depth of penetration on the need for the evidence or on the gravity of the case. The manner of execution, extremely important to the person whose property and premises are being searched, is left largely to the officers' mercy.

I was out one day with a group of RIP cops executing a search warrant. A witness had identified a photo and told us that the suspect in the photograph was wearing the very jacket stolen from the robbery victim. When the cops asked the suspect about it, he claimed it was his jacket and that he had given it to his brother to hold for him. We went out to look for the jacket in the brother's apartment. The brother answered our knock, admitted us, and read our warrant with interest. He said he did not have the jacket and opened the hall closet to prove it. Our cops made a halfhearted effort to look through the clothes packed into the closet, looked briefly under the sofa cushions, and left. On the way back to the House, I asked why they had not conducted a more thorough search. "With a warrant," I said, "you can walk through walls."

"I know," Joey Dean replied. "We could have thrown all the clothes all over the place, turned the furniture upside down, emptied the drawers, and all that. But why should we? He didn't give us a hard time, and besides, the jacket's not there. This perp told his bro we were looking for it and that jacket walked out of that place long before we ever got there—if it was ever there in the first place. So why bother?" They were right, of course, and once more an innate sense of limits prevailed over the broad license allowed by law.

But other circumstances bring out other behavior. A "hard time" from the occupant, or some other frustration, may combine with temperament to produce an aggressive execution even with slight hope of accomplishing the warrant's purpose. And if the police actually believe the evidence is hidden on the premises, and if the threat of a thorough search does not produce the item by surrender, the cops armed with the warrant must decide whether to tear the place apart or simply call off the venture as a failure.

Neither alternative is attractive. One might suppose that, inasmuch as judicial authority has been invoked, the question of the depth of the search appropriate to the objectives of the warrant might be judicially determined at the time the warrant is issued. Since the whole point of the Constitution's warrant procedure is to remove from police discretion such an important decision as whether to penetrate private preserves, it seems foolish to leave to the officer in the field the hard choice of how disruptive and destructive the search by warrant should be.

15

AN ANOMALY: THE CRIME SCENE SEARCH

S ome things you do every day seem hopelessly illegal to me," I told Richie Abbinanti. "The funny thing is, nobody seems to notice." I was talking with Detective Abbinanti sometime after my tour with 9 RIP was over and he, like several of the other RIP cops, had been reassigned to the detective unit in the Ninth Precinct. Although Richie had only good things to say about the robbery task force, crediting the program for bringing the robbery rate down from betwen 200 and 300 per month to 80 to 100 per month, it was clear he was glad to be back in the PDU. He "enjoyed" homicides, he told me, because he felt individually responsible for each investigation.

Richie obviously liked using his head and told me of his pleasure in calling upon the more sophisticated police facilities, such as serology, fingerprint, and lab analysis. He mentioned with diffident pride a conversation he had had with the medical examiner concerning the skill with which a murderer had severed the limbs from his victim's torso. "Enjoyment" might be a surprising word to use in connection with his assignment, but I understood what Abbinanti meant. The work suited his temperament.

Richie looked well. He was, as always, neat and trim in appearance, the Lacoste polo shirt of his RIP garb replaced by the more formal attire of the detective unit. To see his crisp white shirt and the yellow tie firmly knotted at his throat, one would never have guessed the hot, wilting weather outside, much less the scenes of gore and violence he waded through in the course of a day's work. Nor would one have guessed from his bemused detachment that Abbinanti had grown up in the neighborhood he now policed, that the killers he hunted and captured sometimes turned out to be kids he had played ball with as a child.

Abbinanti was trying to explain to me the satisfaction he got when small, seemingly inconsequential clues he picked up at the scene of a homicide led to solid evidence that helped "solve" the crime. He explained to me how the first officers on the scene of a homicide are a special unit, called *crime scene*, who photograph the place and look for fingerprints. Then they turn the scene over to the detective who caught the case. "This," Abbinanti said, "is the best time to find evidence that was left behind by the killer." If there had been a struggle, pieces of cloth or jewelry might have been torn loose that would later prove extremely helpful. Richie had a particular case in mind.

"In 1984 I had a case. It came in about ten minutes to one on December 30," Richie began with his customary precision. "We get a call in the office that they found a dead body. The girlfriend couldn't get in touch with her boyfriend. When she went to his apartment, she opened the door a foot or so and hit the body lying against the door. She called the police. The uniformed men never went in; they saw blood on the jamb and called us. We went around to the window, and we saw blood all over the place and the apartment in disarray. So we called crime scene. They came and photographed everything, then they invited me in. It was a mess. There was blood everywhere in the apartment. It had been a terrible struggle. There was blood in the sink, like someone had washed up. The apartment looked like it was disturbed but not ransacked. There were signs of drugs on tables and some paraphernalia in the garbage can."

I asked Richie how he felt when he came upon the scene of carnage. "My first reaction was 'Why me?' " he said. "But then I began thinking about the case. The door was locked and the windows were closed. It looked liked the victim had invited the killer in. And maybe he had a key; he locked the door behind him when he left. There was blood in the hall outside the apartment, indicating maybe the killer was bleeding too. That's why you need samples and serology. In the kitchen, somebody had been making a fried egg, so it looked like someone got up for breakfast. Talking to the friends of the deceased, I found out that he never got up early. He got up about two in the afternoon. It was obviously an apartment where only one person was living at that time. So that was interesting."

"How do you start on a case like that?" I asked.

"I usually just stand there and try to imagine what happened. Looking at the blood on the couch, looking at how the blood splatters on the walls, furniture that's overturned, and you're trying to get a feeling. It must have made a lot of noise, but nobody heard anything. There was a towel under the head of the body, which meant that the person who killed him knew him. Maybe he was sorry after the act and tried to make the person more comfortable. So I started looking around more carefully and I found a little horn, a gold horn, on the floor near the couch, and underneath the kitchen table I found a little piece of cotton cloth that had stripes in it.

"Next day, when I went to the Medical Examiner's office, after the body was washed off, we saw all the wounds. Actually, we saw the autopsy. There were nine wounds to the head. After talking to the M.E., we found that there was actually an imprint of a pair of scissors on the head, so we vouchered a pair of scissors from the apartment and brought them down, and he said, yes, they could have made the wounds. So we have a lot of evidence. But we still have no suspect."

"Where do you go from there?"

"I went to the funeral and spoke to his family and his friends, and I found out a lot about the deceased. He had been an artist and carpenter, and he sold cocaine, but only to his friends. The deceased himself had a heroin habit. I finally found a person who really knew the deceased, a friend of his who got his drugs from the deceased. I showed him the little gold charm I had found, and he identified it— not as his, but he knew the name of the guy who had worn it. When I first spoke to the person who owned the charm, he was wearing a type of shirt similar to the little piece of cotton fabric I had found at the scene. I spoke to his girl-friend and she said, yeah, he has a shirt that matches the piece exactly."

"Do you think the things you recovered on the scene were important in making the case?" I asked.

"Oh, no question about it," Abbinanti told me emphati-cally. "They led me to the killer and helped get the confes-sion we needed from him. When I showed him the stuff, he told us he killed the guy, he killed him because he insulted his friend. So he picked up a pair of scissors and he stabbed the guy nine times in the head."

"In the *head*?" I repeated.

"He must have hit him really hard," Rich said.

"Well," I offered after a pause, breaking the news gently, "I'm sure no one ever suggested that you might have ac-quired those clues illegally—at least not until now."

"What do you mean?" Rich seemed baffled. "We took them from the crime scene."

"In this case," I conceded, "you probably wouldn't have a problem, because they were taken from the dead man's apartment. And he has no complaint, constitutional or oth-erwise. But if the killer had lived there too, it might be a different story."

Richie was unconvinced. Like every other homicide cop, he thought the scene of a crime, particularly a murder, was exempt from the usual constitutional protection. The crime was serious, the place was a possible goldmine of indis-pensable evidence, and who could possibly object?

Consent, I reminded Richie, even written consent, is a

treacherous substitute for a judicial warrant. It's a tempting alternative—fast, clean, and easy for the investigating officer. "Mind if we come in and have a look around?" These words, pleasantly spoken, open doors for cops like a magic charm. The obliging invitation seems free enough to the officer. But, as I frequently warned the RIP cops, courts see it in a different light. A request from a police officer, with or without an accompanying smile, sounds to the ordinary citizen like a command. "Mere acquiescence to apparently lawful authority," courts are fond of reiterating, "does not amount to operative consent."

Next, I tackled the idea that a "crime scene"—especially the scene of a homicide—is a place somehow exempt from the normal operation of the Fourth Amendment. Here, the argument runs, because of some special necessity, the Constitution tolerates searches and seizures without warrant that would be offensive in other circumstances. That argument was an easy one to bring down. No dice—that's the whole answer. It had been tried in *Mincey v. Arizona*, a gruesome case involving the unmasking and murder of an undercover cop. Furious, brother officers stormed the place, conducting an extensive search without benefit of warrant. The Supreme Court heard the "scene" argument and solemnly said, nice try, but no way. The mere fact that premises were the scene of a crime, even a brutal murder, does not strip them of constitutional protection.

Well, if consent won't work as a waiver, and the place does not lose its Fourth Amendment shield because a murder was committed there, Richie persisted, they would just have to get a search warrant. Surely the warrant could be easily obtained (though Abbinanti could not remember a case where it was needed). Now my job was more difficult. It would be hard to persuade Abbinanti of a fact that students of constitutional law readily accept: The law has gaps in it—large, irrational omissions leaving unclear, perhaps even wrongly resolved, major issues of common occurrence. Even in this overgrown, tangled patch of law governing the criminal process, we occasionally encounter a hole of major proportions.

"Aside from the probable cause, and the oath, and the judge's signature," I began, "the whole thing about a search warrant is that it describes with particularity the thing that the officer is authorized to seize before he goes in and makes the search—right?" Richie nodded. "The requirement is right in the words of the Fourth Amendment itself. You can't get a search warrant unless you can swear in advance that there is probable cause to believe that a particular object is where you want to look for it, and you have to say exactly what it is you are looking for—right?" I repeated. Richie waited.

"Well, you've just been telling me that aside from some blood stains, maybe, you don't know what you'll find on the scene until you go in and look around. Now, you know ordinarily you can't get a warrant from any court to go in and just look around. A crime scene is no different. If you didn't have good reason to believe you'd find that charm or the torn shirting in that apartment, you couldn't get a warrant to search for them. And even if someone might argue that those items were in plain view to the officers who were there lawfully to remove the body and all that, the argument would not cover all the other things you look for on the scene: reading the letters, going through the desk drawers, developing film found in cameras, listening to the messages on the telephone answering tape—all those things you were telling me are standard procedure."

I don't think I convinced Abbinanti that the saving warrant remained out of reach, necessity notwithstanding. He is too good a cop to be bothered about uncertainties in the law covering ordinary daily actions that to him seemed inoffensive and vital to the job. "Look," he said to me, "I hear what you're saying. But if I only do what I have to do, I don't think they're going to throw me out of court. And if they do," he added with a shrug, "we'll just have to find some other way to do it."

The indigestible fact remains: At a crime scene—even a homicide scene—search without a warrant is illegal. And if it turns up evidence against a lawful occupant of the premises, that evidence will be suppressed. And though the purpose of that suppression is to encourage the investigating officers to obtain a lawful search warrant authorizing their intrusion, the warrant is virtually impossible to obtain in the usual case where the police do not know beforehand what clues they will find in the place. Look-around warrants are anathema to the basic structure of the Fourth Amendment.

I do not know if there is a legal way to close this gap in the law and allow the cops to do lawfully what they do anyway. I have had a go at drafting a statute that might withstand constitutional challenge. So far, however, I have had no success in selling it to a champion who might take it through the legislature. I suspect that my idea will lie fallow so long as the anomaly continues to go virtually unnoticed.

16
THE ORDEAL OF
THE WITNESS

There are many things most of us would gladly avoid in this life. Somewhere between a flat tire in a snowstorm and root canal work, I would place the subpoena to give vital evidence in a lawsuit. From time to time, I have counseled friends and others who had received subpoenas of various sorts. However they greeted the prospect initially, all suffered escalating anxiety as the moment of truth (or some approximation thereof) approached, and by the time the ordeal was over, most felt misunderstood, if not maligned. But of course these were novices making their first trip to the witness stand, unfamiliar with the glare of attention focused on them, unaccustomed to the phraseology of lawyers' questioning and the strange demand for precise expression in answering under oath. I assumed that a police officer, in contrast, would be a seasoned and confident witness.

Testifying, I used to think, was a regular part of a cop's job. As the arresting officer, or merely as a witness at the scene or in the stationhouse, the cop would be an indispensable trial witness. Over the course of ten or fifteen years, one might suppose, his arrests and backups would bring him to the witness stand dozens of times. Not necessarily so.

Years ago, when I was trying quite a few cases, I was surprised to discover how many experienced detectives were virgins on the stand. But it's not so strange when you think about it. Police officers rarely make arrests for serious crimes. And of those they do make, a substantial number are dismissed for one reason or another at an early stage of the process. Of those that survive, better than eight out of ten will be disposed of without trial, most likely by a plea of guilty. The cop may testify at a short, rather informal preliminary hearing on the complaint. If he's made a good felony collar, he will tell the story briefly and without cross-examination in the friendly and secret confines of a grand jury room. Today he is also very likely to be called to relate the facts of the arrest at a pre-trial hearing to determine the constitutionality of the seizure of some item of evidence, the reception of the suspect's oral account of the crime, the way in which the suspect was exhibited to the eyewitness for identification purposes, or some other such issue. But after all the hearings are over, plea bargaining is still far and away the most common means of disposing of cases. So cops rarely appear as witnesses at trial. And while testimony at a pre-trial proceeding is serious business, there is nothing like a jury in the box to intensify the experience.

As many cops know to their sorrow, convincing testimony does not come naturally even to an honest and conscientious officer. Nor is a winning personality in the squadroom any assurance of a winning performance in court. A persuasive witness must exhibit a certain professional competence and detachment, a willingness to engage with counsel in the give-and-take of examination without losing the high ground of vantage. He must have human qualities that will appeal to the jurors—wit, perhaps, or modesty or common decency. But he must never appear to pander or to pose. He must meet the lawyers with dignity, without either bristling or fawning. It's a talent that many police officers either have or develop. But not everyone.

The police officer on the stand often holds the outcome of the case in his hands. Eyewitnesses and coconspirators may be effective—if any can be found. Objective, "scientific" evidence can be the most important ingredient of a criminal prosecution and occasionally, especially in homicide cases, the "forensic" was done and done well. But in the ordinary run-of-the-precinct case—the usual robbery, for example, where the victim might not be the community's most upstanding citizen or may have been a bit impaired at the time and somewhat confused or forgetful thereafter—in these cases, it is often the cop who has the telling piece of evidence to relate. It might be the description of the scene or the evolution of suspicion. Sometimes it is the circumstances of the defendant's capture, including, perhaps, a statement he made following his arrest. The manner in which the cop presents these facts to the jury frequently determines the verdict, either sealing the conviction or swinging the jury around to the defendant's side by raising suspicions about the cop's conduct or candor.

Unlike most ordinary citizens, police officers are not neutral figures in this society. While many judges presumptively respect the officer, big-city jurors are a different audience, and, to some jurors, cops start with two strikes against them in the virtue and credibility department. They are, moreover, the favorite targets of a certain breed of defense counsel.

It should be said that the work of most lawyers regularly employed in the defense of accused criminals has few joys. The big bucks come with representation of the heavy drug dealers or members of the underworld. But other grief comes with that clientele. Most criminal lawyers, most of the time, put their energies and talents to work for mean and dangerous people, generally guilty and unappreciative, toward an end whose social value becomes an increasing source of concern and self-doubt to all but the most insensitive of them. Some lawyers have candidly confessed to me that in this fix they take their greatest pleasure in the public humiliation of a cop. Some think it their duty to the "system" to attack cops at every possible point of vulnerability "to keep them honest." Whatever the ultimate effect of these tactics on the jury, whatever their impact on the officer's air of disinterested competence, the combat is often disconcerting, not to say offensive, to the officer who is locked into the unfamiliar role of patient and polite responsiveness.

Unless he is compulsively thorough and orderly in his work or very well prepared by the A.D.A. who calls him, or happens to be gifted in the esoteric repartee known as cross-examination, the police officer on the stand may find himself at a distinct disadvantage. At least one important object of the defense lawyer—and sometimes her only hope—is to make the cop appear unworthy of belief. There are several well-trodden paths to this goal. Defense counsel may try to portray the officer as so sloppy that he could easily have overlooked a crucial piece of evidence that might have exonerated the defendant or so forgetful of the surrounding details of the case that he is not to be trusted on the facts he chooses to relate. Or else counsel may suggest that the cop's story is so sharply at variance with the versions of other witnesses, including his brother officers, or with the written record of the investigation that he may be lying through his teeth. If the defense lawyer manages by insinuating cross-examination to provoke the cop into some intemperate replies, counsel may even argue that the officer is so ill-tempered that he may have brought a baseless charge out of sheer malice.

All that is necessary for a defense victory is a reasonable doubt in the jurors' minds—and doubts on almost any score concerning the police evidence will do it. So the energetic defense counsel will eagerly await the appearance of her prime target on the stand. Lawyers have a number of promising resources with which to arm themselves for the encounter.

For starters, there is the Paper Trail. Unlike other witnesses, police officers are required to paper every case with a variety of forms and memoranda, all of which become available to the defense lawyer to use for impeachment. *Impeachment* is the general term used to describe the lawyer's process of trying to make an adverse witness look like a liar or a fool—or both. Inconsistencies, often trivial, between the notations and the testimony or omissions of certain details are all brought forth with maximum drama. The officer's response to this form of challenge is often significant in the jury's appraisal of his credibility. Does he stonewall it? Does he become too entangled in efforts at explanation? Is he rattled? Does he respond to his tormentor with undue aggression?

Another favorite ploy is to ask the witness endless questions about surrounding minor details of the case in hopes of eliciting as many "I don't recall" answers as possible. What clothing was the suspect wearing? What time was this? Where was the officer standing at that time? Who else was present? Et cetera, et cetera. Sooner or later, the witness may become embarrassed at the number of gaps in his recollection and try to improvise an answer according to his best guess or supposition. Now counsel may have the makings of another conflict between witnesses. At worst, counsel can come up with an argument to the jury that so forgetful a witness is not to be credited in the crucial portion of the testimony.

Then, of course, there is the good, old-fashioned sneer-and-snarl technique. A lazy way, but often effective. "You wouldn't lay a finger on a prisoner, would you, Officer?" "You really don't like black people, do you, Officer?" "Now tell us, Officer, just how many times did you go over your story with your partner until you got it straight?" The variations are endless. And again, apart from the implication counsel hopes to convey to the jury, the response trap is laid: if the officer steadfastly refuses to rise to the bait, the jury may think him arrogant or insensitive; if he does respond, he risks appearing foolish, apologetic, or short-tempered.

There are ways to tread deftly through these minefields and emerge intact on the other side; the ordeal may even burnish the honor of the witness. But it takes personality, practice, and preparation. The officer must exhibit a manner on the stand at once relaxed and official, formal but not stiff; evince a strong sense of duty without getting too defensive about implications of dereliction; appear intelligent but not "wise," deeply concerned but not overly involved. Unfortunately, God-given talent for the role is rare, practice is hard to come by, and preparation is scant. On the one occasion I talked to a couple of RIP cops about a case in which they expected to testify, I was surprised to find that they had done little to prepare for the trip to the stand. I could see after a few questions that the case was dimly and differently recalled by the several officers involved in it. Embarrassment, if not disaster, surely awaited them in court, yet they seemed strangely heedless. If I didn't know better, I might have thought their attitude was born of faith.

One of the most bruising blows to the confidence of the RIP unit came as a result of an unconvincing performance on the witness stand in another case. One day, three of the men had been out on foot for a change. They related that they went into Tompkins Square Park, where Rocco Regina had a brief exchange of words with a bum who did not make the trio as cops. As Joe Byrne stood by, Rocky probably told the man to "take a walk," a common police phrase. Something in his tone ignited an aggressive response, and the man pulled a long-bladed knife and pointed it at Rocky's midsection. "Ya wanna try and make me?" At that point, the park bum could have been shot from three sides at once. Instead, Tom Trepcyk grabbed him from behind, pinning his arms, and the other two quickly and efficiently disarmed him and put a pair of handcuffs on his wrists.

The man was tried for felonious assault with a deadly weapon. The prosecution witnesses were Trepcyk, Byrne, and Regina—three alert, coolheaded, disinterested professionals. The defendant was his only witness. On the stand, he testified that he kept the knife to clean his fingernails and open his mail. Clean his nails with a seven-inch blade? And just what sort of mail did he get on the park bench where he lived? The cross-examination was beautiful. It looked like a piece of cake, until the jury came in with their verdict. The defendant was acquitted.

I later talked to Robert Haft, the judge who had presided at the trial. He shook his head in utter bewilderment. "I can't understand it. The jury just didn't believe the cops, what can I tell you?" (P.S.: Within a matter of weeks, the same man was tried for an unrelated robbery where the only witness against him was a derelict drug addict. The derelict was believed beyond a reasonable doubt and the jury convicted.)

I wondered how the men absorbed the blow—Trepcyk, an experienced cop with about sixteen years on the Job, Byrne, affable, young but very capable, who would soon pass the sergeants exam and be promoted out of RIP, and Regina, a proud, street-tough cop. The implications of the verdict were unmistakable. This was not a hung jury, where one or two of the twelve went off on a tangent or voted some personal bias. Inescapably, the acquittal meant that twelve out of twelve refused to believe all three officers. How does the confident, broad-shouldered ego pick itself up off the mat and reassert the sense of personal integrity that is so important to the way these three cops function on the Job?

They didn't talk much about it, and I noticed that the usual teasing banter among the men made no mention of the verdict. But when I asked what went wrong, they expressed no sense of responsibility. They blamed nobody for the outcome—not the judge, not the A.D.A., not even the jurors. They seemed to regard it simply as another example of the occasionally irrational operation of the "system," mysterious, unavoidable, no one's fault.

I said nothing, not having seen the trial. But if pressed to conjecture, I would probably blame the Assistant District Attorney who had tried the case. From what I gathered, the prosecutor—overconfident, perhaps—spent little or no time rehearsing the witnesses. No conscientious trial lawyer would put a witness on the stand—much less three witnesses—without extensive rehearsal, or "woodshedding," as they call it.

To some, unfamiliar with the trial process, a faint whiff of unethical conduct may emanate from this procedure. But they are confusing legitimate preparation with "coaching." Coaching, in the sense of teaching a witness what to say on the stand is not only highly unethical, it may amount to the crime of suborning perjury. Every decent trial lawyer is very careful not to cross the perilous line dividing preparation from coaching and will conscientiously inform the witness to say nothing from the stand that the witness does not personally know to be entirely true. Having said that, the lawyer should take the witnesses, one at a time, through the testimony they will give, paying meticulous attention to the trivial and peripheral details that could trip them up on cross-examination. The lawyer should stimulate recollection, identify inconsistencies, and attempt to reconcile differences if possible. That is good preparation, not coaching.

Obviously, the mere fact that the lawyer's witnesses happen to be experienced cops does not excuse the omission of this vital part of trial preparation. Cops need woodshedding as much as the ordinary witness does. The prosecutor is, in a sense, the "producer" of the trial and as such must take responsibility for mounting the most convincing presentation. Cases don't try themselves, even when they are composed entirely of police testimony. If, as I suspect, the A.D.A who tried the Tompkins Square fiasco put the cops on cold, the primary fault was the prosecutor's.

17

THE UNWORTHY VICTIM

As we climbed into one of RIP's sagging cars one morning, Joe Dean glanced upward and uttered a brief prayer: "Just send me a good, clean victim today." He turned to me. "I just can't remember the last time I had a halfway respectable complainant."

"What's the matter?" his partner, Izzy Pagan, chided him as we drove off. "You got a gripe about the customers?"

In the Ninth, the cops were accustomed to complainants who were not the most innocent of victims. The Precinct had more than its share of drug addicts, prostitutes, and others with dubious connections to honest society. Their street presence, their weakness, and their lawless lives made them particularly vulnerable to the predators in the Precinct. When they appeared as robbery victims, as they frequently did, they often posed an unpleasant problem to the officers of the RIP unit. While police occasionally turned away from a complaint with hardly a second thought, often they heard a dubious story that presented a hard choice between book duty and common sense.

Operating by the book, a police officer should make an arrest when his complainant's story adds up to a felony and he has reason to believe that an identified person committed the crime. Marty Browne and I often argued the point. "That means," I questioned Marty on one occasion, "any time a person walks up to a cop and says, 'That man just showed me a knife and took my wallet,' the cop should slap the cuffs on the person indicated and take him in, no questions asked."

"You got it," Marty said.

"Even if a search of the guy turned up neither knife nor wallet?"

Marty stood firm. "He could have thrown them away."

"Add two eyewitnesses who tell the cop the victim is lying?"

"They could be the perp's buddies."

I was still at it. "How about a hooker with a drug problem accusing another pros in what looks like a fight over territory?"

"Ah, now you're getting somewhere," Marty admitted with a smile. "We don't have to look ridiculous to do the job right."

I didn't get very far with Browne, but at least I had established the point: somewhere in the process, bad character influences the choice. I remember an incident illustrating the point. One afternoon, I was out on patrol with Rich Abbinanti and a couple of other officers. We were driving down a particularly desolate block when we saw two young women standing near the stoop of a ruined building. One, dressed in black leather with many silver studs and chains, appeared to be in some distress. As we slowed down next to her, I noticed she was at the point of tears. The cops had spotted her as a possible victim from the end of the block and now asked her from the car whether anything was wrong. She told us that a man had come out from under the stoop of the building, took her money at knifepoint, and disappeared back into the cellar with it. "If you're cops, you should go chase him," she added petulantly.

Richie smiled but made no move to get out of the car.

"You gave him the money for drugs, didn't you?" he asked.

"What if I did?" she shot back. "He took it and ran off with it. That's stealing, isn't it?"

Richie shrugged. "You just can't trust these dope pushers anymore," he offered in mock sympathy as we drove off.

Just what was it in that scene, I later wondered, that caused Abbinanti and the others to pass it by? Even if the silver-studded victim had stuck to the knifepoint-robbery version, I am fairly certain the men would not have jumped out of the car and run into the building. They had just decided, instinctively and unanimously, that they wanted no part of it.

To some extent, their decision must have been based on the character of the complainant. They didn't trust her. They didn't trust her to tell them the true story to begin with; they didn't trust her to stick to the story; they didn't trust her to appear in court to follow up; they didn't trust her to maintain an interest in prosecuting the case after the arrest was made. Without a reliable victim, an arrest may turn out to be an empty gesture.

This is not to suggest that the victim's wishes control the pursuit of a criminal complaint. Contrary to popular belief, a complainant has no option to "drop the charges" and call off the dogs. In the American system of criminal justice, prosecution is a public concern and decisions are made by public law enforcement agencies.

It was not ever thus. Centuries ago, criminal law enforcement was largely in the hands of the victims, their kith, and their kin. Crime, short of treason or the like, was regarded as a private injury to be avenged, if at all, by those directly concerned. In several nations today, including some in the English-speaking family, faint echoes of this ancient arrangement can still be heard in the institution known as private prosecution. In places where the institution survives, the private citizen retains the right to hire a lawyer and bring to trial a person who allegedly has violated the criminal laws. It is a right seldom invoked today, and in the United States, private prosecution is anathema. American law has wholly embraced the modern dichotomy between civil and public law, and crime is entirely in the public category.

We do retain a curious relic of the days when citizens were obliged to join in the *posse comitatas,* when the "hue and cry" (as it was then termed officially) was raised to pursue and capture a suspected malefactor. The statutes of most states still empower the private citizen to effect an arrest under certain circumstances. Rarely do we avail ourselves of our antique prerogatives, however, and almost never without the protective presence of an officer. Our wise caution and immediate relinquishment of the captive to official processing render the event a "citizen's arrest" in the most technical sense only. Generally, in criminal cases the victim's role is only that of an injured witness.

On the civil side, a demonstrable injury to an individual is remediable through the courts entirely at the election of the injured party or, in the case of a wrongful death, of surviving heirs. By offering a court system, the state lends itself to the parties' interest in securing compensation or other appropriate remedy for their injuries. But, in most cases, the state's concern is only the provision of a fair, orderly, and expeditious mechanism, available to those injured citizens who choose to use it. Except where it is itself a party, the state has little, if any, interest in whether or not legal remedies are sought for any particular injury or how they are defended.

A crime is something else altogether. Although the action of the defendant may be identical—taking property belonging to another, for example—the act is deemed an offense to the public at large rather than to the private owner of the property taken. A catalogue of conduct, selected and defined by the legislature, is designated *criminal,* that is, of such a peculiar and serious nature that the behavior affronts the norms of the community as a whole, apart from or in addition to being injurious to a particular individual. Theft, for example, not only deprives a private person of a valuable possession; it threatens the general order of property and hence constitutes the public offense or *crime* of larceny.

Thus, it is fair to say that in criminal cases in this country today, the victim surrenders full responsibility for prosecution to public officers once the complaint is made or the state otherwise learns of the commission of the crime. Our public prosecutors are elected or appointed to carry the case against the alleged criminal. These lawyers have no client except the community at large and in no sense represent the victim. They are not responsive to the interests of the victim, therefore, except insofar as they believe those interests coincide with the public interest they serve. Whether to investigate, whether to charge, whom to charge, what crime to charge, whether to settle the case for a guilty plea to a lesser charge—these are all subjects of prosecutorial discretion.

Among the factors affecting the prosecutor's judgment, the attitude of the chief prosecution witness—the victim— surely deserves serious consideration. It is a lot easier to present a convincing case with a fully cooperative star witness. But conscientious public prosecutors must solve a complex equation in deciding their adversarial posture, and the victim's reluctance to pursue a complaint is only one factor. So too, a police officer, while operating in a much narrower field of discretion, cannot be a slave to the victim's wishes. But, like the prosecutor, the cop also thinks seriously about arresting a person the complainant does not want prosecuted.

The victim with unmistakable character defects presents a special problem for the exercise of police discretion. Police suppose, with good reason, that marginal people shrink from courtrooms, whatever their role in them might be. Because of their tenuous hold on stability, they may suddenly disappear, leaving the cop with a suspect in custody and no case. Of course, cops know full well that the operation of the criminal law should not be affected by the dubious station of the victim in the community—in the eyes of the law, the nature of the crime has no regard whatever for the moral or social virtue of the victim. Character does have a bearing on the police decision whether to arrest, however, insofar as character may affect the credibility or reliability of the witness.

So, the hard question is: Should police, in the exercise of discretion, decline a case founded on the uncontradicted allegations of a complainant who is deemed unworthy of belief by reason of bad character or whose story is inherently incredible? *Discretion* is not an easy word to define in this context; in fact, it has been the subject of considerable debate among legal scholars. But we may begin with the fact that police, as public officers, make many decisions based on personal judgment that no higher authority will call wrong. An adequate working definition of discretion, then, might be: an unreviewable choice, based on a variety of factors—often unarticulated—having more to do with justice than with law. Obviously, discretion is a critical factor in the process, requiring a sensitive, incorruptible, and often courageous exercise of professional responsibility. Indeed, by the uses of discretion, the entire legal system may be judged.

I was with three RIP cops—Trepcyk, Regina, and Byrne—when they decided to check out a robbery complaint that Muldoon, a patrol officer, had picked up the day before. Tom Trepcyk had nineteen years on the job. He had been in a number of assignments, including the highly sensitive internal anticorruption unit. Divorced, shaggy, and bearded, he lived with a girlfriend in the West Village, lifted weights, and looked it. On his off time, he carried a leather shoulder bag (usually with his gun in it) and worked as a stuntman in the movies. He often wore a silver satin jacket with the name of one of his movies prominently displayed across his broad back: "The Verdict." Rocco Regina was a tough-talking young cop who knew the back alleys of the Precinct from his days on anticrime patrol. He had recently been promoted to the rank of detective. He drove fast when responding to emergency calls, and he took no back talk from the people on the street. A builder and jack-of-all-trades, he was also a serious cabinet maker. Until he chose to reveal his gentler nature, Rocky easily could be described as the tough guy in the outfit. Joe Byrne was the new man on the RIP roster. He had come up only recently from the

Precinct's anticrime unit and was still getting the feel of the deck in RIP. I did not know him very well yet, but he seemed particularly thoughtful, sympathetic, and good-humored. He has since been promoted to sergeant and assigned to a velvet precinct on the Upper East Side.

We parked outside the fleabag hotel where the complainant lived and followed the clerk through a maze of narrow hallways to her door. She emerged in response to Regina's knock, and we saw a young and somewhat disheveled black woman. As Regina questioned her, wedged in that dim space in front of her door, she recited the facts to us.

The previous afternoon, after cashing her welfare check and secreting sixty-odd dollars in her sock (because, she explained, she wore no underwear), she had decided to go to the movies. She went across the street from her hotel, where a landmark Bowery theater functioned as a porn and horror movie house. Slowly, to make sure we understood, the complainant demonstrated how she had reached down into her sock to get the price of the ticket, all in full view of both the "old lady" selling tickets, the man taking the tickets at the door, and anyone else who happened to be passing by. She then went inside and up to the balcony where, she told us, she was distracted by the unfamiliar sight of two men engaged in sexual activity in the row in front of her.

At that point, according to her account, a flashlight was shone in her face, then on an open knife, and then on the face of the person holding the knife and the flashlight. In the beam, she recognized the man who had taken her ticket a short while before. The man then reached into her sock, took her money, and left. She immediately went out to the theatre lobby, where she saw the robber back at his post. She ran out into the street, where she flagged down a passing radio car and made her complaint to Muldoon.

She told us confidentially that she was aware that some police officers are corrupt, or for other reasons inattentive to duty, and she suggested that Muldoon's failure to arrest the ticket taker on the spot was suspicious. She hotly denied she had been drinking or was under the influence of any drug. She exhibited the insides of her arms as proof that she did not use drugs. I asked her how her attacker had managed to hold a knife in one hand, a flashlight in the other, and still keep one hand free to fish in her sock for the loot. She tried to explain the maneuver again. Regina asked some more questions. But it was soon evident that our victim would not be shaken from her original story, vowing that she would go to court and swear to every detail. We told her we'd be back.

Downstairs, standing next to our car, we discussed it. All of us were thinking the same thing: Was this woman giving us the true story? Regina was not ready to say she was lying, but it was clear that he did not entirely believe her either. After some further conversation, Rocky decided to take his victim across the street to see if she could make an identification. While he was upstairs fetching her, I turned to Tom Trepcyk. "What do you think?" I asked him. "Is Rocky making the right move?"

"Yeah, I think so," Tom answered. "I really don't think he's got any choice at this point."

"But Tom," I persisted, "you don't believe her story, do you?"

"Well, no. But what difference does that make?"

"Aren't there cases when a cop can decide not to take someone even though the victim insists? Are you telling me that you have no room to use your own common sense?"

"Well, sure," Tom now conceded. "There are times when you know someone is just using you for some personal grievance or something. I mean, I'm not going to bust some poor mope just because some bastard has it in for him."

"So what's the difference?" I wanted to know. "You have to judge if there's any truth in the complaint in both cases."

At that point, Rocky returned with the complainant. We all crossed Third Avenue and, as we approached the movie house, our complainant pointed to the ticket booth and announced, "There. That's him in the booth right now." Through the ticket seller's window we could see the face of a middle-aged Hispanic man looking out at us in evident concern. Rocky and I went to the door of the booth, where Rocky talked to the man, obtaining his name and address.

In broken English, assisted by a young man who had quietly appeared in a proprietary manner from inside the theater, he told us that on the previous day this same woman, apparently under the influence of liquor, had bought a ticket and gone up to the balcony. A while later, she had returned to the front door, highly agitated, and accused the ticket taker of robbing her at knifepoint. She had flagged down a passing patrol car, but after hearing the whole story the police had left without taking action. The accused seemed honest and honestly distressed; the young man completely corroborated his version with quiet assurance.

We asked who was in charge of the theater and were led up through the dark auditorium to a tiny, cluttered office behind the projection room, where a small, intelligent, and well-spoken young man, who looked like he would be more at home in an ivy-covered library than in this seedy establishment, identified himself as the manager and fully answered all our questions with care and concern. He told us that the accused man had worked at the theater for three years. He was a steady and reliable worker and was completely trusted with the receipts by the management. He had never been in trouble with the law during his time with the theater and had never before been the subject of any customer complaints. The manager, although obviously concerned, made no attempt to influence the decision the police were struggling with. We carefully followed the dim flashlight beam back to the street.

"Well?" Tom and Joe looked at Rocky.

"I could take him right now," Rocky said.

"You mean take him right out of the ticket booth and lock him up? He'll be in overnight before he gets to court, won't he?" I asked.

"You're right," Rocky told me. "I don't have to take him now. I know where he is, I could come over and get him on my tour tomorrow. He's not going anywhere."

"I don't know if the boss would agree," Tommy put in, "but it's your case."

Generally, Sergeant Browne disapproved of prolonging investigations; a case, he thought, should remain open only so long as the continuing investigation promised new discoveries. The undying hope that something helpful just might turn up to move the case toward clearance by arrest did not justify the designation "active." A closed case could always be reopened, and the closing on paper did not have to close the mind of the assigned officer to new and fresh scents along the trail. And in this instance, Regina was careful to articulate a reason for keeping the case open: "I know Muldoon," he told me. "He's one good cop."

Later that day at the House, I was introduced to Muldoon. He said the woman in the ticket booth had told him that our suspect, the ticket taker, had not left his post during the entire time the complainant had been in the theater. "I would have known if he left, because I had to cover the door when he went away for any reason," she had told Muldoon. Muldoon also told Regina that the complainant had looked a little "strange" to him when he talked to her at the theater the day before.

A few days after that, I learned the conclusion of the matter. Regina had decided to close it. The accused man had agreed to take a lie detector test, and the complainant had lost interest. I talked to Marty Browne about the decision. Contrary to the prediction of his men, the sergeant had not favored the arrest. With a disparaging wave, he said the woman was obviously not credible and the man she accused was an honest working man. Here was a case where the unmistakable bad character of the complainant, at least when contrasted with the evident good character of the man she accused, convinced even Sergeant Browne that the police could exercise their discretion and decline an arrest, notwithstanding an insistent complainant and an identified suspect within reach.

18

CREDENCE AND THE BACKFIRE EFFECT

Marty Browne was growing eloquent one day, telling me once again that in the exercise of discretion, the wise cop should consider the consequences to himself of a backfire. If a cop declines to make an arrest because he thinks the victim is incredible, the person he releases may later commit another crime. Why take the chance? Let the courts and the D.A. decide if the victim is lying, Marty concluded with some heat. That's what they're there for, isn't it? "I don't get paid enough to buy trouble for myself." Marty often quoted the old civil service maxim—"Cover Thine Ass," which reflects the belief that the system does not reward initiative, but it does penalize error.

One might expect that this universal and unchallenged adage would produce by-the-book rigidity. But I suspect that—at least among the better cops—a strong countervailing force keeps the discretionary balance tipped toward initiative and the dictates of common sense. Like most people, cops were raised with a strong sense of justice, and they naturally apply it when the occasion arises. Police—and, preeminently, Browne himself—believe that what they do is meaningful, and (despite their frequent expressions of cynicism about "the system") they want their product to correspond to their concepts of justice, if possible. The reassuring fact is that when making a series of choices, one by one, through unfamiliar terrain, it is far easier to be guided by a sense of immediate fairness than to chart a course based on avoidance of unwarranted bureaucratic blame.

The credibility call is often a tough one for anyone to make. Despite their confidence, cops are frequently groping in the dark when they try to rate the veracity of the people they deal with. The cues are often as subtle as tone of voice or eye contact, and the pieces of the picture rarely fit neatly together. Even in the spontaneous, informal interaction characteristic of early contact with a case, police must overcome barriers to clear understanding. Ethnic differences, unsuspected self-interests, and artfully concealed character flaws may confuse the good sense of even the most dogged and experienced cop. Pegging a decision as important as the commencement of a criminal prosecution on such elusive and disguised clues to credence, and lodging the decision in the largely unreviewable judgment of the street cop seems a risky, if not downright dangerous, arrangement.

Marty Browne is right when he points out that the criminal justice system has provided several veracity filters in and around the courthouse. Is anything important added to the criminal justice system by entrusting the police with discretionary choices at the street level? And do we needlessly require them to expose their vulnerable hindquarters?

Police on patrol, in the ordinary course of a day's work, inevitably encounter situations calling for discretionary choices. The radio car drives by blocks of double-parked cars without so much as a second glance; two rock fans pass a joint back and forth while the cop at the door looks on passively; unlicensed peddlers and three-card-monte players are chased but not arrested; a man on the street obediently opens his fist and displays to the RIP cops a small package of white powder, and they tell him to throw it down the sewer. Small potatoes, perhaps, but a normal part of the cops' daily operation. Acknowledged or not, discretion and judgment are part of the Job. The issue, then, is not whether cops should make arrest decisions but whether credibility factors should influence them.

Timing is also important. If a case should be tossed and will never work its way through the formal end of the prosecution process, when is the best time to toss it? An immediate choice by the police may be of considerable importance to the parties. The complainant may get some satisfaction, a sense of validation, from the credit the police accord the complaint. And to be turned away by a cop, summarily dismissed as a liar or worse, must be a bitter pill. So too the suspect who saunters out of the stationhouse or away from a street fracas feels very different from the person who gets taken in handcuffs to spend hours locked in a miserable cell, uncertain of how he will be treated by the system. Several times I have seen suspects arguing their innocence to the cops as though it were their last chance; clearly they did not altogether trust the fine tuning of the mainframe institution of justice downtown.

Apart from these considerations, allowing the individual police officer to decide whether or not to make an arrest fundamentally affects the nature of police work and the manner in which cops approach the Job.

According to academic analysts, a police force can be designed to resemble one of two models. One is the efficient, anonymous, well-pressed unit, trained to do the job by the book. The advantages are real and attractive. It is relatively corruption-proof. It is crisp and correct in contact with courts and citizens. It generates detailed and impersonal memoranda. The prototype is probably J. Edgar Hoover's FBI. The defects of this model are also considerable. Mindless, bound by steel rules, which are themselves necessarily inadequate to many of the real situations that arise, the impersonal corps is perceived by the people as an alien, if not actually hostile, force. And, like Hoover's FBI, this model readily lends itself to the enforcement of a commander's personal ideology.

The alternative model is the local unit in which the cops police a neighborhood in which they grew up or one similar to it. They maintain relationships with the citizens and merchants and perhaps with the low-life characters as well. They occasionally mete out street justice to the mischievous while according friendly service to the weak or disabled. Informality is the watchword, and individual officers frequently rely on common sense and human reaction. Their conduct, therefore, often satisfies the community's notions of appropriate response.

Historically, these virtues of the neighborhood police force have been overshadowed by clouds of politics and corruption. Experience has shown local stationhouses too often and too closely tied to the local politician and too friendly with the local tavernkeeper. Moreover, rough and ready justice—dispensed from the end of a nightstick, as the expression goes—might well offend contemporary sensibilities.

Which model is better? We may never agree. But must we make the choice? Surely, even a clean, well-trained police unit is improved by encouraging the exercise of the thinking process. And the most avid advocate of "professionalism" cannot wince at the notion that individual police officers are—and should be—concerned with justice along with obedience to departmental regulations.

I am in favor of developing the faculty of judgment, even in police officers. The cops I have watched do much better when they try to figure out what is the best move than when they try to recall and apply what they think the rule requires. So I would try to build on strength and promote the idea that individual cops bear some responsibility for the intelligent performance of the Job. I would like to encourage cops to decline an arrest when they believe, with good reason, that a crucial account is false and that no judge or jury would be likely to weigh it differently.

However, even if the Police Department agreed that encouraging cops to think is a good policy, sooner or later, the Legal Bureau would feel obliged to *guide* the exercise of discretion and, by the inexorable operation of one of those laws of civil service, the published *guidelines* would be read as *rules* in the trenches, where they would probably be reshaped and hardened into unrecognizable forms. The use of ordinary intelligence would again yield to the application of misunderstood rules.

An unfortunate incident put the credibility dilemma squarely on the shoulders of RIP officer Hiram Gonzalez. And he narrowly escaped a devastating backfire. But in the strange way things played out, even had the backfire fired, the court, not the cop, would have had to bear the blame.

It started as a rather dull case. A telephone call was received from a court officer in the criminal court downtown. They were holding a young man who had allegedly manhandled his girlfriend in the crowded courthouse elevator and tried to take her purse. Because the courthouse is not in the Ninth Precinct, the crime (such as it was) had not occurred in our jurisdiction, but the parties resided in the Precinct, and the court officers thought we should take it. It had been a slow afternoon, and our people rarely declined a case, so we said sure, we'll be right down. The cops looked at one another and mentally drew straws. Hiram Gonzalez and Tom Longobardi finally spoke up and said they'd take the ride. I went with them.

We found our way through the labyrinth behind the courtrooms to a cluttered office where a matronly Hispanic woman sat slumped in a chair. In the corridor outside, we could see a clean-cut young man sitting handcuffed to the arm of an old wooden courtroom bench. We asked the woman what had happened. A long, disjointed story poured forth in heavily accented English. The basic facts were that she (call her Rosa) and the man sitting outside (call him Frank) had met at a methadone center and had taken up residence together (what the cops called a "Methadonian marriage"). When Rosa had finally asked Frank to go find another place to live, he had trashed her apartment, tearing her clothes and breaking up the furniture. On another occasion, ten days before the incident that brought us downtown, she had come home alone to find him waiting in the rain outside her house. He had threatened her with a knife and knocked her to the ground. Grabbing her purse, he had taken some cash. She never reported the incident.

On the afternoon of our arrival, she had been on her way to court to answer a court summons (the precise nature of which we could not learn from her at that time). She told us that Frank had been lurking outside her house again and began to follow her, pushing behind her onto the bus. When she got into the courthouse elevator, he had demanded her purse and threatened her. A court officer overheard the struggle and brought them both to the office in which we found them.

When she finished the story, Gonz and Tommy looked at one another for a moment, wondering: What have we gotten into here, a domestic squabble? Who needs it! Still, the story had allegations of a recent knifepoint robbery (in the rain) as well as an attempt (in the elevator). At least, they agreed, a little clarification would be helpful. So they decided to take the problem back to the RIP office. They gave Rosa a dollar and directions to the Ninth Precinct House. Frank would ride with us. As we stood by while the court officer unlocked his handcuffs, Frank looked up at us urgently. "Don't you want to hear my side of the story?" he implored. "Sure," Gonzalez replied, "when we get to the House. Save it."

But Frank couldn't contain himself. "She's lying," he told us as Longobardi expertly dodged through the downtown traffic. No one took the bait, but Frank continued. "We were on our way to court together. We had a little argument and Rosa started shouting. She's very excitable, you know. I never tried to take anything from her. Why would I do a thing like that? We're living together."

This time, Tommy couldn't resist a rejoinder: "Oh? Then why did you trash her apartment?"

"Did she tell you I did that?" Frank shot back, indignant. "That wasn't me, Officer. That was Raoul, her brother-in-law. He thought Rosa's sister was staying with her."

With that hint of the layers of domestic grievance underlying the shove in the elevator, the officers pulled back. "Look, fella," Gonz advised, "Why don't you just hold it till we get there, okay?" After that, the cops talked only about the Mets as Frank sat in obedient silence.

At the House, Frank was placed in the small RIP office without benefit of cuffs. When Rosa arrived, she was escorted to the sergeant's office, separated from her lover by the wide PDU office. We focused our attention on Frank at last. He told us that he had been employed as a maintenance worker until recently, that he had never assaulted Rosa or taken any money from her. In fact, he told us earnestly, he had recently given her two hundred dollars in cash. He had received a tax refund check made out to him and Rosa jointly, he had her endorse it, and after cashing it gave her a part of the proceeds, which she used to buy herself some clothes and a "hot" TV set from a man on the street. The only time he had ever demanded or handled Rosa's purse, he assured us with some vehemence, was one time when he suspected that she was using tranquilizer pills contrary to their agreement to stick faithfully to the methadone regimen.

He appeared sincere, his story was convincing. He also told us that earlier that day he had left their conjugal apartment in Rosa's company to go to court to answer a criminal complaint stemming from an earlier arrest of both of them in the Ninth Precinct for shoplifting. He was determined to get himself straightened out and have nothing further to do with Rosa who, he confided, had been nothing but trouble since he met her. The impression Frank made on us all was favorable. Of the two, he certainly seemed the wronged party. Gonzalez and I went back to Rosa, sitting sullenly in the sergeant's office. This time Gonzalez spoke to her mostly in Spanish. No, she told him, she had never been arrested. No, she had never received any cash from Frank. No, she had never endorsed any tax refund check. No, she had not left the apartment that day in Frank's company.

Gonzalez got the records on the shoplifting arrest. Frank's story checked out. Some further checking disclosed that Rosa had no fewer than three outstanding warrants on her, meaning that on three separate occasions she had failed to appear in court on some criminal charge and the judge had issued a warrant for her arrest.

Gonz was getting angry. "I thought you told me you had never been arrested," he challenged her. "Now let's go over this again, and this time I want the truth." Yes, she admitted, she did remember endorsing that government check and receiving some cash from Frank. Yes, actually, Frank was still living in the apartment, and they had left together to go to court that morning. But, she insisted, he had trashed her apartment, and he had robbed her on that rainy night. "How can I believe you about anything after you lied to me three times?" Gonzalez asked her rhetorically. He moved her from the sergeant's office to the detention pen and notified the warrant squad. But Frank still sat in the RIP office, and Gonzalez was puzzled about what to do with him.

Sergeant Browne was not on the premises, so the first thing Gonz did was telephone the District Attorney's Office for advice. I was surprised when he told me he had done so. RIP cops, in my experience, do not ask for advice very often. Not from anyone. Two or three of them working on a case together will casually check their moves with one another occasionally, though even then I have not often heard one turn to another and ask flat out: "What do I do now?"

The logical person to turn to for advice would be the sergeant in command. In addition to affording insulation against backfire, Sergeant Browne enjoys the respect of his men. Yet when I once asked one of them why they did not consult Marty Browne more frequently, he shrugged and said, "We're police officers. We're supposed to know the Job. We don't want him to think we're afraid to take on the hard ones."

The Legal Bureau of the Police Department also provides machinery for the line cop to get expert advice. Just a phone call away, sergeants and better—often lawyers in uniform—are standing by to answer questions. I have seen that call placed only once. When I ask, "How come?" the reply is a disgusted grunt: "I've never been that desperate. The answer takes a week to come back, and then—often as not— it's so full of ifs, buts, and howevers that I don't know any more than when I started."

Gonzalez's call to the D.A.'s Office was no help; the A.D.A. who got on the line told him it was "a police matter." So as Frank sat, passive and uncertain, in the small RIP office while his erstwhile paramour sulked in a cell, Tommy Longobardi, Hiram Gonzalez, and I stood in the middle of the PDU office and debated the next move. Tommy was noncommittal: it was not his collar. I was not much more help. I only asked why Gonz did not phone Sergeant Browne at home and let him decide. "Don't want to bother him" was the reply.   Gonz shook his head. "I just can't believe that woman. She admitted she lied to me, how can I believe her? Three warrants, three!" "Look," Longo finally offered, "if you don't believe her, why take him in? No D.A. will write this up, you know that. So what's the point?"

Still undecided, Gonz returned to the RIP office. He looked at Frank. "Listen, guy," he said, sounding more assured than he was, "if I let you walk out of here, can I get your word you won't bother this woman any more?" Fervently, Frank supplied his word. "You still have clothes and stuff up at her apartment?" Frank nodded. "Well," Gonz continued, constructing his plan as he went along, "I don't want you going back there to get them, understand?" Frank, afraid to utter a sound that might divert Gonzalez from his developing plan, nodded again. "You come back here. Six o'clock. We'll send a uniformed cop over there with you to get your gear, understand?" Gonz had another thought: "Where do you plan to live?"

"As soon as I get my things, I'm getting on a bus and getting out of this town. My brother's got a place in Middletown, upstate. I'll go stay with him. I should've got out long ago. That woman is no good for me; I can see that now."

Reassured, Gonz put his plan in motion. He let Frank get up and walk out. Frank did not glance in the direction of the detention cell as he left. Gonz looked at me. "I sure hope we did the right thing, buddy."

We didn't. Frank did not show up at the appointed time and two days later went back to Rosa's apartment and tore it apart.

Shortly thereafter, Rocky Regina spotted Frank at the methadone center and locked him up. But he was released again, this time by the court. Some weeks later, someone set a fire in the building where Rosa lived, beneath her apartment. Frank was the prime suspect. The last I heard, he was still at large and wanted for questioning.

Beware the ring of truth.

"You see? What did I tell you?" Marty Browne pursued the familiar argument. "You've got to protect yourself. If Rosa had been in that apartment—maybe with a couple of kids, God forbid—and that fire had got one of them, how would Gonzalez explain why he let Frank go in the first place?"

"Don't you think he has a good explanation?" I countered. "He had an incredible complainant. He wasn't working on a hunch; she admitted several lies."

"I don't care how many lies she admitted," Browne said. "She stuck to the robbery part of the story. It's not the cop's job to decide who's telling the truth. That's for the court or the D.A."

I was not satisfied. "Don't we expect the cop to use a little common sense? If he knows the case is going out as soon as it gets downtown, why spend everyone's time and money to bring it down there."

Browne was unpersuaded. "Listen, there are rules in this department. In a domestic situation, the cop is not supposed to make peace. If one party complains, the cop makes the collar. There's a good reason for that rule, believe it or not. Somebody did an experiment. They tried every way of dealing with these domestic disputes and found that what worked best was the good old-fashioned arrest. It's also safest for the cop. These things can get dangerous—look at what happened in this case. We were just lucky no one got hurt."

I saw the point as well as the futility of arguing it further. But I had to remind Marty that it was not a police decision that led to the arson. "Let's not forget it was the court, not Gonz, that let Frank out before he torched the place."

"And don't think I'm not thankful for that," Marty replied with feeling.

19

TRY A LITTLE TRUTH
FOR A CHANGE

The complainant was a man named Robert, calling himself Roberta, who dressed like a woman and worked as a beautician. "Not bad, either," Tommy Longobardi noted appreciatively. "Could have fooled me." Robert claimed that while sitting in Tompkins Square Park with his portable stereo sound box, a man he had never laid eyes on before threatened him with a knife, threw him to the ground, and took the sound box, which Robert said was worth about two hundred dollars.

Robert told Longobardi that as the thief fled with the radio, he dropped a plastic identification card, which Robert recovered and turned over to the police. Tommy telephoned the person named on the card—call him White—and asked him to come in. White appeared at the appointed hour at the RIP office. He readily told Tommy a remarkable story.

Yes, White said, he had known Robert for some time, although he thought he was a woman named Roberta. He had been up to Robert's apartment a few times and, on the occasion in question, engaged in some amorous activities with him. He was about to leave the apartment when he remembered that he needed to buy Pampers for his baby and had no money. Robert was out of the room and, without telling him, White "borrowed" the sound box and later pledged it to a friend in exchange for some cash. A day or so later, he saw Robert on the street. Robert angrily accused him of stealing the radio and demanded its return. White promised to get it back from his friend and return it to Robert. Robert asked for some "security" to back White's word, and White gave him the plastic identification card from his wallet. To prove his version, White described Robert's apartment to Longobardi. Tommy let him leave, telling him he would telephone him again if he were needed. He then took White's story to Robert, who unequivocally called White a liar and reaffirmed his original account of the incident. He swore he had never seen White before.

I thought the case of the purloined sound box might be a good one for a lie detector test. Tommy liked the idea at once. He had never seen the polygraph test and looked forward to learning how it was done. We had a discussion about the device and whether we should ask both White and Robert to take it.

We had just heard a departmental message encouraging detectives to avail themselves of the police polygraph facility, which apparently was being widely ignored by police who preferred their traditional methods of assessing credibility or who—like Browne—did not think police business included veracity checks on witnesses or victims. Tommy phoned the Department polygraph operator, only to learn (to his disgust) that the facility was suddenly jammed with requests and there would be a two-week wait to have the test performed. "I should have known," Tommy snorted. "They finally get something interesting on line, then they set it up so that no cop can possibly use it. Two weeks! Sometimes I can't escape the feeling that this department is run by morons."

The next day, White was in the office again and I suggested that Tommy have him make a sketch of the layout and furnishings of Robert's apartment. White obligingly drew a careful though crude rendition containing many details: number and location of windows, floor covering, shape and location of the hallway and the rooms off it, position of sofa and table in the living room, and so forth. Tommy went over to the apartment and the sketch checked out. Robert tried to shrug it off. "He must have been in here some other time."

"Robert? He's lying," Tommy told me confidently. "I think he's lying, Harry Childs thinks he's lying, everyone here thinks he's lying. But he sticks to his stupid story." An appointment was finally scheduled with the polygraph unit. "That should solve it," Browne told me.

The polygraph, or "lie-detector," test occupies a decidedly equivocal place in the criminal justice system. One might suppose that in a system fundamentally devoted to finding the truth—an extraordinarily difficult business— any help from the scientific world would be warmly welcomed. Committed as we are to entrusting nearly impossible tasks to the mystical twelve in the jury box, we still recognize that experts are useful when the jury is called upon to make some determination beyond the common ken.

But judging whether a witness is lying or telling the truth, difficult as it may be, is just the sort of decision that courts believe to be within the competence of an ordinary lay jury. Even under relaxed rules that encourage expert testimony, most courts would probably reject an "expert" opinion—from a psychologist, for example—concerning the veracity of a witness who had testified at the trial. Some psychologists, by special training or research, may actually be experts in mendacity, and their opinion might really help an uncertain jury. But courts are wary of usurping the jury's traditional province, and judges remain reluctant to allow witnesses to "interfere" in the process of deciding matters of credibility.

In addition to the problem of invading jury turf, polygraph evidence must cross a barrier of interdisciplinary suspicion. Not every self-proclaimed expert is accepted as qualified to offer an opinion in court. Trial judges gener-

ally follow a set formula for the qualification of an expert:
The witness must be specially educated or experienced in a
subject or technique that has been accepted as valid for purposes other than litigation. The idea is perfectly sensible. If
the procedure or the basis for expert understanding is sufficiently reliable to be employed generally in some recognized
field, it is good enough for jury consideration. A witness
who testifies about blood types, for instance, will be heard
because all serologists use the same system in grouping
blood for medical purposes. One of the reasons asserted for
not allowing the polygraph operator to testify is that no
scientific community exists that can vouch for the reliability of the technique. Polygraphologists belong to no discipline but their own; their work passes no critical peer test of
acceptance.

These reasons are not entirely persuasive. Courts do accept expert opinions on many things that might be thought
to be within the ordinary knowledge or experience of a
layperson. Whether two signatures were written by the
same hand, whether the blow of a hammer can cause a frac-
ture of the skull—questions such as these receive expert
opinions. Too, courts have accepted expert opinion in
much newer and narrower fields than polygraph operation.
Voice print analysis, for example. And experts have been
deemed qualified in test methods that have virtually no
uses outside the courtroom: ballistics, hair and fiber matching, and so forth.

The real reason why polygraph evidence is still not accepted in any court is neither the jury turf problem nor the
technical obstacle to qualifying an expert. The real reason
stems from insufficient confidence in juror skepticism. The
aura of infallibility of the "lie detector," unwarranted in
the estimation of our courts, creates what lawyers call *prejudice*. Prejudice, as lawyers use the term, means that a jury is
likely to accord to an item of evidence greater probative
value than it deserves, or that they will mistakenly consider
the evidence as proof of a fact it does not really imply. For
example, a prosecutor may want to prove that a defendant
on trial for robbery was previously convicted of a robbery

committed in the same neighborhood. The evidence may be relevant inasmuch as it tends to prove that the defendant frequents the area where the crime was committed, but it would be highly prejudicial because the jury might also take the evidence as proof that the defendant is "a robber" and therefore probably committed the crime with which he is charged. In fact, committing robbery A is no evidence whatever of the commission of the unrelated robbery B.

The unwarranted reputation of the polygraph, courts fear, might overwhelm the deliberative process. Juries should not surrender their responsibility for assessing veracity to some "expert" who takes the stand and pronounces the magic words "lie detector." Whether jurors would in fact be so overwhelmed by the information that a person passed or flunked the lie detector test as to abdicate their sworn duty is a matter of pure conjecture. But it does seem likely that the credibility-judging mission is so perplexing that at least some jurors might turn too eagerly to any "scientific" rescue.

Just how reliable is the polygraph? We really have no idea. Listen to the polygraph lobby, and the device is virtually infallible. (The saving feature, according to the polygraph people, is the "inconclusive" category. An uncooperative subject or skillful liar, they say, can put himself into this slot, but he can't actually fool the black box.) Most other commentators will say such things as "A great deal depends on the skill of the operator, and we have no control for that" or "While we can count a certain number of liars discovered, we can never measure the false results and, so as long as we posit a less than perfect performance (as we do), we can never know the actual level of accuracy."

If for these reasons there is universal rejection in a courtroom, why does the Police Department encourage its use by investigative officers? The fact is that, notwithstanding its unsuitability for jurors, the polygraph is widely employed by both government and the private sector for questions of employee honesty and the like. And law enforcement agencies, including prosecutors' offices, occasionally use the polygraph to check the veracity of a questionable witness.

Frequently, the mere suggestion is enough to produce some modification in a witness's story.

The polygraph did the trick in the Robert/Roberta case, but indirectly. "The lie detector test came up inconclusive," Browne told me a few days later. "But the cop who runs it is pretty sharp. He thought White was lying, so he didn't even tell him the result. He just played on the guy's guilt. After the test was over, he simply said, 'You're lying,' and White admitted the whole thing to him. Easy as that—and after all the time Tommy spent on it. White just shrugged and said, 'Yeah, you're right. I am lying.' I guess he decided to try a little truth for a change."

"Did he give the polygraph man the whole story?" I asked.

"He told him how he saw Robert in the park, knocked him down, and took the radio. Didn't admit to the knife, but he gave us enough to lock him up on a robbery." Marty smiled. " You see? Who was the only one around here who said from the beginning, 'Let's not try the case in the squadroom; make the collar and let the court decide.' "

I was astounded. "But Marty," I protested, "the diagram! How did White know the layout of Robert's place if he was a stranger?"

Marty laughed. "I asked Tommy about that. He said he was so disgusted when the mope came out and admitted the whole thing, he didn't think to ask him. I can't blame him for being fed up. The way this guy jerked him around, he was in no mood to ask him any more 'how comes.' "

I looked at Marty, bewildered. "I know," he said. "It seems kind of funny to me too. White must have been up there some time to draw that sketch. But as I told you before, no one ever gives us the whole truth. I usually end up not knowing what the hell really happened."

Of course, the conclusion of a credibility contest does not always leave an infuriating strand loose. And sometimes the cops know the true story all along and the only problem is finding a way to get the complainant to come out with it.

The little black box with its awesome reputation is only one device available to persuade the cagey customer to try a little truth.

Consider, for example, the day I arrived to find Marty Browne interviewing a tearful young white woman at one of the desks in the PDU office. He looked as though he was about to drop off to sleep, or maybe rouse himself, throw down his pen, ask the young woman what kind of fool she took him for, and heave her out of the office. Instead, as I approached, he stared at her blankly, and said in an uncharacteristically flat tone, "So tell me again how it happened." The victim described how she had been approached by two black women, one very pregnant, who asked for directions. One of them then opened her purse, displayed a knife, and demanded money. The victim surrendered what little she had, together with her watch. They asked her whether she had a bank account and, when she confessed she did, they took her to the bank and made her withdraw her meager savings and turn the money over to them. Marty grunted and wrote it all down. Behind her, offering an occasional reassuring pat on the shoulder, was the distraught victim's boyfriend.

A few minutes later, out of earshot in the RIP office, Marty told me wearily, "Con game. Obviously. She's ashamed to admit she was such a fool in front of her boyfriend." A couple of the other RIP cops who had heard the story nodded in agreement. Pocketbook drop, no doubt.

"What are you going to do?" I asked, "Write it up as a robbery?"

"That's what she's giving me," Browne replied.

"But you don't believe her story," I pressed.

"Look," Browne said patiently, "there's a lot of stories I hear on this job I don't believe. But I'm not the jury. People don't take an oath when they talk to me, and I'm not the one supposed to decide who's telling the truth. You know that, Professor." He smiled.

"Say, Boss," Joe Sweeney put in mildly, "let me talk to her alone for a few minutes. What do you say?"

"Help yourself," Browne replied with a shrug. Sweeney,

middle-aged and overweight, collects old glassware and other thrift shop items, carefully checking them off in catalogs, as absorbed as any patron of Sotheby's. He had once told me that in all his years on the Job, his greatest satisfaction had been to help a troubled young person straighten out his life. To the amusement of the others, I had dubbed this gentle and soft-spoken detective our staff psychologist. Now he was closeted in the lieutenant's office with the complainant. I also noticed a quiet conversation going on in the corner between one of our cops and the boyfriend.

Twenty minutes later, I watched as the young woman, now thoroughly composed, recounted how she had lost her money in a classic confidence swindle known as the *pocketbook drop*. The knife disappeared from the story, to be replaced by the usual dialogue with a stranger about a found purse containing a large stack of cash that the loser, for some reason, could or would never reclaim. Flashing the currency, the woman tells the victim that some respected person—a former employer, perhaps—had advised her that it was perfectly legal for them to keep the money. At this point, a second woman comes on the scene, pretending to be a stranger to the first. Her opinion is solicited and she suggests that, since they do not know each other, they should each post "good faith money" as a condition for obtaining a share of the windfall no one would miss. They both then turn to our trusting victim who readily agrees to a plan the other two think is the right way to proceed. The mark then goes to her bank (nearby, since she had been spotted by the con artists only minutes before as she emerged from the bank), and withdraws her life's savings. In exchange for being dealt in on the split, she posts the money as her bond of "good faith" only to see it disappear with her new partners. She is left, literally, holding a paper bag, which now contains a well-wrapped bundle of newspaper cut to the size and shape of currency.

It was a familiar tale, even to me, and Browne looked much happier taking her revised story, as the rest of us guessed the usual details, and offered reassurances that many others had lost a good deal more money than she had in similar traps. Obviously, our complainant felt much better telling the truth, and even the boyfriend seemed relieved that she had abandoned her contrived tale. Maybe that's worth something in Joe Sweeney's terms.

To me, the case was a rare and dramatic instance of a complainant who turned truthful before our very eyes. We didn't do it with the little black box; we had Joe Sweeney. But however it was accomplished, her conversion—like White's—was a momentous event in a criminal justice system starved for veracity.

20

THE PRECIOUS
CONFESSION OF GUILT

Agents of law enforcement everywhere have a long-standing and well-known appetite for words acknowledging guilt from people suspected of committing crimes. Particularly at the culmination of a long and difficult investigation, there is nothing so gratifying as the prisoner's confession. Contrite or defiant, the contribution of the perpetrator is ardently solicited, delicately elicited, and warmly appreciated.

The process of identifying, locating, and capturing a suspect taps many of the primal energies of the hunt that seem so firmly embedded in the human unconscious. The sense of triumph in bringing down the quarry is even more deeply satisfying when the last gasp of total surrender is forthcoming: "You got me, I give up. I lay down my defenses, my bluffs, my evasions. I'm yours." It has to be a glorious moment, even for the most seasoned hunter.

In addition, the confession provides confirmation of suspicion, which also seems important to the pursuer's peace of mind and urge for completion. Not every case is clear, and a cloudy picture makes the investigator's sense of rectitude uneasy. For many law enforcement people—police and prosecutors—the confident belief that they are doing the right thing is a vital ingredient in the undertaking. Even if the confession is excluded from evidence at a subsequent trial, it contributes that needed assurance. With all the frustration, the ugliness, and the hazards of the Job, the feeling of being right is an enormously important reward to take home after a day's work.

A particularly dramatic (and ironic) example of the hunger for confession occurred some years ago following a shockingly brutal double murder of two young women, Emily Hoffert and Janice Wylie, on Manhattan's posh Upper East side. A specially composed team of detectives fruitlessly pursued tips and leads for months. Coming to a near standstill, amid periodic press lashings, the investigation received a bad reversal when a dull-witted drifter named Whitmore, arrested in Brooklyn on an unrelated charge, suddenly gave a long and detailed confession to the Manhattan murders. A conscientious young Assistant District Attorney in Manhattan was suspicious. He conducted a thorough investigation and finally disproved the confession. The indictment against the hapless young Whitmore was immediately dismissed (he said he had given the false confession because the police had treated him so well), and the investigation—now seriously bruised—resumed.

Some time later, long after every clue had been chased to a dead end, a couple of drug addicts were arrested. They offered the police valuable information in exchange for lenient treatment. They said they would give up the murderer of Janice Wylie and Emily Hoffert. The parched investigators eagerly worked out the deal and were given the name of a professional flat burglar, Ricky Robles, who, the informants said, had come to them on the night of the murders, his clothes soaked with blood. They had listened to his account of the double murder and helped him destroy the incriminating evidence. The cops took the information to the same young prosecutor who had exonerated Whitmore.

After some preliminary checking, both the A.D.A and the police were inclined to believe that Robles had murdered

Hoffert and Wylie. But they knew they could never convict
him on the highly suspect account of the accessories, tendered to buy leniency. Corroboration was needed. So arrest
was deferred and every device was tried to obtain some additional evidence, including repeated attempts by the informants to lure the suspect into conversation about the crime,
while eager investigators listened secretly (with the informants' consent, of course) by means of hidden micro-
phones. All to no avail.

Eventually, Robles learned of the interest of the police,
and the effort to trap him into a self-inculpatory move became a farce. Their hand forced, the police finally moved in
and made the arrest. They had one last hope: a confession.
From the moment he was taken into custody, the suspect
had only one thing to say to the officers (showing them a
card): "I want to talk to my lawyer." The cops knew, and
certainly the young Assistant D.A. directing the operation
knew full well that any statement, no matter how detailed
and reliable, given by the suspect after requesting to consult
counsel could not be used as evidence against him in the
courts of New York. Nonetheless, with the prosecutor's con-
nivance, the police ignored the request, and for hours they
tried every trick in the book to induce Robles to utter the
acknowledgment. Threat, cajolery, false promise, prayer,
and the supposed last wish of a dying mother—all conveyed
by a battery of the department's most skilled interrogators—
were met with the same cool response: "I want to see my
lawyer, here's his phone number."

I later asked the young prosecutor (now a judge) why he
had allowed the protracted effort to obtain a confession to
continue when he knew it could not possibly produce a
piece of usable corroborative evidence. "We wanted to hear
it from his own mouth," he told me simply. "After all we'd
been through in that case, with the false confession and all,
we just wanted to hear him tell us that we had the right guy
this time. For our own peace of mind. It seemed very important to us all at the time."

The ironic twist came after the police team finally gave
in and called the suspect's lawyer, who came down to the

stationhouse and conferred privately with his client. The lawyer left the room to use the public phone down the hall. A cop who had known the suspect from the neighborhood years before sauntered in and offered the suspect a bite of the sandwich he was eating. The cop sat on the table and said one sentence: "Rick, did you ever think it would wind up like this?" In the same tone, Robles replied, "I don't know— I went to pull a lousy burglary and I wound up killing two girls."

And it all came pouring out. The cops tried to slow the torrent of confession, to write it down, to get a stenographer, to call a superior officer, but there was no halting it once the floodgates had opened. The confession contained verified details unknown to the police up to that moment (unlike the previous discredited "confession," the recited details of which were all known to the interrogating officer), and Richard Robles was convicted for the crimes.

Psychological gratification, however, is not the only power driving police to press for a confession. Cops know that whatever other evidence may be at hand, if the jury learns that the defendant freely admitted his participation in the crime, that evidence will count heavily when the jury considers its verdict. And if, for some reason, the other evidence in the case weakens, the confession may make the difference between conviction and acquittal. Richard G. Denzer, former prosecutor and retired judge, once wryly wrote:

> Said the cop as he viewed with contrition
> The defendant's bloody condition,
> "For the case that's not sure
> There is really no cure
> Like a solid, substantial admission."

Sometimes police press a suspect for information simply for the value of the information. One Monday, while visiting another RIP unit, I noticed a small, unprepossessing man sitting disconsolate in the squad's detention cage. Eventually I discovered what he was being held for. On the preceding Friday evening, a merchant, Sidney Blum, was closing up his shop. He told the police that in the shop with him at that time were his brother, Myron, and a man who had been hired at the beginning of the week as temporary help. His name was Sonny and his job was to keep the store swept out and tidy. Sidney Blum was licensed by the Police Department to carry a handgun, which he kept in a holster on his belt. Myron was locking up in front of the store as Sidney counted the receipts in back. Suddenly Sidney felt a hard object shoved in his ribs from behind, and Sonny demanded, "Give me your gun." As Sidney later told the police, he took it off his belt, still in its holster, and handed it over to Sonny, who immediately left by the back door, which led to an alley. Sidney shouted to his brother and both gave chase, but they soon lost sight of Sonny.

The police notified the agency from which Blum had hired Sonny and, surprisingly, Sonny showed up for another work assignment the following Monday morning. The police were called, and they arrested him without any trouble. "Just to be sure" (as they explained to me), the police held a lineup, and each of the Blums separately picked out Sonny at once. That was the state of affairs when I walked in.

After filling me in, the sergeant's interest in Sonny seemed to reawaken. He unlocked the cell and took Sonny out. Telling the others he wanted to have a talk with Sonny, the sergeant headed to the line-up room at the other end of the PDU office. I went along and took a chair in one corner as the sergeant seated himself across the table from Sonny.

"Look," the sergeant said without preliminaries, "I'm going to level with you, Sonny. I'm going to tell you right off what I want, okay? I want that gun, that's what I want. That's all I want. I don't care about you. I don't care if you go to jail or whatever. I gotta get that gun back, and I'm going to get it. You understand what I'm saying to you? Now are you going to tell me like a gentleman what you did with it?"

Sonny looked steadily and sadly back at him. "I'm sorry, Captain," he said slowly. "I don't have no gun."

"I know you don't have the gun on you now." The sergeant allowed a flicker of impatience to suggest that he was having difficulty holding his temper under control. "I want to know what you did with it. If you hid it somewhere, or gave it to some dude, I want to know about it. I've got to get that gun back before someone gets hurt. Look, you're not a bad guy." The sergeant's voice softened as he tried a new tack. "You don't want someone to get hurt out there with that gun. Because if someone gets shot, it'll be on you—you know that, don't you?"

Sonny paused a long time, before answering, raising our hopes. "I told you, Captain—I mean Sergeant. I don't know nothing about no gun."

The sergeant had Sonny in that room almost two hours. As he later put it to me with a laugh, he tried everything he knew. He asked Sonny to tell us his version of what happened and listened attentively to a largely incoherent account of events having nothing to do with the incident. We looked at each other. Clearly, Sonny was not playing with a full deck. Patiently, the sergeant told him that he couldn't believe that story after hearing the complainant's version. After all, Sonny's employer, Blum, was an established merchant in the area who had been carefully checked out by the police before he had been issued the gun license (untrue); Sonny just shook his head sorrowfully. The sergeant appealed to Sonny as one Catholic to another. Silence. Suspecting from some phony ID that Sonny carried that he might be a "buff," the sergeant solemnly swore him in as a "Special Deputy" assigned to the recovery of the gun. Nothing.

The sergeant found out that Sonny sometimes stayed with an aged mother and told him he was going to get a search warrant and "go out and tear her house apart." And he warned, lacing his voice with menace, if he found the gun in Sonny's mother's house, she would have to serve a year in jail for it. He opened the door and called to one of the men, asking whether the warrant had been drawn to search the "old lady's place." He suggested that if Sonny told him what he wanted to know, they might forget about the charge of robbery altogether.

For all his effort, the sergeant got nowhere.

Finally, he began to share some of my doubts about the complaint. Our prisoner did not look like the kind to pull such a bold stunt. And then too, the sergeant wondered out loud, why had he left the money untouched after he had the gun in hand? Was it possible that Blum had lost the gun some other way—negligently, perhaps—and, rather than report it as it had happened, concocted the robbery story? Possible, the sergeant conceded. But why bother with such an elaborate and risky story when all he had to do was say his house or car had been broken into and the weapon stolen? A good point, too.

I hated to leave the case in such a state of uncertainty. Who was the liar, the Blums or Sonny? I never learned the outcome; I was only visiting for the day, and when I phoned to ask, the sergeant told me he had dropped the case into the "system" and lost track of it. The sergeant's heavy-handed interrogation might well have been excessive, but his only purpose seems to have been the recovery of the weapon. He didn't need a confession for the case; he had a creditable (though probably dishonest) witness plus a solid identification. But in terms of energy and persistence, he appeared to be pressing a good deal harder in pursuit of the goal of recovering the gun than he might have had the confession been his primary object. Or maybe he was only showing off his skills as an interrogator for the benefit of a visiting professor.

Mainly, of course, the confession is sought for its incriminating content. As evidence, however, the confession suffers from peculiar infirmities. By nature, evidence in this form must be given secondhand. The physical object in evidence speaks for itself; the testimony of an eyewitness, who testifies under oath and subject to cross-examination, is the live repository of matters personally perceived. The significance of the object may be disputed. The credibility of the witness or the meaning of his or her perception may be a subject of disagreement. But the evidence is there before the fact finder for examination.

The defendant's self-inculpatory declaration, by contrast, usually comes before the fact finder from the mouth of someone else, generally a police officer. Traditionally, the rules of evidence take a dim view of such secondhand reports of important verbal communications. It is called *hearsay*, but there are a number of exceptions to the rule against admitting such evidence in court. The confession is one of the oldest and most firmly established of those exceptions.

Although the law allows it, the oral report of the police officer carries several intrinsic weaknesses when it finally arrives in court. The first—and far from the least of these—is not a hearsay problem at all. It is the question of credibility. Every juror understands that the easiest way for an eager cop to win his conviction is simply to testify that the defendant, having been properly advised of his rights, ruefully acknowledged that he was the perpetrator. Tendered in oral form, evidence of confession is, therefore, often suspect.

Even assuming that the jury is ready to believe that the defendant made a statement admitting his guilt, spoken words are an especially unstable form of proof. It is difficult—really impossible—for even the most conscientious person to recall the precise words used by another to express an idea. Great phrases adhere to the memory, often immutable in form. "Fourscore and seven years ago" remains indelible in the mind in that particular language and the exact phrase "Wherefore art thou Romeo?" is probably better known than its meaning. But the conversations and narratives of our fellow creatures are usually remembered only by substance and paraphrase.

When it comes to a confession, however, the precise expression may be more important than the general import. There is a world of difference, for example, between: (a) "She told me that she killed him but she claimed she acted in self-defense," and (b) "She said, 'I was standing with my back against the kitchen wall. George flipped open his knife and lunged at my belly. I am six months pregnant, remember. So I swung the iron and hit him on the side of his head.' " In this instance, it is obviously important to the defendant to have her words reported fully and accurately. In other cases, the prosecution may suffer by paraphrase. Persuasion, after all, is the burden of the prosecutor, and the cop's testimony reporting only the gist of the defendant's statement rarely carries the impact of a verbatim rendition.

The age-old response of law enforcement officers to this age-old problem has been the written confession. But it is a poor device. Most defendants do not express themselves easily in writing. A cop cannot say to the average suspect, "Here's a pad and pen, my good man. Please write down just what happened, and don't spare us the crucial details." Nor do most people talk well while someone else is writing it all down. Or trying to. Cops don't take shorthand. And verbatim notes, preserving the suspect's words while not slowing the flow, are too much to ask. So what comes out is usually a rather crude police effort to capture the essence of the story, maybe even keeping some of the original flavor, but often betraying its unmistakable authorship. I saw one such statement purporting to be in the suspect's own words and discovered that the *dramatis personae* were all identified as "FB," and "MWH," and the like, cop shorthand for "female black" and "male white Hispanic." Even if signed (and even the most talkative suspect somehow balks at signing a piece of paper), a statement in the officer's language may later be attacked as words put in the suspect's mouth by an overzealous cop.

Ancient history, one might think. Once again technology has come to the rescue. Hearsay and the written confession are obsolete; video is here. Would it were so.

I suppose that today most major police or prosecutors' offices boast some video equipment. But few cities have cameras at the ready in the interrogation rooms of local stationhouses. Notwithstanding the proven superiority of the recorded image of the defendant coolly recounting his crimes—unbeaten, unthreatened, and often unprodded—economic considerations invariably prevail. In Manhattan, virtually no crime except murder is serious enough for the prosecutor to send out the video crew. The Police Department itself has apparently never been able to scrape up the cash to purchase video equipment of its own.

For one reason or another, there was clearly no way 9 RIP was going to put any of its customers on videotape. When I mentioned it to Marty Browne, he just laughed, "Hey, are you kidding? We can't even get color film for the Polaroid."

I would have been happy with electronics of a far simpler—and less expensive—sort. While an ordinary tape recorder might not reassure the jury that the suspect was speaking with untwisted arm, surely an audiotape is far superior to any other device in use. Sergeant Browne and all the men to whom I made my suggestion agreed heartily.

"If it makes such good sense and costs so little," I asked, "why doesn't the department do it?"

"You just answered your own question," Marty replied dryly. "Now you're beginning to understand the way this department works. If it's simple, cheap, and effective, the brass gets very nervous and everybody changes the subject."

21

MIRANDA EXPLAINED (AT LAST)

Since the founding of the Republic, courts have rejected evidence of confessions obtained by torture. The actual words of the famous *privilege against self-incrimination* of the Fifth Amendment to the Constitution are that no person "shall be compelled in any criminal case to be a witness against himself." And no one ever doubted that applying physical force to induce a person to utter self-inculpatory statements amounts to compelling that person to be a witness against himself. Nor was any specially constructed exclusionary rule thought necessary to bar the subsequent use at a criminal trial of a statement thus obtained against the person from whom it was forcefully extracted. Thus, the court's reaction to a violation of the Fifth Amendment contrasts with the hands-off attitude toward unreasonable searches and seizures which were unlawful under the Constitution's Fourth Amendment but—for 172 years—admissible in state courts where most criminal cases are tried.

One might easily guess that the reason for the courts' longstanding rejection of forcefully extracted confessions derives simply from judicial understanding that innocent people may confess falsely in order to avoid or terminate physical pain. Since reliability of evidence—that is, its actual tendency to prove what it purports to prove—is the basis upon which admissibility is normally judged, the dubious probity of a coerced confession seems an obvious reason it should be excluded at a trial.

The guess would be wrong. We were carefully and clearly instructed by the Supreme Court, speaking in the pedagogical tones of Justice Felix Frankfurter, that reliability is a wholly irrelevant consideration. In a case called *Rogers v. Richmond*, Frankfurter wrote in the strongest terms that a court should not take into account the probable truth or falsity of a confession in passing upon its admissibility in evidence at the trial. The implication of the decision, and the unwavering line in the Court since, is that the constitutionality of the police action must be assessed by the methods employed and not the effects produced. Many people give demonstrably true confessions under torture; they are not on that account acceptable in a court of law. Torture is itself intolerable, and the product is irremediably tainted, however probative.

From physical coercion to the threat of it is only a small step, and threats were assimilated unnoticed into the rule against compelled confessions. From there, little extension was required to include psychological coercion. *Psychological coercion* refers to pressure that neither inflicts nor threatens direct physical harm. Incessant and protracted interrogation, for example, or deprivation of food or sleep for twenty-four hours, while not really damaging to physiological health, have the forbidden tendency to overbear the will and induce nonvoluntary "cooperation." The analogy to physical coercion is strong and the result is the same.

Unfortunately, however, the category of psychological coercion is not always so clearly marked as simple brutality. False statements by the interrogating officers, for example, are particularly troublesome. A police officer's lie may precipitate an admission, but it does not necessarily compel it. For instance, the false statement that an eyewitness who had a good clear view of the perpetrator has just been located may move the recalcitrant suspect to admit his guilt, but it would be difficult to call the admission "compelled" in the constitutional sense. On the other hand, if a suspect succumbs to an officer's contrived threat to tear his mother's house apart in search of a missing weapon, any resulting statement can easily be recognized as compelled by *fraud*, a form of psychological intimidation.

The mark of intolerable deception is not falsity alone but the coercive impact of the false threat. A false *threat*, after all, is different from a false *statement of fact*. And some courts and legislatures have drawn the line of admissibility on the basis of whether the deception was so threatening that it might induce even an innocent person falsely to admit guilt. Because this standard of coercive deception does not take account of the actual reliability of the particular statement made, focusing rather on the nature of the trick that induced it, the rule probably does not disturb the ghost of Felix Frankfurter.

The standard conforms to our sense of justice too; we're not likely to get a false confession from a false statement that a good set of prints had been found at the scene, and if we get a true one, the lie does not seem altogether deplorable. Inducing true admissions of culpability—even by misleading statements—seems to most of us far less troublesome than inducing false ones. Only the purest idealists would argue that all police deception is unacceptable and the suspect under interrogation must have a factually true and complete account of the state of the case against him to allow him to make an informed, and therefore free, choice to cooperate. It is doubtful that this is the teaching of *Rogers v. Richmond* and in 1986, in similar though not identical circumstances, Justice Sandra Day O'Connor wrote in *Moran v. Burbine*: "[W]e have never read the Constitution to require that the police supply a suspect with a flow of [accurate] information to help him calibrate his self interest in deciding whether to speak or stand on his rights."

So, on the eve of the Great *Miranda* Decision, here's where we stood: any proven police conduct that overcame the suspect's freedom to resist the police hunger for confession, any interference—whether by torture, threat of physical abuse, or psychological coercion—with the suspect's free will to choose whether or not to supply his own acknowledgment of culpability, resulted in the suppression of the suspect's statement along with any other evidence acquired by the police as a direct consequence of it. *Miranda* hasn't changed this doctrine, but it has enlarged it.

The cornerstone of the *Miranda* decision was the Court's discovery of another variety of coercion. Let's call it *inherent coercion.* Citing some rather questionable data (the sort of thing that raises eyebrows throughout the gallery of conservative jurisprudents), the Court found that police generally employ subtle, often undetectable methods of persuasion calculated to obtain the outcome they seek. Principally, the Court relied on a "manual" by Professors Inbau and Reid, who are described as officers of the Chicago Police Scientific Crime Detection Laboratory with extensive lecturing experience. This and another text, the Court noted, had "rather extensive" use and total "sales and circulation" of 44,000.

The Court then devotes several pages of the opinion to a recital of the books' various recommendations such as being "alone with the person under interrogation," depriving the subject of "every psychological advantage," suggesting the "invincibility of the forces of law," displaying "an air of confidence," and minimizing the "moral seriousness of the offense." The officer should "interrogate steadily and without relent, leaving the subject no prospect of surcease," according to one manual, adding that sympathetic questioning might be alternated with "a show of some hostility" in the classic "Mutt and Jeff" act. The Supreme Court (fascinated or outraged) details this and other techniques, quoting at length the colorful language of the police guides.

In addition to the effects of police employment of techniques specifically designed to induce anxiety or to establish false trust, the Court cites the atmosphere of the ordinary police station—isolated, police-dominated—as a factor that conveys to the subject a feeling of hopelessness and foreboding. This pervasive climate, the Court found, inevitably causes some erosion of the sense of personal sovereignty underlying freedom of choice. Thus, coercion to confess is implicit in the situation of custody and common in the process of interrogation. Moreover, this inherent duress undermines voluntary choice even in the mind of an experienced or case-hardened suspect. So, the Court ruled, whenever any person is held by the police, regardless of how gently he is treated and how sophisticated he may be, the fact of custody itself is coercive and the will to decide to cooperate is never free.

Despite the Court's customary protracted effort to explain and justify its conclusion, it is easy to take issue with the intermediate conclusion that coercion is implicit in custody. For one thing, even if the books were circulated or used in training, as the Court claimed, no one—and certainly not the Court—could know whether the recommended techniques were generally, or even frequently, employed.

More important, the Court's psychological assumption concerning the motivation to confess and the will to resist is vulnerable. Even accepting the Court's finding that the "atmosphere" of custodial interrogation is inherently coercive, it is difficult to believe that every suspect, even the streetwise and prison-hardened felon, suffers an appreciable loss of will the instant he finds himself in a police station. While good interrogators may, and occasionally do use interrogative ploys to loosen the tongues of people sitting across a table from them, it seems doubtful that the custodial circumstance of the conversation would so much as nick the confidence of the ordinary suspect, much less overwhelm his power to decide whether to talk and what to say.

I have sat in on a number of sessions at which cops tried—usually without much success—to get a confession and I have no doubt that the police-dominated atmosphere of which the Supreme Court wrote does induce most subjects to moderate aggressive or resentful reactions they might ordinarily exhibit. The cops demand both passivity and respect. But whatever implicit coercion might emanate from the handcuffs or other trappings of custody, I have never seen a suspect's will collapse because of the custodial circumstances in which he was questioned. On the contrary, the cops joke about the impediment of the badge in the quest for truth. "Listen," Joey Dean, who grew up among street toughs and petty criminals on the West Side, once told me, "the people in this Precinct were raised to lie to us. They wouldn't tell us what we wanted to hear even if it would help them. That's the way I was raised myself. I would never tell a cop the truth about anything, would you?"

Nevertheless, the Supreme Court's discovery of *inherent coercion* was generated by legitimate misgivings. As dissenting Justices have indicated, the majority position probably proceeds from an unstated distrust of confession evidence as such. Unstated but not irrational. History and common sense require suspicion concerning the actions of unsupervised police on their own ground, in a head-to-head confrontation with a person they believe to be guilty. Every advantage, including credible deniability, is unmistakably on the police side of the room. The situation presents too easy and tempting an opportunity for the natural affinity of interrogation and torture to reassert itself in some form, however subtle. The notorious police appetite for a confession sometimes—not invariably, but sometimes—leads to oppressive exploitation of an inherently unequal situation.

Moreover, once it takes hold, police license has an unfortunate tendency to expand, all at an inestimable cost to hard-won human liberties in this society. Although there is nothing wrong with confession evidence in itself, the unrestricted opportunity accorded police to obtain such evidence from the uncounseled and isolated person under total domination of arrest is obviously cause for concern. Thus, one might justly say (as did the majority in *Miranda*) that the threat of secret and unlawful force is implicit in the fact of custody and necessarily affects all the acts of every prisoner, including his utterances.

A second argument in support of limiting police access to a suspect for purposes of interrogation is best stated in an aphorism by Sir James Fitzjames Stephens who, speaking of the investigative practices of Indian police, commented that they would much prefer to sit in the shade rubbing pepper in some poor devil's eyes than to go mucking about in the hot sun looking for evidence. So reliance on confessions is sometimes said to encourage police sloth. With full regard to Sir James's research, however, my own experience does not suggest that the opportunity to obtain a confession materially discourages the quest for other evidence.

But whatever might be said either way about the Court's discovery of the debilitating effect of inherent coercion, the truly remarkable thing about the *Miranda* case is the means constructed to resolve the dilemma. The force of its own argument brought the Court to the very edge of a major revision of American criminal process. If custody in and of itself creates a morally intolerable pressure to confess, logic would seem to require the conclusion that every such "coerced" statement uttered in custody is constitutionally inadmissible as trial evidence. Thus, the Court, by its own reasoning, seemed poised on the brink of total rejection of all confessions made by persons under arrest.

From where we now stand, it may seem strange to contemplate a system of criminal law enforcement virtually stripped of confession evidence, but one could muster both principle and logic amply to support that idea. The Constitution provides that no person shall ever be forced to bear witness against himself, and the introduction against him, over his objection, of his own "testimony" given under police interrogation before the trial is, in effect, just that. Moreover, no person in police custody is capable of a truly free decision. And, as a matter of principle, the unfree mind of an unfree person is an impermissible source of evidence for use against that person. Thus, we might conclude, we should tolerate criminal punishment only on evidence of some other kind.

But, having come to the edge, the Court swerved, interrupting the force of its own logic by a second great discovery. In a stroke of inspired alchemy, the Court concocted an antidote to the atmospheric coercion inherent in custodial interrogation. The Court found the ingredients in a British administrative advisory known as the *Judges' Rules* and familiar to any aficionado of English crime fiction. When placing a suspect under arrest, British police are required to speak these words: "You are not obliged to say anything unless you wish to do so, but whatever you say may be put in writing and given in evidence." With a little rewording and two added stanzas, the Judges' Rules became the famous four-part warning that bears the name of the case that created it and is now equally familiar to the fans of domestic crime fiction.

Miranda requires that before beginning interrogation the police officer must advise the suspect in custody that (1) he has a right to remain silent, (2) anything he says may be used against him, (3) he has the right to have counsel present, and (4) if he has no funds to retain counsel, a lawyer will be provided for him free of charge. The officer administering the warning must get an acknowledgment that it was understood, and before questioning can begin, he must obtain an express waiver of both the right to silence and the right to have counsel present. No pressure, trick, or cajolery may be employed to induce a waiver. If either waiver is withheld or revoked, questioning must stop at once. A request for counsel operates exactly like a refusal to be questioned at all.

The wonder of the Court's miraculous rescue of the custodial confession is the notion that the mere utterance of this four-part litany instantly dispels the pall of coercion and permits the suspect to make a free, and therefore operative, choice of whether or not to cooperate with his interrogators.

Should he elect to allow the questioning to go forward, his responses will not be deemed the product of inherent coercion.

It is too late in the game to reargue the anomalies of the *Miranda* solution to the troubling problem of confessions. We can do little more than marvel at where our cultural ambivalence toward this sort of proof has brought us. Confessions from uncounseled prisoners are available as evidence, but only if police first perform a ritual cleansing of the atmosphere. Police, the felon's natural adversary, are converted by the Constitution into disinterested advisors—even counselors—suggesting that he refuse their demand for cooperation. All players must solemnly pretend to a meaningful exchange of words, though the ritual has likely lost all real meaning to both parties. From the mere recital of this catechism, appellate courts are comforted to believe that uncoerced choice is suddenly possible in the previously oppressive interaction between police and suspect, that isolation and police domination have miraculously lost their coercive influence, and that in this newly purged atmosphere the cornered felon may freely forego his right to silence and make a voluntary confession. Truly, acceptance of this myth is an act of faith beyond the bounds of reason.

To me, the resolution of the *Miranda* case seriously impugns the integrity of its premises: if a confession given in police custody is necessarily coerced, so is a waiver. I heartily appreciate the Court's reluctance to outlaw all confessions given by suspects in custody; the cost to law enforcement would be far too great. But if noncoercive custodial interrogation is to be permitted (as it is), the famous warning adds little to the suspect's protection. Those suspects actually intimidated by the circumstances of custody are hardly reassured by hearing the ritual incantation from their inquisitors.

Some argue that the true value of the *Miranda* warning is not in the advice communicated to the suspect but in the implicit assurance that the cop himself recognizes that the suspect need not cooperate in the interrogation. It's a nice twist on the asserted function of the litany, but I doubt that it offers much comfort to most suspects. A truly noncoercive situation provides more substantial assurance that the suspect is in control of the decision to talk than does any form of words read from a little plastic card. So I tend to think that for doctrinal as well as practical reasons, we probably would have done better to confine the operation of the Fifth Amendment privilege to those situations in which true coercion of the pre-*Miranda* variety could be discerned and leave ritual purges of chimerical demons to the witch doctors.

22

MIRANDA
IN THE FIELD

While some few of us remain eager to debate flawed assumptions and logical warps in the *Miranda* reasoning, the question nearly everyone asks is: What effect has the decision actually had in the daily operations of law enforcement? The question may be addressed at more than one level. On a rather elementary reading, the question is manageable. Even a casual observer can furnish some field observations on matters like: Do the cops really give the warnings, and do they give them completely and dispassionately? Do they give them early enough? And do they scrupulously honor an expressed disinclination to talk or a request for a lawyer? Much harder to answer and, I think, more important is the crucial question: Do the warnings significantly discourage confessions and, without the confessions, are important prosecutions lost? Hard data on this one are impossible to obtain. Who can count the number of suspects who would have otherwise told the police a true story but held their peace after hearing the articulation of their right to silence? In this empirical desert, all I could do was watch how the RIP cops behaved with suspects and guess at the effect of the *Miranda* factor in their exchanges.

Cops talk to suspects as a matter of routine, but I was surprised to find that interrogation—at least the structured, purposeful variety—is not universal. When I was out with the street narcotics enforcement team, for example, I never heard a suspect asked a question seeking to obtain evidence. Here's how that unit worked. Our "catch car" waited around the corner from a concealed observation team. When they saw a transfer of narcotics, they radioed a description of the buyer to us and as soon as we spotted the described person turning the corner, we swooped down and grabbed him. The cops swiftly and silently went through their prisoner's pockets, ignoring his loud protests of injured innocence, until they came up with the packets of recently purchased dope (as they invariably did). They then handcuffed the suddenly silent buyer and put him in the car. When the car was full, we all rode to the House.

Not only did the arresting officers not question their prisoners, they brushed aside any conversational openings by the people under arrest. Even after reaching the House and while going through the paperwork, the only exchange was name, address, and the like. They obviously didn't expect or need any confession and had no patience for the tales of woe they expected to hear. Nor were they interested in adding bribery charges to the misdemeanor narcotics bust, as they clearly could have done in several cases merely by hearing out the netted buyer's tentative "Can't we take care of this, Officer?"

With cops like the RIP officers, who routinely engage in conversation with suspects, the early exchanges are usually casual and offhand. The likely setting is the car in which the prisoner is being taken to the House. He may or may not be handcuffed during the ride, depending in part upon whether the police are playing out the fiction that he is not "in custody" yet, but more often depending on their assessment of the pacific and submissive disposition of their prisoner. But whether or not restrained, the suspect is experiencing the emotional pressure that in most people, even those who have taken the trip several times before, accompanies the initial realization of capture.

In some people, the twinge of fear, perhaps fear of mistreatment, may be uppermost. Others may experience some relief that the flight is over. Anger, directed at themselves or maybe at suspected betrayers, engulfs some as they feel the presence of their captors. But in all, these first few minutes under police control produce a state of agitated uncertainty. How much do the police actually know? That seems to be the overriding question in the mind of the guilty prisoner. He is trying to sense how the wind is blowing and figure out his best course of escape. Do these guys have me on what I did, or am I about to get framed for some other guy's crime? Are these cops smart, or can I make suckers out of them? Is there still a chance I might talk my way out of this one?

The state of anxiety is not confined to those who fear the police may know the true story. Even in those rare birds, the truly, totally blameless people under arrest, the certainty of innocence sometimes trembles before the uncertainties of accusation. So, in that initial unsureness of where they stand, suspects generally are eager to open a conversational gambit, particularly where the setting suggests informality.

Apart from the hope of making a bribery arrest (which I found rarely aroused much interest), cops exploit the conversational impulse for one of three reasons: they want a statement to cement the case against the person speaking; they just want to confirm their own suspicions; or they are hoping to obtain leads or general information concerning others who might be criminally involved.

Of course, everybody—especially those seasoned by experience in the system—should know that there is no such thing as an off-the-record conversation with a cop. But it is surprisingly easy to forget even one's self-interest in the cozy and casual atmosphere of the squad car headed for the stationhouse. And many people initiate a tentative exchange with an arresting officer as though they were in a sort of legal time-out zone where words don't count.

The exchange between police and prisoner in the police car reflects the ambience of the setting. Rarely are the officer's questions direct or confrontational; rarely are the suspect's answers full or detailed. Although there is no typical conversation, and composites are inevitably false to some extent, the squad car dialog might run something like this:

Perp: What's this all about, Officer? I mean, what are you taking me in for?

Cop: You don't know what this is about?

Perp: I swear, Officer, I don't know nothing.

Cop: We told you. It's a robbery.

Perp: Yeah, I know that. But what robbery are you talking about?

Cop: (aside to fellow officer, chuckling): He means he did so many of them, he can't remember this one. (*To perp:*) It's the shoe store job. Last week. Up near Fourteenth Street.

Perp: I don't know nothing about that.

Cop: Then you got nothing to worry about, my man. But we got a witness, picked out your photo. Said you were one of the dudes that did the place.

Perp: Don't I get a line up, Officer? I mean it could be a bad photo or something.

Cop: That's just what we're going to do when we get to the House, as soon as we can arrange it. We want to find out if you were the guy who held the gun on the lady behind the cash register.

Perp (vehemently): That wasn't me, Officer. I never owned no gun, I swear it. I wouldn't even have gone in there with that guy if I'd'a known he had a gun. Honest, I didn't even know he was fixing to stick up the place.

Cop: Nobody's perfect. And if what you say is true, then you aren't the worst guy in the world, you know what I mean? It would be too bad if you had to take the whole weight here. You might be able to do yourself some good in this case if you helped us locate this other dude. Think about it.

At this point, the hypothetical car arrives at the House, and the hypothetical party moves upstairs.

How shall we characterize this friendly conversation? There was no physical force, no threats, no deception, no protracted or otherwise psychologically debilitating circumstances. Yet the suspect was clearly in police custody, and no *Miranda* warning preceded the conversation. If the exchange can be fairly characterized as "interrogation," no trial court will permit the jury to hear the defendant's partially inculpatory admission, no matter how helpful the evidence might be in resolving a close and difficult issue, no matter how serious the crime.

To the police officer involved, it may not seem like what he would call "interrogation"; after all, he was not really asking questions about the crime—if anything, he was being interrogated by his prisoner. So if one of the cops is later asked at a hearing in court, "Officer, did you or your partner question the defendant during that ride to the stationhouse?" he is likely to reply with perfect sincerity, "No, ma'am. We talked with him, yes. But we did not question him until later." To a lawyer or judge, however, the interrogatory form of the police utterances that elicited the inculpatory declaration is less important. These people are more inclined to examine the purpose and effect of the conversation.

About 4:30 A.M. on a January night in 1975, while on patrol in Providence, Rhode Island, a police officer recognized a man in the street as a person previously identified by photo and wanted for the shotgun murder of a cabdriver less than a week before. The suspect, a man named Innis, was arrested and advised of his rights under *Miranda*. The warnings were repeated twice as higher ranking officers arrived, and Innis indicated he wanted to speak to a lawyer. Under *Miranda*, this election precludes any subsequent interrogation. The captain directed three officers to take Innis to the police station in a car with a mesh screen dividing the front from the rear seats and instructed them not to question or intimidate the prisoner on the way in.

As they drove, two of the cops struck up a conversation with each other. One mentioned that he was familiar with the neighborhood of the crime and that a school for handicapped children was nearby. He said that a lot of handicapped children play in the area. "God forbid," he remembered saying to his buddy, "that one of them might find a weapon with shells and they might hurt themselves." His fellow officer shared his concern. The third officer had a substantially similar recollection of the conversation. Innis then offered to show the police where he had secreted the gun. He was returned to the scene, where a search for the weapon was in progress. He was given a fourth set of *Miranda* warnings and this time responded that he wanted to "get the gun out of the way" to protect the kids in the school. He then led the police to the shotgun hidden under some rocks in a nearby field.

The trial judge allowed into evidence both the gun and the circumstances of its discovery, but the high court of Rhode Island, five to two, set aside the conviction on the ground that the conversation between the police was a disguised and impermissible *interrogation*. Rhode Island appealed to the United States Supreme Court, and we had the first careful exposition by that Court on the meaning of the term *interrogation* for *Miranda* purposes. The court concluded that the word means not only "express questioning" but "any words or actions on the part of the police (other than those normally attendant to arrest and custody) that the police should know are reasonably likely to elicit an incriminating response from the suspect." Applying the new definition to the *Innis* case, the Court found that the conversing officers had no reason to believe that the suspect "was peculiarly susceptible to an appeal to his conscience concerning the safety of handicapped children" and therefore had no reason to think that the suspect would respond with an inculpatory offer to recover the weapon he had hidden. The hope or intent of the police in this seemingly casual exchange, the Court thought, was not determinative, since they had no basis for thinking the incriminating response "reasonably likely." The exchange, they held, was therefore not *interrogation*.

In view of the palpable risk that a talkative passenger might later clam up and the substantial danger that the court might exclude from evidence the suspect's only damaging statement, one would think that the *Miranda* warnings would be voiced to a suspect at the start of every squad car ride. But I have heard many car seat conversations and only once was the prisoner mirandized during the ride—the single instance where I can truly say my presence affected police behavior. "The only reason I gave him his warnings," Sergeant Browne later told me with a smile, "was that I could see you getting all nervous about it so I figured, what the hell." Anyway, we discovered as soon as we got to the House that we had the wrong man, so Marty Browne's rare deviation from common practice was for naught.

In addition to the danger that a car seat confession will be lost, there is a real likelihood (in New York, at least) that a subsequent, fully mirandized confession will be excluded on a cat-out-of-bag theory of *taint*. In the law's usual homey, metaphorical style of reasoning, courts have found that once the cat is let out of the bag by an admission before mirandizing, the suspect realizes the futility of silence and continues the damaging conversation despite a subsequent *Miranda* warning. Under these circumstances, exclusion of the pre-warned statements while allowing the mirandized sequelae, our courts believe, would cheapen *Miranda*. So even the confession freely tendered after a properly administered *Miranda* warning will be excluded as tainted if an unwarned admission preceded it. It's a dire consequence to hang on a friendly and informal conversation.

In 1985, in a case called *Oregon v. Elstad*, the Supreme Court held that the intervention of *Miranda* warnings protected later statements from the virus that infected the first unmirandized declarations. Voicing the incantation, the Court reasoned, supplied what had been lacking and thereby fully made up for its earlier omission. The Justices evidently thought that (to shift the metaphor) though the loose cat cannot be rebagged, the suspect, properly advised, can thereafter freely choose to release no more cats. In a later decision, however, the highest court of the State of New York declined to follow the Supreme Court's view of the matter, electing once again (as they may under our federal system) to maintain the position that the mirandized confession is inadmissible if preceded by an unwarned custodial disclosure.

These developments were subsequent to my tour with 9 RIP, and the troops at the time had little concern with the possible effects of the casual confession on the admissibility of a later statement given under more formal circumstances. If New York law had shown signs of its later development, the message had not yet reached the front lines. Still, even if the danger of infectious exclusion was largely unrecognized, the men understood that the prisoner's first acknowledgment of culpability might be the only one they got, and its admissibility was clearly in doubt. I began asking the RIP cops why they didn't protect the carseat confidence with the *Miranda* verses, a precaution as simple and routine as the warnings they later administered at the House.

I got several answers. Halfheartedly, a cop would venture that the suspect was not really under arrest yet because the witness had not picked him out of a lineup, or another might lamely argue that he was not "interrogating" the prisoner when he conversed casually in the car. To the credit of the 9 RIP cops, these lines of self-justification were readily abandoned. Other replies were subtler and more persuasive.

From several of the officers, I heard an explanation that sounded to me as if they were reluctant to break the relaxed mood of the preliminary exchange. They were concerned that the announcement formalizes the interaction, puts the prisoner on guard (which it is designed to do, of course), and conveys the impression that the arrest is irrevocable (which it is not), all reducing the suspect's hope of talking himself out of trouble (and thereby talking himself more deeply into it). Some cops told me frankly that at that point they are thinking less about the possible courtroom consequences than of the immediate effects on their immediate need for confirmation of suspicion or leads to accomplices or weapons. I found it interesting that in this limited and specific context, at least, a number of experienced line officers believed that the *Miranda* warnings actually do inhibit self-incriminating revelations.

Another rationalization for delayed warnings is composed in equal measure of considerations of convenience and testimonial trepidation. Taped to the wall in the 9 RIP office is an open manila folder on which the *Miranda* catechism is handwritten in large, black letters. Or at least the NYPD version of it. When the RIP cops give the warning, they invariably read it from the sign. I have chided them for this, asking whether they had not yet learned it. No, they tell me, they have not memorized it exactly as printed, and they are afraid they might get some of the words mixed up if they trusted to memory. But the substance, I insist, surely you must remember the essence of the four parts. It's really very simple: (1) You have a right to remain silent; (2) anything you say may be used against you; (3) you have a right to have a lawyer present to advise you; (4) if you have no funds to hire a lawyer, a lawyer will be provided for you free of charge. It doesn't matter what words you use as long as you correctly convey the substance of it.

Really? I detect a moment of polite disbelief—the usual police academy residue: the by-the-book, do-it-right, form-is-substance myth. Tommy Wray laughs out loud. "I can just see it. I'm on the stand, and I say I made up the words of the *Miranda* warning. Defense counsel will have a ball: 'You mean, Officer, you can't remember the exact words you used when you warned my client?' Then he'll ask me to say the warning in my own words, and I'll probably clutch and forget half of it. No thanks! It's safer to read it."

I was also told an infuriating story of a premature warning. In a particularly ugly murder case, the prime suspect had given a long and detailed confession to the detectives of the Ninth PDU, following a good *Miranda* warning and a waiver. The confession was particularly important because the several eyewitnesses were a bit inconsistent and, in any event, not people of the highest credibility rating. Unknown to the detectives who questioned the suspect at the House, however, "some rookie" in uniform had read the

Miranda incantation when he picked up the suspect and put him in the patrol car for passage to the PDU. The prisoner had replied to these initial advisories by saying that he thought he had better talk to his lawyer first.

The cops who told me the story were disgusted. "That overeager sonofabitch killed the case for us." The confession was excluded on *Miranda* grounds, and without it the jury was not persuaded by the witnesses. The defendant was acquitted. A killer walked free because a cop, fresh from the academy, had given the warnings upon arrest rather than waiting for the commencement of *interrogation* by detectives at the House.

It was difficult for the PDU cop to appreciate the reasoning behind the result. After all, why shouldn't the second waiver, freely tendered, prevail over the initial assertion? Ordinary logic would tend to accord controlling weight to the most recent disposition. Even a suspect in custody may change his mind and—provided the mind change was not induced by police pressure or trick—what sound policy forbids the use in evidence of the product of the prisoner's second thought? There are some cases in which courts have allowed the use of statements by mirandized prisoners who initially declined to waive. If a prisoner, altogether spontaneously and without any police prompting whatever, initiates further conversation during which he makes unprovoked admissions, those statements may be received in evidence. The United States Supreme Court has also allowed the use of statements obtained by a different team of police officers on a different investigation following a fresh set of warnings and a waiver, notwithstanding the initial refusal to waive. Despite these rare instances of operable revocation, however, courts generally hold that once the right of silence or the ancillary right to consult with counsel is asserted, no subsequent waiver of the right can cancel that assertion.

So, notwithstanding some uneasiness with the *Miranda* doctrine, most courts have adhered to it firmly, even extending it to invalidate warned waivers following either an assertion of the right to silence or an unwarned admission that let the cat out of the bag. *Miranda* has become part of the legal landscape, part of our evolved sense of justice. Yet we really do not know how it actually affects a suspect's reactions: Does it induce the talkative to clam up? Or perhaps might some fearful and mistrustful person, after being assured that the cops know and respect his rights, let down his guard enough to allow an incriminating utterance to escape? Recall Whitmore's false confession and Robles's true one in the Wylie-Hoffert murder case; think about the mirandized, experienced criminal choosing not to talk to the uniformed patrolmen who picked him up and, a short time later, after repeated warnings, giving a full confession of homicide to a detective in the stationhouse. Such cases illustrate the impenetrable mystery of the choice. But the mere fact that the answer everyone seeks is unknowable does not hinder the formation of opinion. I asked some of the 9 RIP cops what their experience had led them to believe on the subject.

The most unhesitating and unequivocal contribution came from Sergeant Marty Browne. "The *Miranda* warnings do not make a particle of difference," he told me with assurance. "It's just plain silly. In the first place, nobody we're interested in talking to believes a word we tell them. Whether it's for their own good or not."

"Nobody?"

"Okay, some people may believe we're on the level and trying to help them out, but those aren't the people who have anything to tell us that we really need to know. Second," he continued, "do you think any one of these people we bring in doesn't know already that he doesn't have to talk to us? Or that what he says to us may be used against him?"

"But does he know the part about the lawyer?" I asked.

"As far as getting him a lawyer, free of charge, and bringing the lawyer in here to sit with this mope while we're questioning him, you're right," Marty conceded, "he probably didn't know about that. And he doesn't believe it when he hears it. Of course, no cop is going to get up and go out, to court or wherever, to find a lawyer and bring him back so he can continue with the interrogation. It never has happened, it never will. And the Supreme Court is making us lie when we say it will. So you see, the perp is perfectly right not to believe what we tell him in the first place."

I pressed, "But Marty, don't some of the guys think that the warnings put a little distance between the cop and the perp and make it harder to get conversation going? In the car, for example, the warnings must make *some* difference or the guys would give them."

"Oh, sure," Browne acknowledged, "I know they think it makes a difference. But I don't believe it for a minute. If a perp wants to talk about the crime for whatever reason, he talks to us. Nothing we say to him, in the car or anyplace else, will stop him. And if he starts out giving us some bullshit story, like he just went in to the store to buy himself some Adidas and he didn't know he had a gun in his jeans, and later he decides to tell us the truth, he's not going to remember what we told him in the beginning."

"So if it makes no difference, what's your objection?" I asked.

"Look, if they want us to give them their rights, we'll do it. It doesn't bother me to say the words. I just don't like to see the perp walk because some cop forgot part of it, or because some judge doesn't believe the cop when he testifies that he read the magic words before the questioning began. If you want my candid opinion, I think *Miranda* is just another way for the courts to throw out perfectly good cases."

I witnessed what might be regarded as collateral support for Sergeant Browne's position when I heard him quite unself-consciously issue a most peculiar dictum to a prisoner. I have come to think of it as *Browne's contra-Miranda advisory*. Sitting in the RIP office was a person who had earlier turned aside RIP's effort to question him by stating that he wanted to talk to a lawyer first. The men went about their work; he sat silently waiting—not for the lawyer who, everybody knew, would never arrive at the House, but for conveyance to Central Booking downtown. Browne looked long and hard at him; then, yielding to that inner need for confirmation, he addressed him as follows: "Now listen carefully to what I tell you, my man. You have asked for a lawyer, and I now advise you that nothing you say to me at this time can ever be used against you. Do you understand? It means that even if you tell me that you helped Lee Oswald assassinate the President of the United States, no one can ever use that statement against you. Understand? Now, having advised you of your rights, do you want to tell me about this case before your lawyer gets here? You have nothing to lose, I promise you." Good try, Marty, but the suspect remained mute, probably because he didn't believe a word you said.

Others agree with Sergeant Browne that the warnings have a comparatively slight impact on the suspect's disposition to communicate. "Some of these perps have heard that *Miranda* warning so many times they know it by heart," Harry Childs told me. "I'm just going through the motions; the words have lost all their meaning for the average guy we pick up." But the position is not unanimous. Joe Dean once confided, "I feel funny reading those warnings. It sounds to me like I'm telling the guy to keep his mouth shut. Anybody who stops and thinks about it has to know that he's hurting himself by admitting to a crime, right? So how come I'm telling this guy to think about it? That's not my job."

Though I did not witness any full confession, I watched several interrogations and I discussed with a number of the 9 RIP officers their techniques and the reactions of persons under interrogation. The cops recalled a variety of sessions that had produced confessions. But the pattern, if any, eluded me. They had some cases in which they knew from the start a confession would be forthcoming, while in others the suspects persisted in patently false denials that they seemed on the perpetual verge of abandoning (Sonny's gun case was one example). They had cases in which a sudden change of heart came unexpectedly at the end of a long and fruitless interrogation (like Richard Robles's confession). In others, they said they had correctly predicted in the first moments that they would come up dry in the end. I asked, but they were unable to describe the signs of a fruitful or frustrating outcome.

When it came to discussion of what techniques of questioning they had found most productive, I heard some general agreement, mostly on the proposition: "It all depends."All agreed that sympathy and friendliness were more effective than hostility, for example, but a feel for the individual suspect determined whether to play on the seriousness of the charge or to stress the suspect's comparatively minor culpability. Some perps responded to talk of guilt and shame ("Would you want your momma to hear about this?"), others to honor and manliness ("You tell your son to stand up and tell the truth like a man, don't you? Now look at you sitting here and lying to me about what you did. What would your kid say if he could see you now?"). But the RIP cops all believe that the most common motivation to confession is either pride or self-justification. Thus, a skillful interrogator may provoke an inculpatory rejoinder by deriding the crime or the criminal as sloppy or stupid. Or he might stimulate agreement by venturing that the victim probably had it coming to him/her.

All the cops I spoke to agree that it is well for the police officer to learn as much as he can about the details of the crime before he starts talking to the suspect. Having some facts against which to check the suspect's first account frequently allows the cops to confront him with the true version and induce a shift in the story, perhaps toward truth. In addition, I discovered that police customarily tell the suspect a great deal about the crime and about what others have told them. Accustomed to the guarded courtroom disclosure of such facts, I was somewhat surprised at the free transmissions at this stage. Browne explained that he sought to convey to the suspect the impression that the police already had so much evidence that the suspect's cause was all but lost and he might as well try to do himself some good by talking.

"Telling the suspect what you know about the crime is one thing," I said to Tommy Wray one day, "but do you ever make up some fake facts to stimulate a statement?"

Tommy was interested. "You mean I can lie to him?" he asked.

"Sure," I said. "Tell him you found some fingerprints on the scene and you sent them down to the lab. See what that produces."

There was some danger, Wray thought. If the suspect thought the cop was faking, the edge might be lost. But in many cases, he told me, a false fact could be very useful in getting a conversation going. "But, are you sure I can do that?" He was still dubious. "Wouldn't it violate his rights?"

"No," I assured him. "Once the suspect freely agrees to talk to you, he has no right to have you tell him the whole truth about the case. And if the lie you tell him is not the sort that is likely to make an innocent person confess, you have nothing to worry about."

Tommy was evidently pleased, if still somewhat incredulous. While *Miranda* may inhibit some exploitations of custody, it clearly leaves the police as free as ever to try every psychological ploy in the battle of wits to induce the suspect to furnish the evidence for his own conviction.

23

A HELPFUL DISPOSITION TO INCREDULITY

D o cops always assume that whomever they put the cuffs on is the guilty person? In common speech, they usually say "perpetrator" when they mean "suspect"; are the two words somehow equated in the cop's mind? As an officer sits down to talk to his prisoner, does he believe that the truth he is after will turn out to be an admission of complicity? Should the artful interrogator, then, maintain an undaunted attitude of disbelief no matter how seemingly persuasive the story of innocence, persisting by various means to try to discredit all but the incriminating statements? Or does police credulity vary according to the circumstances?

At the outset, it must be said—as every good trial lawyer knows—that excessive credulity is not an asset in the business of interrogation. Those disposed to believe that most members of the human race are generally honorable in behavior and truthful in speech are not destined for greatness in the practice of criminal law. And people who tend to believe the stories of strangers, even when they conflict, especially when delivered with some emotion and accompanied by earnest oaths taken on the heads of close relatives, such people should probably look for careers that do not entail examination of suspects or witnesses in criminal investigations. For those who do enter the law enforcement trades with a generous view of human nature, a few years of work on the ugly side usually obliterates that outlook.

I think police officers come to the task of interrogation with a fairly strong disposition to believe inculpatory statements and disbelieve claims of innocence. As we have noted, police are not in the business of separating truth from falsehood in close cases, and they usually apply fairly broad precepts somewhat like the following:

1. Criminals are often the most persuasive liars.
2. When a crime has been committed, someone did it, and the suspect is the most likely candidate.
3. Self-serving statements, regardless of vehemence, are less likely to be true than self-damaging statements.
4. "Respectable citizens" (e.g., local merchants, middle-aged married people, conventionally employed people) are more likely to tell the truth than other sorts, but even honest people rarely tell cops the whole truth.
5. Friends and family members can be expected to lie to corroborate the story of a person in trouble.
6. Hope of monetary gain, fear of reprisal, and the settling of old scores are powerful inducements to fabrication.
7. Stories that fit the physical facts in some respects are entitled to careful consideration in all particulars.
8. Stories that are contradicted by the physical facts in some particular are likely to be false in all respects.

Applying this basic set of axioms, a cop will ordinarily approach a suspect predisposed to believe him guilty. This disposition, however, is affected by the particular circumstances of the case as it stands at the moment of arrest. The character and motivation of the complainant, the prior relationships of the parties and witnesses, if any, the certainty with which the suspect or his photo was identified by the witness—all of these and similar factors will affect the cop's willingness to credit the suspect's expected initial denial. Other aspects of the case, along with the personality and weariness of the cops, will affect the energy they will expend on trying to shake the disbelieved denial. Thus, in the ordinary case, with a bad prisoner unequivocally identified by a clean victim, a relatively fresh team will approach interrogation with a strong set to discount exculpatory stories, and they will devote considerable time and energy to dislodging facially credible claims of innocence.

It is equally important to emphasize that even so set, many officers can become dubious during the course of questioning, or even be convinced otherwise. In other cases, the cop may open the conversation with the suspect less than fully persuaded by the story he has heard from his complainant, which also affects his skepticism quotient.

A case in point: I was sitting in the 9 RIP office one summer afternoon talking with Joe Byrne and Tom Trepcyk when we noticed a frail young man being searched by one of the PDU detectives and put into the holding cage outside our doorway. I don't know what alerted Byrne that it was a case for us, but he stepped outside and returned a moment later to say, "Here's a good one. The victims of this robbery picked up the perp and brought him in."

"There you are," Trepcyk said to me triumphantly, "our first citizen's arrest. I hope it's a better collar than the ones we've been getting from our own troops. Come on, Joe, let's see if there's anything to enhance on this one."

We all walked out and there, sitting just outside the swinging gate to the PDU room, was the couple who had brought in the suspect. The woman, who appeared to be about forty, could hardly be called lithe, but the man looked for all the world like a Japanese sumo wrestler. His features were vaguely Asian in cast, his hair straight and black. A sparse beard of straight black hair curved over his chin. His arms were the diameter of my thighs, and his midsection appeared to be a perfect sphere.

They smiled at us as we approached. I was eager to hear their story. Both spoke English poorly, but through the heavy Spanish inflection we could understand them. But about all Joe and Tom got from them at that point was that they had been robbed earlier that morning in their apartment in the Projects by two men with guns, one of whom they had later seen on the street and brought into the stationhouse. The report of the crime was made to the Housing Police, and Joe and Tom were more concerned initially with getting the paperwork in hand than in developing the story from the witnesses. They took their address and telephone number and, to my disappointment, let them go with a promise to contact them later.

With several deprecatory remarks about the inefficiency of the Housing Police, Joe, Tom, and I rode down to their office to fetch the 61. "They should have delivered it to us by the end of the tour. If we don't go and get it, we probably won't have it till tomorrow. Now they know we're coming over for it, they're probably just typing it up," Tom told me.

A Housing Police officer was indeed typing up the 61 as we walked into their office fifteen minutes later. Jealously we noted that the Housing cop was using an electronic typewriter far more sophisticated than anything I had ever seen in any regular police facility. When we read the 61, we found it as sketchy on the facts as most patrol reports, but it did describe in some detail the three pistols with which the robber was allegedly armed. Pistols, plural, but robber, singular. No mention of an accomplice. Driving back to the Ninth, I suggested we stop by the Projects, pick up our complainants, and give them a lift to the House. The others agreed, and it turned out to be one of the best moves we made all day.

We found the complainants' apartment on the top floor and rang the doorbell. We were admitted into a tidy, well-furnished place. In the entrance, a large, clean, illuminated fish tank displayed a variety of colorful tropical fish. The living room, crowded with furniture, had a glass-topped coffee table in the middle of the room, a large color television set, and an enormous portable stereo box on the mantelpiece over a false fireplace. The kitchen was small and cluttered but contained a washing machine and a number of other appliances. A bathroom and two bedrooms lay beyond. In addition to our two complainants, now half undressed, we found a young man and a young woman with a baby. The female victim identified them as her children and grandchild. Looking around, we went over the facts in some detail, this time with the help of the young man, who had been present during the robbery and spoke better English. His sister hung back and offered no help.

As the story emerged, a man had appeared at their door about 8 A.M., awakening them and demanding entry. He displayed a star-shaped badge and a piece of paper that he said was a search warrant. Thinking he was a police officer, they admitted him to the apartment. They gave us a very complete description of his physical appearance and equipment. He carried, they said, three pistols stuck in his belt. They showed us where he had each and supplied a surprisingly knowledgeable description of them. He also carried a two-way hand-held radio and wore a police-style baseball cap with the insignia of the Housing Police Auxiliary. He said he was looking for narcotics and put the family into the bathroom, threatening to "blow their heads off" if they came out. The victims were now suspicious—it did not seem to them the way the police would conduct such an operation.

Still, there was no mistaking the armament, and they remained in the bathroom. They did look out the window and, twelve floors down, they soon saw their visitor emerge from the building, meet another man who was standing outside, and walk away with him. The family came out of the bathroom and discovered about $200 in cash and trinkets missing from the bedside table. Later, while driving around looking for the robbers, our complainants saw the man whom the robber had joined as he left the building. We learned that they had previously seen that person "around the neighborhood," although they didn't *know* him. They took him into their car without difficulty (girth may have been persuasive here), and brought him in to us.

With this story in hand, we asked them to return to the stationhouse with us, which they did. Leaving these large people in the RIP office, Tom and Joe and I led our frail prisoner into Lieutenant Kennedy's office and closed the door. Byrne sat behind the lieutenant's desk. First he asked Tom to bring him the *Miranda* sign from the RIP wall, which he read slowly and carefully to the prisoner, whom we will call Francisco. Francisco immediately denied having had anything to do with any robbery or being in the vicinity of the complainants' building that morning. He said he had slept in the park and gone swimming at a park pool when he awoke. "Besides," he said confidently, "why would I do that? I know those people."

"What do you mean, you know them?" we asked. "You mean you've seen them around, right?"

"Naw. I mean I know them."

"Well, they say they don't know you, Francisco. And they're going to get up in court and say they saw you meet the guy who stuck them up and walk away with him. So you must know this guy."

"Where do they say I met him?"

"On the street. As he was coming out of the building after doing the job."

"How are they going to recognize me from all the way up on the thirteenth floor, tell me that?"

We looked at each other. "Who told you they live on the thirteenth floor?" Byrne asked.

"Like I told you, Officer. I know those people."

"How well do you know them?" Byrne was now interested. "Have you ever been up to their apartment?"

"I watched their apartment for them when they went to Puerto Rico."

"What do you mean, you watched it?"

"They left me money. They left me the keys. I would go in and like pay their bills for them, you know, the rent and the electricity, and like see everything was all right. And feed the fish."

I couldn't resist putting in my two cents: "Describe the apartment."

"Well, when you first walk in there's this big fish tank," Francisco began. He described the glass coffee table in the living room and other furniture, the washing machine in the kitchen, the layout of the rooms. He got it all right.

"Wait here, Francisco," Byrne told him. He and I crossed the RIP office where our complainants were waiting. Byrne questioned them closely. No, they insisted, Francisco had never been up to their apartment. They could not explain how he would know about the fish tank. "Did you go down to Puerto Rico this year?" Byrne asked.

"Yes," the woman said. Her mother had died, and there was some property. She had to go down to "sign some papers."

"Who did you leave to watch your apartment while you were gone?" Byrne wanted to know.

"My daughter," she said. She wouldn't trust anyone else.

For about another hour, Byrne, Trepcyk, and I shuttled back and forth between the two rooms. We asked about our complainants' sources of income and wondered how they could afford $76 worth of fish for the tank (we were shown the bill). They insisted their only income was public assistance. Francisco told us about the car, the van, and the Lincoln that the complainant drove. The complainant told us he had sold the Lincoln to buy the van. Francisco said they must be doing drugs to afford the luxuries. They denied it and told us that drugs were being sold from an apartment two floors beneath them.

We caucused. Joe and Tom looked baffled. Joe said, "Look, I'll have to cut this guy loose anyway, right? Even on what they say I don't have enough to hold him for robbery." He was right. "But," Joe added, "I think they are telling the truth about getting robbed."

Trepcyk agreed. "Still," Tom added, "there's no doubt in the world Francisco was up in their place."

I asked Byrne (who had once been in a narcotics unit) whether he thought our complainants were dealing drugs from the apartment. "Not likely," Joe said without hesitation, "The place is too clean."

"But Francisco might have thought they were doing drugs up there," Tom put in. "He still thinks so. Probably thought they had stuff and cash there so when he and his buddy got talking about doing a job, he sends the guy up there."

"Makes sense," Byrne agreed.

"But how did he get into the place to begin with?" I asked. "You don't believe that story about watching the place while they were away, do you?"

"Maybe the girl," Joe suggested.

"He might have had a little thing going with her while her momma was away," Tommy noted.

Possible. Everybody walked out—separately. Byrne gave the complainants the RIP card and told them to keep a sharp eye out for the robber. "Please give us a call if you see him," he urged. "Don't try to bring this guy in yourself. He just might be carrying a couple of those pistolas."

That was the last we saw of the case.

24

THE STRENGTH AND THE WEAKNESS

It always seemed to me that 9 RIP operated like a small pocket of anarchy in the midst of a vast, paramilitary, bureaucratic structure. After working with them for months, I was still unable to distinguish the white-shield police officers from the gold-shield detectives, though in other respects the men accorded great importance to the difference in rank. From the way they dealt with one another and the way they went about their work, I couldn't tell the hot shots from the drones, the vets from the rookies. Half the time I didn't even know which officer was in charge of what case. Everybody worked on everything, it seemed, and nobody gave orders to anyone. Even Marty Browne rarely directed anyone to do anything and, to my knowledge, never challenged a member of his command for the way he went about his work.

In many ways, the informal, unstructured character of the unit was its strength. The casual organization fostered a communal spirit of group enterprise which contributed to the energy of the unit. People worked—individually and cooperatively—because they felt a sense of personal responsibility. No one ever said, "That's not my job." No one ever said, "Why bother." Nothing was ever bucked to another level of authority. Too, their operational mode seemed well suited to RIP's mission. Many times, the free, uncompetitive exchange of information and the extra effort of reinforced persistence provided the factor that ultimately made the difference.

Ordinarily, RIP's work is uncomplicated. The men are looking for, or processing, a particular person on a particular case. It is an effort that relies primarily on insight, happenstance, perseverance, and lucky breaks (perhaps in the reverse order). A loosely structured, egalitarian outfit like 9 RIP, operating on diffuse resources and self-generated energy, is well suited to develop and react most effectively to such assets.

But the informal structure has its weaknesses too. It is not designed to deal with complexity, and it may buckle when confronted with a large, unclear case involving multiple defendants and crimes with uncertain connections to one another. Under pressure of confusion and fatigue, the men may get in each other's way and the lack of structure or clear responsibility may reduce the opportunity to build a case. I remember one such instance. Though the case was not entirely lost, the failures of the RIP method weakened the prosecution position in court.

First from Marty Browne and later from Izzy Pagan, Tommy Wray, and Joe Dean, I heard a particularly irate account of the District Attorney's intransigence. A gang of six young suspects had been arrested, and after a long and, I gather, somewhat disjointed night's interrogation, the RIP cops were satisfied that among them the group had committed no fewer than fifteen robberies in the Precinct. Two of the victims had made positive photo identifications and seven others had been uncertain. No live lineups had yet been had, though they were planned for the future. One of the young men had admitted twelve robberies for which the cops had 61s on file, the female suspect had admitted to three, and the others had confessed to between four and eight crimes each. It was a major arrest.

I can imagine the scene that night in the cramped quarters of the RIP office, spilling out into the PDU space. The tired cops encourage their youthful captives to remember the details of their exploits so the police can match up their accounts with the open 61s. They're taking statements, trading information, typing arrest forms, betraying no emotion that might discourage cooperation. The hours drag on, fatigue and frustration steadily creeping up on them. And through it all, they try to remain conscious that they are compiling a case. Clearing open 61s is important, but it is *evidence* they are accumulating, the stuff of prosecution, a product bound for close and critical review in court. Izzy even made a chart, they told me, laboriously collating the statements of the particular suspects with the specific robberies described in the 61s. The kids talked through the night, but in the morning the cops discovered the evidence had evaporated.

Baffled, angry, the cops told me that when they finally had the investigation wrapped up and took the case downtown, some Assistant D.A. looked at their work with scorn and told them, "Forget it." Not one confession, not one word told to the cops during that long night could be presented to the grand jury.

I examined Izzy's chart, I read the reports of the interrogation typed on the "fives," I asked for their notes (they had not had time to take notes, they told me), I asked them who said what about which robbery. Sadly, I shook my head and told them I could understand why the Assistant had trouble finding a clear, discrete case in the heap of fragmentary data. I explained that the D.A. could not try a case of robbery on the police officers' incomplete recollection that the defendant "admitted" participating in the crime. That's a conclusion, the opinion of the officer concerning the gist of the suspect's statement. Without the words of the suspects themselves, clearly relating to a specific crime, the D.A. had correctly pronounced the confessions unusable.

The cops were indignant. What did they want, a ribbon tied around it? In disgust, they told me that the D.A. had complained that the cops had not asked the perps, "Who held the gun, who was standing where, who grabbed the victim first, shit like that." A couple of the cops darkly confided that they had actually heard the D.A. say it was too much trouble to try to match up the interlocking admissions of the suspects and the complaints.

It is no reflection on the honesty of the cop who was satisfied that the felon had acknowledged culpability. But in court it is not the cop who must be satisfied, it is the jury. And they will want to know: Just what did this suspect say, how did he put it, what detail and specificity did he supply, how spontaneous was the admission, did he accept the cop's description or did he furnish his own, was he really admitting to the particular robbery charged in the indictment or to some other like it? These aspects of a statement do more than provide shading to make the admission persuasive, they are vital ingredients of the statement without which the mind of the confessing person is unintelligible and the sense of the confession cannot be discerned.

The men seemed to understand—even accept—what I was saying. Then they told me something they said they had not yet revealed to the Assistant District Attorney: Izzy Pagan had secretly recorded on his personal cassette recorder a substantial portion of the questioning of the most loquacious of the suspects. Did I want to hear the tape?

For the next hour or more, interrupted from time to time by other RIP business, Wray, Dean, Pagan, and I listened to the voices of Izzy and Tommy in the foreground and Joe delivering his piece from the corner of the room. I heard enough to recognize that technology is not everything; the recording was clear but the quality of the interrogation was deficient.

I wish I had a transcript; it's not easy to recreate the form and mood of that conversation. I suppose one of the cops would pick up a 61 and open by saying something like "Okay, now let's talk about that stickup over on Fourth between C and D. Were you in on that one?" A long and inconclusive discussion would follow, trying to pin down the incident:

"I dunno. Which one was that?"

"It happened around 11:10 P.M. on the twelfth. One of the guys showed a gun."

"The twelfth you say? Uh, lemme think."

"Yeah, think about that, we don't want you to tell us you did it if you didn't. We got plenty of others to talk about. This dude was taken for fifty-seven dollars in cash and a gold chain—does that ring a bell?"

"Wait a minute, I'm trying to remember. Fourth near D, huh? Yeah, I think I was there."

"He says there were three guys, one was wearing a suede jacket."

"A bomber jacket, like? Yeah, that musta been Pee Wee. Yeah, I think that musta been us."

"Okay. Now let's talk about this one. Four guys with a knife on 5th between B and C. That was the fourteenth. A young woman. One of the guys grabbed her and threatened to rape her or something."

Laughter. "Yeah, man. That sounds like Ace. I bet that was us out there."

And so it would go. From one incident to another. Dates meant nothing to the suspects and precise locations little more. Frequently the 61s contained no unusual features to jog the suspect's memory, and usually the acknowledgment of participation was phrased as "I guess so," "it musta been," or nothing more than grunted agreement. In their effort to cover the sheaf of complaints, the cops accepted these equivocal admissions as confessions; their intuition was to avoid further pressure to elicit the detail that would have nailed the suspect on at least one or two of the crimes. It would have consumed precious time, the suspects might have balked and clammed up, and in any case it seemed doubtful that the young thugs really recalled specific details differentiating one of their many robberies from the others.

To the tired crew trying to sort things out, the extra push must have seemed an overwhelming and foredoomed undertaking. But now, as we listened to the tape, the men realized that without at least one explicit confession clearly related to a specific attack, the night's work had been largely wasted. The prosecution had to depend entirely on unsupported eyewitness identifications.

When we were through, Tommy and Izzy had lost much of the anger they had voiced at the start. The mood was regret, and we began to talk of how training in interrogation would be a welcome project in the unit. I'm sure some training would be helpful, but it's not the whole story. Most of the men in RIP were, in fact, well trained and thoroughly experienced. Many years on the Job, countless successful interrogations, and a good street "feel" for the mentality of the suspects are about the best training the department offers. These men were qualified to instruct others in the business of interrogation.

What, then, went wrong during that long night? I raised the subject with Marty Browne. He came back to the old problem of space. "How can you expect these guys to do a careful job in this madhouse?" he asked. "Everybody is climbing all over each other, the phones are going off, people are wandering in and out on other cases. If you want a thorough and careful interrogation, we have to have a room where you can sit down with these perps one at a time and go over it slowly with him. Otherwise it's just ridiculous." I agree, but cramped quarters is not a full answer either. Nor can the failure be attributed to a lack of stenographers or electronic recording equipment which might have facilitated the process and preserved the product—such as it was.

What happened, it seems to me, was a direct result of the sort of impulsive, responsive approach that characterizes the RIP operation generally. Their usual method, so effective in the usual case, actually impeded the effort in this one. If an organization accustomed to dealing with complex and uncertain facts—a law firm, for example—had confronted the problem that faced 9 RIP that night, its approach would have been very different. Most likely, one person would have been in charge. Taking a structured approach, he or she would have divided responsibility, assigning a suspect or a group of crimes to each investigator. The lawyer in charge might have developed a checklist containing the precise matters each investigator should try to learn from each suspect. At a central review of the investigator's reports, collated into a chart somewhat more detailed than Izzy Pagan's, connections as well as gaps could be spotted for follow-up interview.

Some such hierarchical, organized approach might have elicited a few useful confessions. To be fair, perhaps no method, however well structured, would have saved the day. Even the most meticulous organization cannot produce order and detail from hopelessly vague and fragmentary recollections. But it seems to me that whatever chance there might have been that night of eliciting a complete account of a single crime may well have been lost in the shuffle of papers and perps.

And it was the hopelessly unintelligible "confessions" that put the prosecutor in the position of taking the case to court exclusively on the strength of the eyewitness identifications. Only a few of the many robberies could be proved by a solid identification and, as Joe Dean told me later, the complainants in those cases were frightened and reluctant to testify at a trial. As a result, the prosecutor was lucky to get guilty pleas to reduced charges and a prison term with a maximum of four or five years for the worst offender. In the final analysis, the interesting thing about the incident was the disclosure of the weakness in the RIP method. The improvisational style that serves RIP so well in other contexts, a style so unexpected within an agency as highly structured as the Police Department, sometimes fails.

25

THE MAKING OF A
BRUTE-HERO

Few of us feel neutral about the police. Perhaps more than most collections of people, police are readily invested with heavy symbolic significance. The uniforms, the cars, their way of talking to the rest of us erase their individuality. If you post yourself outside a precinct stationhouse between 3:30 and 4:30 in the afternoon, when the tour changes, for example, you will witness the transformation of real people into anonymous figures. A diverse assortment of young men and women enter, and a short time later cops emerge. But something in our nature will not accept ambiguous figures like these. Neutrality baffles our urge to react to the creatures around us, and so we are quick to ascribe to police officers characteristics with which to replace their lost humanity, characteristics that we choose according to our own experience, imagination, and anxiety.

From myth and the media, from youthful fantasy and political rhetoric, from a variety of obvious and forgotten sources, we draw the attributes to hang on the inviting cardboard figures in uniform. To some, the cop is the symbol of oppressive force. Armed and dangerous, the cop looms as the emblem of state power at its worst. To others, the police officer seems more the embodiment of security, a symbol of rescue and protection. For many of us, the police represent at the same time the best and the worst of human nature: brute and hero. We readily invest our police with the attributes of vice and virtue writ large.

The real world affords ample reinforcement of both sides of the ambivalent ascription. In uniform, with gun, stick, and military insignia, the urban police officer is the natural object of our uneasiness toward state force. As we read daily of the outrages of domestic police aggression in foreign lands around the world, we cannot help but cast a suspicious glance at our own domestic warriors. Given a different local climate, how would they behave? And even today, how far should we credit the persistent tales and the occasional revelations of abuse of power?

Perhaps our fears are not altogether unfounded. I have heard otherwise sensitive cops speak with relish (and perhaps a bit of exaggeration) of beatings they had administered to unruly or threatening people. I have heard the word *napalm* used only partly in jest when talking about the problems of ineradicable street crime in certain areas of the Precinct. I have heard cops express anger at the neighborhood "liberals" who frustrate their desire to cleanse the parks of the drug hawkers and other undesirables by the simple expedient of the nightstick, purposefully applied. And if you happen to be of the racial or ethnic group upon whom police attention is most often focused, some personal experience may engrave lifelong hostility on your attitude toward police in general. Not many of my white students report having been stopped by suspicious cops as they walked innocently on the streets, but a remarkably high— and highly resentful—number of blacks and Hispanics have felt demeaned by what they took to be racial antagonism from the police.

In addition to the actual and feared oppression of which we think our police capable, we hate to be thought blind on the subject of "human nature." Here are all these cops, raising families on small incomes, prowling around with all that power hanging from their belts, daily uncovering nests of criminals wading in illicit profits. Corruption under such tempting circumstances, we believe, is only human nature. What citizen, what journalist does not instantly believe the worst at any hint of police corruption? And of course, even in the best of times and the best of departments, some tangible evidence of corruption will occasionally surface, leading the citizen to smirk knowingly at what is believed to be the fatal corrosion of the moral armor of the badge.

The symbol of the police attracts equally strong positive ascriptions. Cops are the people we call when we need help. They are our brave alter-egos: they move toward dangers from which we shrink. A stealthy stranger in a deserted park, a knot of aggressive young men on the corner, an unseen intruder in a darkened house, a drunk and abusive man waving an open knife in a fouled hallway—these and countless other situations that fill most of us with sudden terror attract cops. Unflinching, guns drawn, they crouch behind cars and exchange fire with desperate men. Over the rooftops, down the fire escape, into the dark cellar, these courageous men and women move with confidence and skill. This is the stuff of heroism. Daily, routine, commonplace heroism.

And for the most part, these heroes seem also a wholesome, likable lot of young people. With their long-suffering, proud wives and attractive children, they are the very essence of the tough-but-gentle masculine type beloved of American mythmakers. Just how the newer female cop will fit into our role Rolodex is not yet clear. So far, she doesn't. But several TV series are hard at work constructing the appropriate feminine-tough image for this recent entrant in our cast of stock characters. She may soon enjoy a distinctive place in our national consciousness as well as an accepted position in the patrol cars of the nation.

The brute-hero figure of the cop in our private mythology is reflected in the social role we assign our police. As a society, we demand essentially two performance duties: effective anticrime activity and restraint. We want them eager but not overeager, aggressive but not oppressive, tough but friendly, involved but detached, "human," but "professional." We want our cops out in the streets as a visible deterrent force as well as a crime-solving and criminal-apprehension battalion, while at the same time we want them law bound, rule observant, and inoffensive to vocal community leaders. In short, the job calls for tempered zeal.

This split social stance of the cop as a gun-slinging crime fighter and the cop as a judicious creature of constitutional integrity is virtually unique. We rarely make such dramatically opposed demands upon our public servants. For all the stress they suffer, neither teachers nor firefighters, not even judges and prosecutors, are pressed to the extremes of duty that police must obey. Nor do we so regularly and severely test opposed obligations in other officials as we do with our police officers who face challenges in court and administrative tribunals for both under- and overzeal.

The burden of conflicting signals, moreover, is not merely a peripheral part of the job description: it is central to the role of police officer. The discrepant calls of duty add more than subconscious strain—they amount to a visible, daily puzzle, a conflict to be solved repeatedly in many of the police officer's most important decisions. Consciously or not, the officer on the line knows that inherent in the authority he enjoys is the balance of power and restraint, a balance to be finely tuned according to some inarticulate standard of the "good cop." It's a difficult assignment, particularly as it must be carried out in an unpredictable variety of situations, many of them emotionally charged and often highly visible and subject to meticulously critical review.

Not that the conflicting commands of the Job induce any outward signs of stress or uncertainty. In their carriage and conversation, cops characteristically reveal no sign of emotional strain. Confidence is worn on the chest with the badge, at least in meetings with strangers.

So the cop goes about his daily tasks, denying an encroaching sense of burnout, gradually succumbing to the lethargy that makes contemplation of retirement more exciting than the prospect of another collar, unwittingly adopting a cynical attitude that blurs the vital distinctions between similar cases. The endless messages that restrain his impulses now seem a tiresome, unrealistic burden on his energy. In his best years, the cop dares the highwire drawn between the opposing poles of aggressive, energetic response and respectful, deliberate restraint. He takes his daily rewards in the respect and authority he feels on the beat. But frustration is inevitable. The Job will never succeed. The system will never deliver justice in every case. And, especially for the cops who care, reality tarnishes the bright metal of the shield.

ENDWORD

Many months had passed since my tour with 9 RIP was over, my experiences were just beginning to form themselves into sentences and paragraphs when I heard the familiar short beep of a police siren behind me one morning as I was walking into the campus at 116th and Broadway. I turned (as I always do) and saw a nondescript car with two mustached men in the front seat. Police. The car pulled up to the curb, the door opened and Tommy Wray jumped out smiling. "I'm up here in the two-six now," he told me. He asked how it felt to be back at school and wanted to know how "the book" was coming. However I ducked the question, the men of 9 RIP never had the slightest doubt that I had a book in mind all along. I told Tommy I had a few pages in the grinder; whatever came of it, I was grateful for the hospitality of the unit.

"It was mutual," Tommy said, smiling. "It was good to have you there."

I was a bit surprised. "How so?" I asked.

"Well," he said, "I learned a few things from all those

conversations we had. In fact, I learned something I didn't even know I was learning."

"Like what?" I asked.

"About the Job," he said, thinking about it. "I guess I used to think the law was for the lawyers to worry about. The things that happen on the street, they're real, and they're the things that make your heart pump."

I nodded.

"If I thought about it at all," Tommy continued, "I figured that the law is just another problem we had. But talking to you, I began to think it's the law that makes the Job interesting. I really never knew that before."

He could not have said anything I would rather hear.

We chatted a bit longer, then he got back into the car. As he pulled away with a wave, leaving me standing outside the gates of my University, I felt I had said goodbye at last.